HOW TO FORM A

NEVADA

CORPORATION

FROM ANY STATE

HOW TO FORM A NEVADA CORPORATION FROM ANY STATE

with forms

Mark Warda
Attorney at Law

Sphinx® Publishing
A Division of Sourcebooks, Inc.®
Naperville, IL • Clearwater, FL

First Edition, 2000

Published by: **Sourcebooks, Inc.**®

Naperville Office
P.O. Box 4410
Naperville, Illinois 60567-4410
630-961-3900
Fax: 630-961-2168

Clearwater Office
P.O. Box 25
Clearwater, Florida 33757
727-587-0999
Fax: 727-586-5088

Cover Design: Andrew Sardina/Dominique Raccah, Sourcebooks, Inc.®
Interior Design and Production: Amy S. Hall, Sourcebooks, Inc.®

This publication is designed to provide accurate and authoritative information in regard to the subject matter covered. It is sold with the understanding that the publisher is not engaged in rendering legal, accounting, or other professional service. If legal advice or other expert assistance is required, the services of a competent professional person should be sought.

From a Declaration of Principles Jointly Adopted by a Committee of the
American Bar Association and a Committee of Publishers and Associations

This product is not a substitute for legal advice.

Disclaimer required by Texas statutes.

Library of Congress Cataloging-in-Publication Data
Warda, Mark.
   How to form a Nevada corporation from any state : with forms / Mark Warda.— 1st ed.
        p.   cm.
   Includes index.
   ISBN 1-57248-101-3 (pbk.)
   1. Corporation law--Nevada--Popular works. 2. Incorporation--Nevada--Forms. I.
   Title.

KFN813.Z9 W37 2000
  346.793'06622--dc21

                                  99-052426
                                  CIP

Printed and bound in the United States of America.

HS Paperback — 10 9 8 7 6 5 4 3 2 1

CONTENTS

Using Self-Help Law Books

Whenever you shop for a product or service, you are faced with various levels of quality and price. In deciding what product or service to buy, you make a cost/value analysis on the basis of your willingness to pay and the quality you desire.

When buying a car, you decide whether you want transportation, comfort, status, or sex appeal. Accordingly, you decide among such choices as a Neon, a Lincoln, a Rolls Royce, or a Porsche. Before making a decision, you usually weigh the merits of each option against the cost.

When you get a headache, you can take a pain reliever (such as aspirin) or visit a medical specialist for a neurological examination. Given this choice, most people, of course, take a pain reliever, since it costs only pennies; whereas a medical examination costs hundreds of dollars and takes a lot of time. This is often the most logical choice: it's rare to need anything more than a pain reliever for a headache. But in some cases, a headache may indicate a brain tumor, and failing to see a specialist right away can result in complications. Should everyone with a headache go to a specialist? Of course not, but people treating their own illnesses must realize that they are betting on the basis of their cost/value analysis of the situation; they are taking the most logical option.

The same cost/value analysis must be made in deciding to do one's own legal work. Many legal situations are very straight forward, requiring a simple form and no complicated analysis. Anyone with a little intelligence and a book of instructions can handle the matter without outside help.

But there is always the chance that complications are involved that only an attorney would notice. To simplify the law into a book like this, several legal cases often must be condensed into a single sentence or paragraph. Otherwise, the book would be several hundred pages long and too complicated for most people. However, this simplification necessarily leaves out many details and nuances that would apply to special or unusual situations. Also, there are many ways to interpret most legal questions. Your case may come before a judge who disagrees with the analysis of our authors.

Therefore, in deciding to use a self-help law book and to do your own legal work, you must realize that you are making a cost/value analysis. You have decided that the money you will save in doing it yourself outweighs the chance your case will not turn out to your satisfaction. Most people handling their own simple legal matters never have a problem, but occasionally people find that it ended up costing them more to have an attorney straighten out the situation than it would have if they had hired an attorney in the beginning. Keep this in mind while handling your case, and be sure to consult an attorney if you feel you might need further guidance.

INTRODUCTION

While most states are jumping on the big government bandwagon and finding new ways to tax and keep records on their citizens, one state stands out for supporting low taxes and citizen privacy—Nevada.

Always a little freer than most states with legalized gambling, prostitution and easy divorces, Nevada has now decided to be at the forefront of low taxation and privacy. In recent years, Nevada has liberalized its corporation laws and decided to offer itself as a haven for those seeking to avoid the high taxes of most states.

Thousands of businesses around the country decide to incorporate or form an LLC in Nevada every year. This has spawned a growth industry of registered agent companies which helps Nevada keep its low tax status.

Anyone who is thinking of forming a corporation or LLC should consider the benefits of Nevada and weigh them against the small costs involved.

The main reason people incorporate or form an LLC is to avoid personal liability. While sole proprietors and partners have all of their personal assets at risk, corporate shareholders and LLC members risk only what they paid for their stock or membership interests. With so many people ready to sue for any reason or for no reason, the corporation and LLC are two of the few inexpensive protections left.

Creating a simple corporation or LLC is very easy and it is the purpose of this book to explain, in simple language, how you can do it yourself. A simple corporation or LLC as used in this book is one in which there are five or fewer participants and all of them are active in the business. If you plan to sell interests to someone who is not active in the business or to have many more participants, you should seek the advice of an attorney. However, some guidance is provided throughout this book as to what some of the concerns will be in these circumstances.

If your situation is in any way complicated or involves factors not mentioned in this book, you should seek the advice of an attorney practicing business law. The cost of a short consultation can be a lot cheaper than the consequences of violating the law.

If you plan to sell shares to outside investors, you should consult with a lawyer who specializes in securities laws. Selling a few thousand shares to friends and neighbors may sound like an easy way to raise capital for your business, but it is not! Since the stock market crash of 1929, there have been federal laws regulating the sale of securities. There are harsh criminal penalties for violators and the laws don't have many loopholes. The basic rules are explained in chapter 7.

This book also explains the basics of corporate taxation, but you should discuss your own particular situation with your accountant before deciding what system to use for your business. He or she can also set you up with an efficient system of bookkeeping which can save both time and money.

Good luck with your new business!

Should You Incorporate in Nevada?

1

Before you take the big step of organizing a Nevada corporation or LLC, you should understand the advantages and disadvantages of corporations and LLCs in comparison to the advantages and disadvantages of using the state of Nevada. For simplicity, when we say "incorporate" in this book, we will be referring to forming either a corporation or LLC.

Advantages of Corporations and LLCs

For nearly any type of business, the corporation or LLC is preferred over the sole proprietorship or partnership. Except for the smallest home-based business, it is foolish to operate without the protections these entities offer. This section will review the advantages of using a corporation or LLC as your business entity.

LIMITED LIABILITY

The main reason for forming a corporation or LLC is to limit the liability of the owners. In a sole proprietorship or partnership the owners are personally liable for the debts and liabilities of the business, and creditors can often go after their assets to collect business debts. If a corporation or LLC is formed and operated properly, the owners can be protected from all such liability.

EXAMPLES

☞ If several people are in partnership and one of them makes many large extravagant purchases in the name of the partnership, the other partners can be held liable for the full amount of all such purchases. The creditors can take the bank accounts, cars, real estate, and other property of any partner to pay the debts of the partnership. If only one partner has money, he or she may have to pay all of the debts accumulated by all the other partners. When doing business in the corporate form, the corporation may go bankrupt and the shareholders may lose their initial investment, but the creditors cannot touch the assets of the owners.

☞ If a person runs a taxi business and one of the drivers causes a terrible accident, the owner of the taxi can be held liable for the full amount of the damages. If the taxi driver was on drugs and killed several people and the damages amount to millions of dollars more than the insurance coverage, the owner may lose everything he owns. With a corporation, only the corporation would be liable. The owner couldn't be touched even if there was not enough money or insurance. One true example was a business owner who owned hundreds of taxis. He put one or two in each of hundreds of different corporations which he owned. Each corporation only had minimum insurance and when one taxi was involved in an accident the owner only lost the assets of that corporation.

WARNING

Note: The corporation will not protect him from the consequences of his own act or from the debt if a corporate officer or shareholder does something negligent himself, or signs a debt personally, or guarantees a corporate debt. Also, if a corporation does not follow the proper corporate formalities, it may be ignored by a court and the owners or officers may be held personally liable. The formalities include having separate bank accounts, holding meetings, and keeping minutes. When a court ignores a corporate structure and holds the owners or officers liable, it is called *piercing the corporate veil.*

CONTINUOUS EXISTENCE

A corporation or LLC may have a perpetual existence. When a sole proprietor or partner dies, the assets of their business may go to their heirs but the business does not exist any longer. If the surviving spouse or other heirs of a business owner want to continue the business in their own names, they will be considered a new business even if they are using the assets of the old business. With a partnership, the death of one partner could cause a dissolution of the business.

EXAMPLES
☛ If a person dies owning a sole proprietorship, his or her spouse may want to continue the business. That person may inherit all of the assets but will have to start a new business. This means getting new licenses and tax numbers, registering the name, and establishing credit from scratch. With a corporation or LLC, the business could continue with all of the same licenses, bank accounts, etc.

☛ If one partner dies and no prior agreements allow continuation of the business, the partnership may be forced to close. The heirs of the deceased partner may be able to force the sale of their share of the assets of the partnership even if the surviving partner needs them to continue the business. If he does not have the money to buy out the heirs, the business may have to be dissolved. With a corporation or properly drawn LLC agreement, the surviving member could be allowed to buy out the interest of the deceased one.

EASE OF TRANSFERABILITY
A corporation and all of its assets and accounts may be transferred by the simple assignment of a stock certificate. An LLC may be transferred with an assignment of a membership interest. With a sole proprietorship, each of the individual assets must be transferred and the accounts, licenses, and permits must be individually transferred.

EXAMPLE
☛ If a sole proprietorship is sold, the new owner will have to get a new occupational license, set up his own bank account, and apply for a new taxpayer identification number. The title to any vehicles and real estate will have to be put in his name and all open accounts will have to be changed to his name. He will probably have to submit new credit applications. With a corporation, all of these items remain in the same corporate name. As the new shareholder, he would elect himself director and as director, he would elect himself president, treasurer, and any other offices he wanted to hold.

Note: In some cases, the new owners will have to submit personal applications for such things as credit lines or liquor licenses.

TRANSFER OF
OWNERSHIP

By distributing stock or different types of membership interests, the owner of a corporation or LLC can share the profits of a business without giving up control. This is done by keeping a majority of ownership or by issuing different classes of ownership some with and some without voting rights.

☛ If a person wants to give his children some of the profits of his business, he can give them stock and pay dividends to them without giving them any control over the management. This would not be practical with a partnership or sole proprietorship.

EASE OF
RAISING CAPITAL

A corporation or LLC may raise capital by selling stock or membership interests. A corporation or LLC does not pay taxes on money it raises by the sale of stock or membership interests.

☛ If a company wants to expand, the owners can sell off ten percent, fifty percent, or ninety percent of the stock and still remain in control of the business. The people putting up the money may be more willing to invest if they know they will have a piece of the action than if they were making a loan with a limited return. They may not want to become partners in a partnership.

Note: There are strict rules about the sale of stock with criminal penalties and triple damages for violators. See chapter 7.

SEPARATE RECORD
KEEPING

A corporation or LLC has all its own bank accounts and records. A sole proprietor may have trouble differentiating which of his expenses were for business and which were for personal items.

TAX ADVANTAGES

There are some tax advantages that are available only to corporations or LLCs. Some of these are:

☛ medical insurance for your family may be fully deductible;

☛ a tax deferred trust can be set up for a retirement plan; and

☛ losses are fully deductible for a corporation, but an individual must prove there was a profit motive before deducting losses.

EASE OF ESTATE
PLANNING

With a corporation or LLC, shares of a company can be distributed more easily than with a partnership or sole proprietorship. Different heirs can be given different percentages and control can be limited to those who are most capable.

PRESTIGE

The name of a corporation or LLC sounds more prestigious than the name of a sole proprietor to some people. John Smith d/b/a Acme Builders sounds like one lone guy. Acme Builders, Incorporated, or Acme Builders, LLC sounds like it might be a large operation. No one needs to know that it is run out of a garage. One female writer on the subject has suggested that a woman who is president of a corporation looks more successful than one doing business in her own name. This probably applies to everyone.

SEPARATE
CREDIT RATING

A corporation or LLC has its own credit rating, which can be better or worse than the owner's credit rating. A corporation or LLC can go bankrupt while the owner's credit remains unaffected, or an owner's credit may be bad but the corporation may maintain a good rating.

DIFFERENCES BETWEEN CORPORATIONS AND LLCs

The limited liability company is the newest form of business entity and some have suggested that every business should adopt the form today. However, a closer look at the entities will show that they may offer advantages for some businesses, but for others, the corporate form may be better.

ADVANTAGES OF
CORPORATIONS

The main advantages that a corporation has over an LLC are:

History. The corporation has a long history and many thousands of court cases have decided the rights and obligations of the participants. Since the LLC was only invented a few years ago, there have been few court cases to spell out those rights. Thus a large business, especially one which plans to go public, might prefer the certainty of a corporation.

Taxes. The main advantage of an S corporation over an LLC is that profits taken out other than salary are not subject to social security and medicare taxes (15.3% of the first $68,400 and 2.9% of amounts over at the time of publication); whereas all profits of an LLC are subject to these taxes. However, there are proposals before Congress to end this benefit of S corporations.

There would not be much difference for a large business where the owners take out salaries of $68,400 or more plus profits. But for a smaller business where an owner would take out say, $30,000 salary and $20,000 profit, the extra taxes would be over $3,000.

Reorganizations. An S corporation is allowed under I.R.C. § 368 to have a tax-free merger or asset divestiture under certain circumstances, but an LLC is not. However, an LLC may switch to a corporate structure prior to reorganization to use these benefits.

ADVANTAGES
OF LLCs

The main advantages that an LLC has over a corporation are:

Asset protection. In some states, the interest a member owns in an LLC can be protected from the rights of that member's creditors. While corporate stock can be seized and sold by a creditor, in some states an interest in an LLC is only subject to a creditor's *charging order*. This means that the creditor only gets what the other members of the LLC decide to give him. He cannot sell the interest because the interest is not assignable. The creditor cannot vote in place of the former member and he cannot require the LLC to dissolve.

Formality. It is presumed by most legal experts that an LLC requires less formality than a corporation. While improper procedures in a corporation may allow a creditor to *pierce the corporate veil* and hold shareholders liable, the LLC is clearly meant to be a safe harbor to protect business owners from liability.

Taxes. An LLC can make special allocations of profits and losses among members [as long as the tests of Treas. Reg. § 1.704(b) are satisfied]; whereas an S corporation cannot. An S corporation must have one class of ownership in which profits and losses are allocated according to the percentage ownership.

In an LLC, money borrowed by the company can increase the tax basis of the owners (and lower the taxes); whereas in an S corporation, it does not.

Contributing property to set up an LLC is not taxable even for minority interest owners; however, for a corporation IRC § 351 only allows it to be tax free for the contributors who have control of the business.

An S corporation may lose its favorable tax status for five years if an interest is acquired by a foreign person, another corporation, or a certain kind of trust, and it may not have more than seventy-five shareholders. An LLC has no such limitations.

When an LLC buys out a member, it may increase its basis in a portion of the receivables and tangible assets, but an S corporation may not. When a third party buys the interest of a member the LLC may make an election under I.R.C. § 754 to increase its basis in assets. An S corporation cannot.

Upon death of an owner, the person inheriting an S corporation interest may need to pay taxes on more income (under I.R.C. § 691) than a person inheriting a similar LLC.

Newness. Another advantage may be psychological. The LLC is a new entity, and in the twenty-first century it may look more up-to-date to be an LLC than an ordinary corporation.

ADVANTAGES OF NEVADA

The state of Nevada and many promoters have lists of the advantages of Nevada corporations over those in other states. Not all of these work for everyone, so we'll review each of them.

SECRETARY OF
STATE

The Secretary of State of Nevada lists the following as advantages:

No corporate income tax. Most states impose a corporate income tax, although many exempt S corporations. If you need a C corporation or live in a state which does not exempt S corporations, then a Nevada corporation can offer substantial tax savings.

One method for saving taxes is to form two corporations, one in Nevada and one in your home state. Your local corporation engages in business and is subject to state taxes, but is has no assets and makes no profit. Any assets can be leased from the Nevada corporation or subject to a lien by the Nevada corporation. Any income of the local corporation would be paid to you as salary or to the Nevada corporation as lease payments, purchases of supplies, etc. See the next chapter for more information on this.

No taxes on corporate shares. Many states tax corporate shares either initially (on issuance) or annually. If you are in one of these states, Nevada can save you money.

No franchise tax. This is an annual tax that some states assess on the "privilege" of having a corporation. (California charges a minimum of $800 a year which rises to thousands of dollars for larger businesses.)

No personal income tax. Since most states impose a personal income tax, forming a Nevada corporation would not exempt you from your home state's tax on your personal income. However, you may be able to leave profits in your Nevada corporation and avoid paying your state income tax on them.

No I.R.S. information sharing agreement. The governor of Nevada once held a press conference to announce that the state of Nevada refused to share information with the I.R.S. This was a nice publicity stunt, but there is also the possibility that the I.R.S. will look more carefully at Nevada corporations, if it thinks they are being promoted as vehicles for tax fraud.

Nominal annual fees. Nevada's $85 per year fee is lower than most states, but there are a few states which have lower annual fees.

Minimal reporting and disclosure requirements. Nevada's annual report is short and requires disclosure of the names and addresses (which may be P.O. boxes) of the president, secretary, treasurer, and directors, but not of other officers (vice-presidents, assistant secretary or assistant treasurer). Many, but not all, states require more information to be disclosed. Some commentators suggest that a corporation hire a person in Nevada (whom the commentator can usually supply) to be the directors/president/secretary/treasurer. Since this person is never available, the corporation's "real" owner serves as vice-president, acting secretary, and acting treasurer. See the warning on the next page.

Stockholders are not public record. In some, but not all states stockholders are public record, so if this is true in your state then a Nevada corporation would offer more privacy.

Directors need not be stockholders. In some states, however, directors must be stockholders.

Trade for stock is allowed. Nevada corporations can issue stock in exchange for services, personal property, or real estate. Also, the directors' determination of the value of these is final. Some other states do not allow such exchanges. However, you should keep in mind that for tax purposes, the valuation must meet I.R.S. guidelines.

PROMOTERS Some other promoters of Nevada corporations have suggested that the following are also benefits of the Nevada corporation:

Bearer stock. The advantage of bearer stock is that if you do not possess it, you do not own it; therefore, if you are put under oath and asked if you own any stock, you may be able to answer no if you gave the certificate to someone else. However, a smart lawyer will ask you to name any stocks you have owned in the recent past. Failure to disclose this information under oath would be perjury. Also, Nevada law requires that a corporation keep a list of its shareholders, either at their Nevada registered office or at a location which is listed at the Nevada registered office. Thus a corporation which did not require shareholders to disclose their ownership would itself be in technical violation of Nevada law.

No interim filings. Some states require that the current directors or officers be kept on record with the state. Nevada requires only that such information be filed once a year. The theory is that you can hire someone to be a director and officer for the one day the filing is made, then fire him and elect yourself for the next 364 days until the next filing is due, and never have yourself on record. *Warning:* While tactics such as this are legal under the technical reading of the statutes, you should keep in mind that courts have a wide leeway in redressing wrongs. If someone uses technically legal tactics to defraud people, a court could still hold him liable. Sometimes these things can be fit into criminal statutes such as "conspiracy" or "scheme to defraud." And there are legal principles which are not always in the statutes which allow courts to reach what they feel is a just result even when someone followed all the technical rules.

DISADVANTAGES OF NEVADA

For most people, the advantages of a Nevada corporation outweigh the costs; but for people in states with no income tax and minimum corporate requirements, they may not. Here are the disadvantages of incorporating your business in Nevada rather than in your home state.

NEVADA REGISTERED AGENT AND OFFICE

First, as a Nevada corporation you will need to have a registered agent and registered office in the state of Nevada. If you incorporate in your own state, you can usually use your own business office as the registered agent and you or one of your employees could be the registered agent.

However, the fee to hire a Nevada registered agent and registered office is around $100 a year so this is not a burden except for the smallest enterprise. A list of corporate agents is included in this book in appendix C.

HOME STATE
REGISTRATION

Second, as a Nevada corporation, you may need to register as a "foreign corporation" in the state in which you are actually doing business. However, this is usually a simple procedure of filing a form and paying a fee each year. In some states, this is a small fee but in others it is considerable. A list of state offices with which you must register is included in this book in appendix B.

One exception is if the corporation is not actually "doing business" anywhere. If it merely owns real estate or passive investments, it may not have to register. Some people form a Nevada corporation to own their assets and then form a second corporation to engage in business in another state. The Nevada corporation loans money or assets to the local corporation and sometimes sells goods or services to it. The local corporation never has any net worth or makes a profit and is therefore judgment proof and tax free. Meanwhile, the Nevada corporation is not subject to income tax if far away and not involved in any risky activities.

LAWSUITS

A third disadvantage is that as a Nevada corporation, you can be sued in Nevada. If you are doing business with anyone in or near Nevada, it would be easier for them to sue you and harder for you to defend yourself far away from where you reside.

TAX CONSIDERATIONS 2

CORPORATION TAX ISSUES

A corporation has a choice of how it wants to be taxed. It can make the election at the beginning of its existence or at the beginning of a new tax year. The choices are as follows:

S CORPORATION Formerly called a *Subchapter S corporation*, an *S corporation* pays no income tax and may only be used for businesses with a limited number of shareholders. All of the income or losses of the corporation for the year are passed through to the shareholders who report them on their individual returns. The corporation files an *information return* listing all of its income, expenses, depreciation, etc. at the end of each year and sends a notice of his or her share to each shareholder as determined by percentage of stock ownership.

Advantages. Using this method avoids double taxation and allows pass-through of losses and depreciation. The business is treated like a partnership. Since many businesses have tax losses during the first years due to start-up costs, it can be advantageous to elect S status in the beginning and switch over to C corporation status in later years. Once a corporation terminates its S status, there is a five year waiting period before it can switch back.

Disadvantages. If stockholders are in high tax brackets, their share of the profits will be taxed at those rates. Shareholders who do not "materially participate" in the business cannot deduct losses. Some fringe benefits such as health and life insurance may not be tax deductible in an S corporation; whereas they would be in a C corporation or LLC.

Requirements. To qualify for S corporation status the corporation must:

☛ have no more than seventy-five shareholders, none of whom are non-resident aliens or corporations, all of whom consent to the election (shares owned by a husband and wife jointly are considered owned by one shareholder);

☛ have only one class of stock;

☛ not be a member of an "affiliated group" of companies;

☛ generate at least twenty percent of its income in this country and have no more than twenty percent of its income from "passive" sources (interest, rents, dividends, royalties, securities transactions); and

☛ file Form 2553 before the end of the fifteenth day of the third month of the tax year for which it is to be effective and have it approved by the IRS.

Multiple Corporations. The IRS has approved the use of two or more S corporations in partnership to increase the number of allowable investors in a venture. It may also be possible for an S corporation to form a partnership with a C corporation.

C CORPORATION

A C *corporation* pays taxes on its net earnings at corporate tax rates. Salaries of officers, directors, and employees are deducted from income so they are not taxed to the corporation, but money paid out in dividends is taxed twice. It is taxed at the corporation's rate as part of its profit, and then the stockholders must include the amounts they receive as dividends in their income.

Advantages. If taxpayers are in a higher tax bracket than the corporation and the money will be left in the company for expansion, taxes are saved. Fringe benefits such as health, accident, and life insurance are deductible expenses.

Disadvantages. Double taxation of dividends by the federal government is the biggest problem with a C corporation. But this tax does not apply to money taken out as salaries, and many small business owners take all profits out as salaries to avoid double taxation. But there are rules requiring that salaries be reasonable and if a stockholder's salary is deemed to be too high, in relation to his or her job, the salary may be considered dividends and subject to the double taxation.

Requirements. There are no requirements to incorporating. All corporations are C corporations unless they specifically elect to become S corporations.

LLC TAX ISSUES

When LLCs were first started a few years ago, they had to follow strict rules in order to qualify for advantageous tax treatment. Single business owners could not qualify for pass-through taxation because it wasn't considered logical to treat a single person as a partnership.

Fortunately, common sense prevailed and there are now no hoops to jump through. You merely obtain form 8832 and check the box indicating whether you wish to be taxed like a corporation or to pass the income through to the owners and have them declare it on their personal returns. Form 8832 is included in this book in appendix D.

Since one of the reasons LLCs were developed was to allow businesses to enjoy partnership taxation with corporate protections from liability, not many LLCs will select to be taxed as corporations.

Using Dual Corporations

As mentioned in the previous chapter, an advantage of the Nevada corporation is that Nevada has no corporate or personal income taxes. One way to take advantage of this if you are doing business in a state which does have a corporate income tax is to form two corporations, one in Nevada and one in your state, and have the Nevada corporation make the profits and the local corporation break even.

For example, suppose you were a painting contractor who owned a building and equipment. You could incorporate in your home state as a painting contractor but put the building and equipment into a Nevada corporation. The Nevada corporation would then lease these to the local corporation. After paying the workers, buying supplies, paying your a salary, and making lease payments to the Nevada corporation, your local company could break even with no taxable profit. The profit would all be in the Nevada corporation which does not pay taxes in your state.

From a federal tax standpoint, there would seldom be an issue because taxes would have to be paid on the profits of any corporation, whether or not it was a Nevada corporation.

There would be a couple issues from a state tax standpoint. One is whether the Nevada corporation was "doing business" in your state. It might not even need to register as doing business in your state if the acts of the Nevada corporation are passive enough. For example, if it just loaned money to your corporation it would not have to register (especially if you happened to go to Las Vegas to sign the papers). In most states, merely owning rental real estate does not require a corporation to register.

A second issue would be whether your state has any catch-all tax laws which would prevent this kind of setup. If you are going to start two corporations for this purpose, you should meet with a local tax specialist to be sure that it is done correctly under your state requirements.

EMPLOYER IDENTIFICATION NUMBER

Prior to opening a bank account the corporation must obtain a *employer identification number*, (EIN), sometimes called a taxpayer identification number. This would be the corporate equivalent of a social security number. This is done by filing form SS-4, which is included in this book as form 3. This usually takes two or three weeks, so it should be filed early. Send the form to the address on page 2 or 3 of the instructions.

If you need the number quickly, you may be able to obtain it by phone by calling the IRS and reading the information on your form. The telephone number depends upon the state you are in and is listed on page 2 of the form. Be sure to have your SS-4 form complete and in front of you when you call.

When you apply for this number, you will probably be put on the mailing list for other corporate tax forms. If you do not receive these, you should call your local IRS forms number and request the forms for new businesses. These include Circular E explaining the taxes due, the W-4 forms for each employee, the tax deposit coupons and the Form 941 quarterly return for withholding.

SALES AND USE TAX ISSUES

IN STATE   In most states, you will need to collect a sales and use tax on each sale if your business will be providing goods or services to the public. Most states exempt various items such as food, medicines or certain types of services. You should contact the state department of revenue in each state in which you do business to register as a collector of the tax and to obtain the rules and regulations. Your business is liable for the tax even if you do not collect it and must remit the taxes even if the state does not send you the forms on time. If your registration materials do not arrive in time for your first filing, you may be able to get temporary forms from your local tax office to avoid a penalty for late filing.

OUT OF STATE   In 1992, the United States Supreme Court safeguarded the rights of small businesses by ruling that state tax authorities cannot force them to collect sales taxes on interstate mail orders (*Quill Corporation v. North Dakota*). This means, for example, that a business in Iowa that sells something by mail to someone in New York does not have to figure out New York tax laws, collect New York taxes and send them to New York tax authorities. If this case had ruled the other way, every small business would have to keep track of taxes in all fifty states (and many cities), many of which require annual fees and that a bond be posted. This would have put all but the biggest companies out of business.

Unfortunately, the court left open the possibility that Congress could allow interstate taxation of mail order sales, several bills which would do so have since been introduced. One, introduced by Arkansas senator Dale Bumpers, was given the Orwellian "newspeak" title, *The Consumer and Main Street Protection Act*. And in 1999, the American Booksellers Association began a national campaign to force mail order and internet sellers to collect sales taxes.

At present, companies are only required to collect sales taxes for states in which they *do business*. Exactly what business is enough to trigger taxation is a legal question and some states try to define it as broadly as possible.

If you have an office in a state, clearly you are doing business there, and any goods shipped to consumers in the state are subject to sales taxes. If you have a full time employee working in the state most of the year, many states will consider you doing business there. In some states, attending a two-day trade show is enough business to trigger taxation for the entire year for every order shipped to the state. One loophole that often works is to be represented at shows by persons who are not your employees.

Because the laws are different in each state, you will have to do some research on a state-by-state basis to find out how much business you can do in a state without being subject to their taxation. You can request a state's rules from its department of revenue, but keep in mind that what a department of revenue wants the law to be is not always what the courts will rule that it is.

BUSINESS TAXES

Being subject to a state's income or other business taxes is even worse than being subject to its sales taxes. For example, California charges every company doing business in the state a minimum $800 a year fee and charges income tax on a portion of the company's worldwide income. Doing a small amount of business in the state is clearly not worth getting mired in California taxation.

Some trade shows have been moved from California for this reason and this has resulted in a review of the tax policies and some "safe-harbor" guidelines to advise companies on what they can do without becoming subject to taxation. Write to the department of revenue of any state with which you have business contacts to see what might trigger your taxation.

INTERNET TAXES

State revenue departments are drooling at the prospect of taxing commerce on the Internet. Theories have already been proposed that websites available to state residents mean a company is doing business in a state.

Fortunately, Congress has passed a moratorium on taxation of the Internet. This will hopefully be extended and will give us a new tax-free world, but don't count on it. A government has never let a new source of revenue go untapped. It would take a tremendous outcry to keep the Internet tax-free. But perhaps the Internet can be used as a new "enterprise zone" to encourage business growth. Keep an eye out for any news stories on proposals to tax the Internet and petition your representatives against them.

If laws are passed to tax the Internet, there may still be ways around them. For many types of businesses, especially companies which can provide their goods or services over the Internet, it would be possible to set up the business on a tax-free Caribbean island. With no state presence, no taxes would be due to any state.

CANADIAN TAXES

Apparently oblivious to the logic of the U.S. Supreme Court, the Canadian government expects American companies, which sell goods by mail order to Canadians, to collect taxes for them and file returns with Revenue Canada, their tax department.

Those that receive an occasional unsolicited order are not expected to register, and Canadian customers who order things from the U.S. pay the tax plus a $5 fee upon receipt of the goods. But companies that solicit Canadian orders are expected to be registered if their worldwide income is $30,000 or more per year. In some cases, a company may be required to post a bond and to pay for the cost of Canadian auditors visiting its premises and auditing its books! For these reasons, you may notice that some companies decline to accept orders from Canada. So much for the benefits of NAFTA.

YOUR BUSINESS NAME 3

The very first thing to do before starting a new business is to choose a great name and thoroughly check it out to be sure that no one else already has legal rights to it.

CHOOSING YOUR BUSINESS NAME

While the quality of your goods or services will improve the value of your name, having a great name can give the initial image of your company the boost it needs for people to give it a try. Consider if you were looking for a flight to Paris and the two airlines you had to choose from were Air International and Barney's Airline and Baitshop! Or if you needed a repair to your office computer and two computer repair shops were called Heather's Techsters on Wheels and Micro Systems Services.

These are exaggerations of course, but you get the idea that when all you have to go on is a name, one that sounds more knowledgeable or established will probably attract more business.

Some people have started a business as a lark, used a silly name and watched it grow so big that the name became embarrassing. You may think that if you are lucky enough to have your business explode, you won't mind changing the name. Perhaps a silly name can be used to challenge fate. You can just hope to get so big that the name has to be changed.

But changing a business name is more complicated than you think. After years of establishing a name and reputation, changing it can be costly, both in time and expense and in lost business.

GUIDELINES   In choosing a name, you should use the following guidelines.

Use the right suffix. Nevada law requires that certain words or suffixes be a part of the name of a company. In chapter 4 is a list of those required for a corporation and in chapter 5 is a list of those required for an LLC.

Don't use forbidden words. Certain words are not allowed to be used as part of a company name without approval or special licensing. See the following chapters for more details.

Don't be too similar. While there might seem to be some advantage to having your name sound like a more successful competitor, it may be more trouble than it is worth. If a name is found by a court to be confusingly similar, it can order the user to stop using it and to pay damages. The legal costs of fighting a large corporation with deep pockets can bankrupt a small business.

For example, Toys 'R' Us® sues any company that it finds using "R Us" in its name (Insurance R Us, Flowers R Us). Their claim was not strong, because legally, using the same name in another field of commerce was not an infringement of a trademark. They won because little companies could not afford to spend $50,000 or $100,000 fighting them in court. Now, however, the law protects famous trademarks from anyone using similar names.

On the other side, if you are looking for some free publicity for your fledgling business, you're sure to get written up in the local papers if a international corporation threatens to squash you for innocently using a similar name.

Be sure it's not confusing. Many words, especially in the English language, are spelled differently from how they sound. Be sure that the name you choose is easy to spell and for people to look up in the phone book, on the Internet, or elsewhere. Someone once published a list of all the remaining English words which had not yet been registered with ".com" and most of them were hard to spell or had confusing homonyms.

SOFTWARE   There is computer software available which is claimed to be helpful in the process of choosing a name. While it is costly for a one-time use, it may be worthwhile if you plan to name several products, or you may be able to find someone who will let you use it once for a fee.

CONSULTANTS   There are consultants who offer their services in choosing an ideal name; however, for a new business, the fee is usually too high. A business magazine once ran a story about a major corporation that paid a consultant $50,000 to come up with a name for a new breakfast cereal. The magazine also polled its own staff for suggestions based on the criteria given to the consultant and their staff produced the same name!

SEARCHING THE NAME

Once you have chosen the perfect name, you need to be sure that no else has established legal rights to it. Many business have been forced to stop using their name after spending thousands of dollars promoting it.

Legal rights can be established by registering a name as a trademark or by merely using the name. Consequently, you can't be sure no one has rights to a name just by checking registered names. You need to check to see if anyone is using the name who has not yet registered it.

The following are places you should check:

DIVISION OF   You should first check with the Nevada Division of Corporations to see CORPORATIONS   if there is another corporation with the same name. They publicize a nine-hundred number you can use to reserve up to three names for thirty days for $10 (900-420-8042). You can call their regular line first at no charge to find out if the name is available (302-739-3073).

TRADEMARKS   Next, you should check the United States Patent and Trademark Office to see if anyone has registered it as a trademark. There are several ways you can do this:

Online search. The records of the trademark office were put online in 1999. You can now search every registered and pending trademark at the following site: http://www.uspto.gov/tmdb/index.html.

If you do not have access to the Internet at your home or office, you may be able to access it on a computer at a public library. If you are not familiar with how to get online, you may be able to have someone at the library perform the search either for a small fee or for free.

Federal depository libraries. You can also search trademarks at the numerous federal depository libraries around the country. These are usually connected with universities. Either your local public or university library can tell you where the nearest federal depository library is located.

Search firms. If you would rather have someone else do the search, you can hire a professional search firm. In addition to a trademark search, they can check other records around the country and give you a more accurate answer as to whether the name is being used anywhere. The cost can range from about $100 to over $500 depending on how thorough the search is and who is doing it. The following are a few firms that do searches. You can call them for a quote.

> Government Liaison Services, Inc.
> 3030 Clarendon Blvd., Suite 209
> P. O. Box 10648
> Arlington, VA 22210
> (800) 642-6564; (703) 524-8200
>
> Thomson & Thomson
> 500 Victory Road
> North Quincy, MA 02171-1545
> (800) 692-8833
>
> XL Corporate Service
> 62 White Street
> New York, NY 10013
> (800) 221-2972

TELEPHONE
LISTINGS

Since some businesses neglect to properly register their name (yet still may have superior rights to it), you should also check phone books and business directories. Some libraries have phone books from around the country as well as directories of trade names, but using the Internet is much easier.

If you have a computer with Internet access, you can search every yellow pages listing for free. Just search for "yellow pages" with any web search engine (e.g., Yahoo, WebCrawler, Lycos, etc.). You can select a state, enter your business name, and it will tell you if any other companies are listed with that name. One site that allows you to search all states at once is: http://www.switchboard.com.

If you do not have access to a computer, you may be able to use one at your public library or have the search done at your library for a small fee.

REGISTERING YOUR NAME

Once you have chosen the right name for your new company, you should register it before someone else does.

DIVISION OF
CORPORATIONS

By forming your corporation with the state of Nevada, you have insured that no other person can register a company with the same name. However, this does not stop someone from registering the name with another state or getting a trademark for it.

FEDERAL
TRADEMARK

A federal trademark gives the owner the right to use the name anywhere in the United States and to stop most others from using it.

☛ Suppose you want to start a motel chain and find that no one has registered the name Rip Van Winkle Inns as a trademark. You checked the Internet, business directories, and yellow pages listings and no one is using it. One you register a federal trademark, you can stop anyone else from using the name except those who have previously used it. Suppose a small motel in Arizona has used the name, but it didn't show up in your search. Because they used the name first, they have legal rights to it in their area. You have rights everywhere else. You can't use the name in their immediate area in competition with them, but they can't expand outside of their area now that you own the name.

Before attempting to register the name, you should know that the following rules apply to federal trademarks.

☞ You cannot register the name of a business. A trademark is a name symbol, or other device use to identify goods; and a service mark is the same as used to identify services.

☞ You cannot be fully registered until you actually use the mark. You can file an application indicating your intent to use a mark, but you must actually use it before registration is accomplished.

☞ In order to qualify for federal registration, you must use your mark in commerce, which means between states or with a foreign country. The use must be bona fide, meaning you can't just mail a copy to a relative or friend.

☞ You can register your trademark with each state. If you plan to get a federal trademark immediately this is not necessary, but if you plan to limit your business to one state or don't plan to expand out of state for a number of years, state registration is faster and cheaper than federal.

☞ Trademarks are registered according to classes of goods. If you plan to use your mark on such different products as tires, lubricants and window glass, you will need to register (and pay a filing fee of $245) for each class.

Registering a federal trademark is beyond the scope of this book, but you have get more information from the USPTO website (http://www.uspto.gov). You can also find all the forms and instructions in the book *How to Register Your Own Trademark* by the author and publisher of this book.

FICTITIOUS NAMES	Sometimes it seems like every good name is taken. Nonetheless, a name can sometimes be used if it is modified slightly or used on a different type of goods.

☛ If you want to use the name "Flowers by Freida" in San Francisco and there is already a "Flowers by Freida, Inc." in Los Angeles, you might incorporate under the name "Freida Jones, Inc." and then register the corporation as doing business under the fictitious name "Flowers by Freida." Unless "Flowers by Freida, Inc." has registered a trademark for the name either in California or nationally, you will probably be able to use the name. *Note:* You should realize that you might run into complications later, especially if you decide to expand into other areas of the state. One protection available would be to register the name as a trademark. This would give you exclusive use of the name anywhere that someone else was not already using it.

SUBCLASSES	If someone else is already using a trademark you want to use and in the same class in which you plan to use the mark, it is possible to register the mark if your goods are different enough.

☛ For example, if you wanted to use the word "bud" (as in buddy) on on an electronic game for boys, but someone else had registered bud (picturing a rosebud) as the name of a doll, you might be able to register in the same category (#28 games and playthings) since the products are different and are aimed at different audiences. However, being so close is just inviting trouble and if you were in the same category as Bud in Budweiser®, it would be suicide.

Corporate Paperwork 4

This chapter explains the specific paperwork you must file to form a corporation. If you are forming an LLC, you should skip this chapter and go on to chapter 5. After completing the paperwork in this chapter, you should continue to chapter 6 for the rest of the start-up procedures.

Articles of Incorporation

The act which legally creates the corporation is the filing of the articles of incorporation with the Secretary of State. Some corporations have long, elaborate articles that spell out numerous powers and functions, but most of this is unnecessary. The powers of corporations are spelled out in Nevada law (See § 78.060 in appendix A) and do not have to be repeated. The main reason to keep the articles of incorporation short is to avoid having to amend them later. Putting all but the basics in the bylaws of the corporation makes altering the corporate structure much easier. The articles included in this book (form 8) are as simple as possible for this reason.

Nevada law requires that only five things be included in the articles of incorporation, these items are as follows:

1. the name of the corporation;

2. the name and street address of the registered agent;

3. the number of shares authorized;

4. whether the people on the governing board are called directors or trustees, and the names and addresses of the first board; and

5. the names and addresses of incorporators (may be post office box).

Some of the rules you must follow when preparing the articles are:

Name of the corporation. If the name of the corporation looks like the name of a person, it must include one of the following words, abbreviations, or other words which identify the business as not being a natural person.

company	co.
corporation	corp.
incorporated	inc.
limited	ltd.

While it is not required by the statutes, it is wise for all corporations to use one of these words or abbreviations. If it does not, someone may successfully argue in court that they did not know they were dealing with a corporation and that the owners should be held personally liable.

One cannot use the words "bank" or "trust" or other words indicating that the company is a financial institution without approval of the commissioner of financial institutions (NRS 78.045). The company must get the approval of the commissioner of insurance if the name of the company or anything else in the articles indicates that the company will be in the insurance business. Except for publicly traded companies which are not in the professional engineering businesses, no business may use words such as "engineer" or "engineering" unless the principals of the company are certified to be licensed or exempt from licensing by the state board of professional engineers.

Name and address of the registered agent. The name and street address of the address in the state of Nevada of the registered agent must be provided. If the mailing address is different than the street address, this must be provided as well. If you will not be using your own office in Nevada, you will need to make arrangements with a registered agent in the state. Some of those that provide this service are listed in appendix C. The registered agent must either sign the articles accepting the position or sign a separate paper stating that he accepts.

The classes of stock. If more than one class is authorized, the classes, the series, and number of shares of each class or series must be included unless the articles give the directors the power to set classes, series and numbers of shares under NRS 78.195 and 78.196.

Whether there are directors or trustees. A Nevada corporation may call its controlling board either trustees or directors. The members of the first board must be listed with their addresses which can be home, business, or post office box. They must all be at least eighteen years of age. If you wish to have provisions for changing the number of directors as provide in NRS 78.115, they should be included here.

The name and address of the incorporator(s). The address can be home, business, or post office box. The incorporator is usually one of the parties starting the business, but it may be any person, even if that person has no future interest in the corporation. For people who need to be incorporated quickly, there are companies in Nevada that can, on a moment's notice, have someone sign and run over to the Division of Corporations to file a certificate of incorporation which is later assigned to the real parties in interest. Each incorporator must sign and the signature(s) must be notarized.

FORMS The Secretary of State provides a form for the articles of incorporation (which is included in appendix D), but it is not required that you use this form. You can type the document on blank paper.

FEES According to the schedule provided on the next page, the filing fee is a minimum of least $125.

<u>Stock with no par value</u>

$1 per share

<u>Stock with par value</u>

Capital $25,000 or less	125.00
Capital $25,001 to $75,000	175.00
Capital $75,001 to $200,000	225.00
Capital $200,001 to $500,000	325.00
Capital $500,001 to $1,000,000	425.00
Each additional $500,000 over $1,000,000	225.00
Maximum fee	$25,000.00

You must also include $10 plus a photocopy of the articles for each certified copy you need. You will need at least one copy because one certified copy must be kept with the registered agent in Nevada.

The return time for the articles is usually a week or so. If there is a need to have them back quickly you may request expedited filing for an additional $50 fee. A complete fee schedule is included in appendix A.

FILING   Your articles can be filed with the Secretary of State of Nevada by fax, mail, courier or over the counter. To pay by credit card use form 1 in appendix D. The fax number is 775-684-5725. The address is:

New Filings Division
101 N. Carson Street #3
Carson City, NV 89701-4786

ANNUAL
REPORT   After your articles have been filed, you will received an annual report which must be filed on or before the first day of the second month after filing of the articles. There is an $85 filing fee for this report. It must include the names and addresses of the president, secretary, treasurer, directors, and registered agent.

Bylaws and Minutes

Every corporation must have bylaws and must maintain a set of minutes of its meetings. The bylaws must be adopted at the first meeting and the first minutes of the corporation will be of the organizational meeting.

The bylaws are the rules for organization and operation of the corporation. Two sets of bylaws are included with this book; form 9 is for simple corporations and form 10 is for professional associations. In order to complete them, you should fill in the name of the corporation, the city of the main office of the corporation, the proposed date of the annual meeting (this can be varied each year as needed), and the number of directors to be on the board.

Nevada law allows corporate officers to execute incorporation papers without a meeting, but it is better to have a formal meeting to prove to possible future creditors that you conducted the corporation in a formal manner.

Shareholder Agreement

Whenever there are two or more shareholders in a corporation, they should consider drawing up a *shareholder agreement*. This document spells out what is to happen in the event of a disagreement between them. For example, the minority shareholders in small corporations have a risk of being locked into a long term enterprise with little or no way to withdraw their capital. A shareholder agreement is a fairly complicated document and you should consider having it drawn up by an attorney. This may be costly but the expense should be weighed against the costs of lengthy litigation should the parties separate. A less expensive alternative is to sit down and decide what will happen in the event of a shareholder's death, divorce, retirement, or decision to sell out, then write it up and have everyone sign. Some of the things which may be addressed in such an agreement are as follows:

Veto by minority shareholder

Greater than majority voting requirement

Cumulative voting

Deadlocks

Arbitration

Dissolution

Compulsory buy-out

Preemptive rights

Restrictions on transfers of shares

Refusal of a party to participate

IRS FORM 2553

If your corporation is to be taxed as an S corporation, you must file Form 2553 with the IRS within seventy-five days of incorporation. As a practical matter, you should sign and file this at your incorporation meeting; otherwise, you may forget. Form 2553 is included in this book as form 11. To make the S corporation status "official," you should also adopt a corporate resolution (form 15) electing to be taxed as an S corporation and keep it in your minute book.

CORPORATE SUPPLIES

A corporation needs to keep a permanent record of its legal affairs. This includes the original charter; minutes of all meetings; records of the stock issued, transferred, and cancelled; fictitious names registered; and any other legal matters. The records are usually kept in a ring binder. Any ring binder will do, but it is possible to purchase a specially prepared *corporate kit* that has the name of the corporation printed on it and usually contains forms such as minutes, stock certificates, etc. Most of these items are included with this book so purchasing such a kit is unnecessary unless you want to have a fancy leather binder or specially printed stock certificates.

Some sources for corporate kits are:

Ace Industries, Inc.
54 NW 11th St.
Miami, FL 33136-9978
(305) 358-2571
(800) 433-2571

Midstate Legal Supply Co., Inc.
P. O. Box 2122
Orlando, FL 32802
(407) 299-8220
(800) 432-8309

Corpex
480 Canal Street
New York, NY 10013
(800) 221-8181

One thing that is not included with this book is a *corporate seal*, which must be specially made for each corporation. Most corporations use a metal seal like a notary's seal to emboss the paper. These can be ordered from many office supply companies. In recent years, many have been using rubber stamps for corporate seals. These are cheaper, lighter, and easier to read. Rubber stamp seals can also be ordered from office supply stores, printers, and specialized rubber stamp companies. The corporate seal should contain the full, exact name of the corporation, the word "SEAL" and the year of incorporation. It may be round or rectangular.

Corporations are no longer required to issue stock certificates to represent shares of ownership. As a practical matter, it is a good idea to do so. This shows some formality and gives each person tangible evidence of ownership. If you do issue shares, the face of each certificate must show the corporate name; that the corporation was organized under Nevada law; the name of the shareholder(s); the number, class, and series of the stock. The certificate must be signed by one or more officers designated by the bylaws or the board of directors.

If there are two or more classes or series of stock, the front or back of the certificate must disclose that upon request and without charge the corporation will provide to the shareholder the preferences, limitations, and relative rights of each class or series; the preferences of any preferred stock; and the board of directors' authority to determine rights for any subsequent classes or series. If there are any restrictions, they must be stated on the certificate, or a statement must be included that they are available without charge.

The stock certificates can be fancy, such as with engraved eagles, or they can be typed or even handwritten. Stock certificate forms are included in appendix D. For professional associations, the following statement should be typed on the certificate: "The transfer of the shares represented by this certificate is restricted by the bylaws of the corporation."

LLC PAPERWORK 5

This chapter explains the specific paperwork you must file to form a limited liability company. If you are forming a corporation, you should ignore this chapter, use the instructions in chapter 4, and then go on to chapter 6.

ARTICLES OF ORGANIZATION

The act which creates a limited liability company is the filing of articles of organization with the Secretary of State in Carson City. Some LLCs have long, elaborate articles that spell out numerous powers and functions, but most of this is unnecessary. The powers of LLCs are spelled out in Nevada law (see NRS 86.281 in appendix A) and do not have to be repeated. The main reason to keep the articles of organization short is to avoid having to amend them later. Putting all but the basics in an operating agreement makes altering the structure much easier. The articles of organization included in this book (form 26) is as simple as possible for this reason.

Nevada law requires that only the name, address, registered agent, and management be listed in the articles of organization. These are the specific rules:

Name of the limited liability company. The company must include one of the following designations or abbreviations as part of the name:

Limited-Liability Company	L.L.C.	LLC
Limited Company	L.C.	LC
Limited	Ltd.	

The word "company" can be abbreviated "Co."

Name and address of the registered agent. The name and street address of the address in the state of Nevada of the registered agent must be provided. If the mailing address is different than the street address, this must be provided as well. If you will not be using your own office in Nevada, you will need to make arrangements with a registered agent in the state. Some of those that provide this service are listed in appendix C. The registered agent must either sign the articles accepting the position or sign a separate paper stating that he accepts.

The name and address of the organizer(s). The address given for the organizer can be from the home, business, or post office box. The organizer is usually one of the parties starting the business, but it may be any person, even if that person has no future interest in the company. For people who need to form their business quickly, there are companies in Nevada that can, on a moment's notice, have someone sign the articles of organization and run over to the Division of Corporations to file it. Each organizer must sign and the signature(s) must be notarized.

Management. The articles must specify whether the company is to be managed by the members or separate managers.

FORM   The Secretary of State provides a form for the articles of organization (which is included in appendix D), but it is not required that you use this form. You can type the document on blank paper.

FILING   The filing fee is $125. You must also include $10 plus a photocopy of the articles for each certified copy you need. You will need at least one copy because one certified copy must be kept with the registered agent in Nevada.

The return time for the articles is usually a week or so. If there is a need to have them back quickly, you may request expedited filing for an additional $50 fee. A complete fee schedule is included in appendix A.

Your articles can be filed with the Secretary of State of Nevada by fax, mail, courier, or over the counter. To pay by credit card, use form 1 in appendix D. The fax number is 775-684-5725. The address is:

> New Filings Division
> 101 N. Carson Street #3
> Carson City, NV 89701-4786

Operating Agreement

As mentioned in the previous chapter, an LLC must decide if it will be managed by all the members or a limited number of managers. If it is to be run by managers, there may be one or more and he or she may be a member or not a member.

In either case, it is important to have a written agreement spelling out the rights and duties of the members and managers if any. This is also a good document in which to include other rules governing the LLC. Even if an LLC has only one member, a membership agreement should be signed to formalize the LLC and make it clear that the member is not personally liable for the debts of the business.

The law of LLCs is very new and since corporations that do not follow procedures can be pierced (and their shareholders held liable), it is possible that a court may try the same on an LLC. Therefore, following the old formula is the safest. Of course, if you set up procedures and do not follow them, this could backfire, and a court could use that as a reason to impose liability.

Membership Operating Agreement

Form 28 in appendix D is a generic member-managed operating agreement. Use this form if your LLC will have one member or if it will have two or more members and be managed by all the members.

This form has basic terms which can be useful to most businesses. If all of the terms apply to your business, you should execute a copy and keep it with your company records.

If there are other terms you would like to include in your agreement, you can add them in paragraph 21 or you can draw up an addendum to the membership agreement.

MANAGEMENT OPERATING AGREEMENT

Form 29 in appendix D is a generic management operating agreement. Use this form if your LLC will have two or more members and be managed by a limited number of members or by someone who is not a member.

This form has basic terms which can be useful to most businesses. If all of the terms apply to your business, you should execute a copy and keep it with your company records.

If there are other terms you would like to include in your agreement, you can add them in paragraph 21 or you can draw up an addendum to the membership agreement.

Both operating agreements use a "Schedule A" to include the specific information for your company (form 30 in this book).

IRS FORM 8832

Form 8832 is used by the IRS to allow LLCs to chose their tax status. It is basically a choice between partnership taxation and corporate taxation. For a single-member LLC, it is a choice between sole proprietorship taxation and corporate taxation.

The difference between the two is that a sole proprietorship or partnership is not taxed at all, but a corporation is treated like a separate taxpayer. A sole proprietorship or partnership just reports its income and expenses and the proprietor or partners report the net profit or loss on their personal tax return. A corporation files a tax return and pays tax on any profits. If it distributes any of the profits to the members, those profits are taxed again. Therefore, in most cases, it is better not to choose corporate taxation.

One way around the double taxation is if all of the profits can be paid to the members as salary they are deductible and then the corporation has no profit on which to pay tax. The problem arises when the company make more money than would be reasonable to pay as salaries and the IRS can then impose extra corporate taxation on the excess amounts.

If you are unsure how you wish to be taxed, you should consult a book on taxation of businesses or check with a tax professional. Once you decide, you should file IRS Form 8832 (form 27 in this book). This form must be filed withing seventy-five days of starting your LLC.

Start-Up Procedures 6

This chapter contains the steps to start your Nevada business after you have prepared either the corporate forms in chapter 4 or the limited liability company forms in chapter 5.

Nevada Business License

Nevada does have one annoying little tax that doesn't fit into their usual free-wheeling scheme, the quarterly state business tax of $25 per employee. Fortunately for Nevada corporations and LLCs that do not do business in Nevada, the fee only has to be paid once.

Once you have formed your Nevada corporation or LLC, you should use the Business License Application (form 7 in appendix D) to register.

Registering with Your Home State

Once you have formed your Nevada corporation or LLC, you must register it as a foreign corporation in the state in which you will have your main office (and any other states in which you will be doing business). This usually requires filling out a simple form and paying the filing fee. You must contact your state corporation division (usually the Secretary of State) to obtain this form. The addresses of these offices for all fifty states are included in appendix B of this book.

For some states, you can download the forms from the Internet, others will send them if you call, and the more backward ones require you to send a letter. You should send for this material right away because some states take weeks to send it.

Check to see exactly what your state requires for registration (it might be a certified copy of your corporate or LLC documents, or a certificate of status) and be sure to get the right form from Nevada. Once your company has been successfully registered in your state, you will be legal to do business.

ORGANIZATIONAL MEETING

The real birth of the business takes place at the organizational meeting of the corporation or LLC. This is when the payment is made for the stock or membership interests, and the officers and directors or members are named.

As discussed earlier in the book, the idea behind an LLC is that not as much formality is need as for a corporation. However, the more formal an LLC conducts itself, the less likely that the members will have to face questions of liability. So it is best to use formal procedures for the LLC whenever it is not too inconvenient.

Usually minutes, tax forms, and other forms are prepared before the organizational meeting and used as a script for the meeting. They are signed at the end of the meeting. Otherwise, they may be forgotten until it is too late.

AGENDA FOR A
CORPORATION

The following is the usual agenda for a corporation:

1. Signing the waiver of notice of the meeting (form 12)

2. Noting persons present in minutes

3. Presentation and acceptance of a copy of the articles of incorporation

4. Election of directors

5. Adoption of bylaws (form 9 or form 10)

6. Election of officers

7. Presentation and acceptance of corporate seal

8. Presentation and acceptance of stock certificate (form 17)

9. Designation of bank (form 4)

10. Acceptance of stock offers (form 14) (Use form 6, Bill of Sale, if property is traded for stock.)

11. Resolution to pay expenses(form 5)

12. Adoption of special resolutions such as S corporation status (forms 11 and 15)

13. Adjournment

At the end of the meeting, the stock certificates are usually issued; but in some cases, such as when a prospective shareholder does not yet have money to pay for them, they are issued when payment is complete.

To issue the stock, the certificates at the end of this book should be completed by adding the name of the corporation, a statement that the corporation is organized under the laws of Nevada, the number of shares the certificate represents and the person to whom the certificate is issued. Each certificate should be numbered in order to keep track of them. A record of the stock issuance should be made on the stock transfer ledger (form 16).

AGENDA FOR LLC

The following is the usual agenda for an LLC:

1. Note persons present in minutes

2. Presentation and acceptance of a copy of the articles of organization

3. Presentation and acceptance of operating agreement or management agreement(form 28 or form 29, plus form 30)

4. Presentation and acceptance of IRS Form 8832 (form 27)

5. Designation of bank (form 4)

6. Resolution to reimburse expenses (form 5)

7. Adjournment

RECORDS BOOK

After the organizational meeting you should set up your company records book, sometimes called the minute book. As noted on pages 38 and 39, this can be a fancy leather book or a simple ring binder.

CORPORATION   The minute book for a corporation usually contains the following:

1. A title page ("Company Records of _____")

2. A table of contents

3. The letter from the Delaware Secretary of State acknowledging receipt and filing of the articles of incorporation

4. Copy of the articles of incorporation

5. The letter from the local Secretary of State acknowledging registration as a foreign company doing business in the state.

6. Copy of the document filed with the local state to register as a foreign corporation able to transact business in the state

7. Copy of any fictitious name registration

8. Copy of any trademark registration

9. Waiver of Notice of Organizational Meeting

10. Minutes of Organizational Meeting

11. Bylaws

12. Sample stock certificate

13. Offers to purchase stock

14. Tax forms:

   Form SS-4 and Employer Identification Number certificate

   Form 2553 and acceptance

15. Stock ledger

LLC   The minute book for an LLC usually contains the following:

1. A title page ("Company Records of _____")

2. A table of contents

3. The letter from the Secretary of State acknowledging receipt and filing of the certificate of formation

4. Copy of the certificate of formation

5. The letter from the local Secretary of State acknowledging registration as a foreign company doing business in the state

6. Copy of the document filed with the local state to register as a foreign LLC able to transact business

7. Copy of any fictitious name registration

8. Copy of any trademark registration

9. Copy of the operating agreement

10. Tax forms:

    Form SS-4 and Employer Identification Number certificate

    Form 8832

11. List of members names and addresses

BANK ACCOUNTS

A corporation must have a bank account. Checks payable to a corporation cannot be cashed; they must be deposited into an account.

Unfortunately, many banks charge ridiculous rates to corporations for the right to put their money in the bank. You can tell how much extra a corporation is being charged when you compare a corporate account to a personal account with similar activity.

For similar balance and activity, an individual might earn $6 interest for the month while a corporation pays $40 in bank fees. Surely the bank is not losing money on every personal account. Therefore, the corporate account is simply generating $46 more in profit for the bank. This money will probably be used to buy more art objects or corporate jets for the bank's officers.

Usually, there is a complicated scheme of fees, with charges for each transaction. Many banks today are even bold enough to charge companies for the right to make a deposit! (Twenty-five cents for the deposit plus ten cents for each check that is deposited. Deposit thirty checks and this will cost you $3.25!) Often the customer is granted an interest credit on the balance in the account, but it is usually small and if the credit is larger than the charges, you lose the excess. The officers in some banks cannot even tell you how the fees are figured because the system is so complicated.

Fortunately, some banks have set up reasonable fees for small corporations such as charging no fees if a balance of $1,000 or $2,500 is maintained. Because the fees can easily amount to hundreds of dollars a year, it pays to shop around. Even if the bank is relatively far from the business, using bank-by-mail can make the distance meaningless. But don't be surprised if a bank with low fees raises them. The author knows of one company that changed banks four times in one year as each one raised its fees or was bought out by a bank with higher fees.

As the banking industry got deeper into trouble, fewer and fewer banks were offering reasonable fees for corporate checking accounts. Even with their balance sheets improving, they are not eager to give up this new source of wealth. But you can usually find loopholes if you use your imagination. One trick is to open a checking account and a money market account. (Money market accounts pay higher interest and do not charge for making deposits. You can only write three checks a month, but you can usually make unlimited withdrawals.) Make all of your deposits into the money market account and just pay bills out of the regular checking account, transferring funds as needed. Banks are catching on to this and starting to charge for deposits into money market accounts. However, you can then switch to a stock brokerage company which offers money market accounts!

Another way to save money in bank charges is to order checks from a private source rather than through the bank. These are usually much cheaper than those the bank offers because the bank makes a profit on the check printing. If the bank officer for some reason says it can't be done when you are opening the account, just wait until your first batch runs out and switch over without telling the bank. They probably won't even notice, as long as you get the checks printed correctly. While most "business checks" are large (and expensive), there is no reason you cannot use small "personal size" checks for your business. They are easier to carry around and work just as well unless you want to impress people with the size of your check.

A study reported in *Business Week* in 1999 showed that attempts by banks to raise fees didn't work and that when fees were raised customers switched banks, thereby lowering the banks' income. If we keep at it, perhaps fees will stabilize at a reasonable level.

All you should need to open a corporate bank account is a copy of your articles of incorporation and your federal tax identification number. Some banks, however, want more, and they sometimes don't even know what it is they want. After opening numerous corporate accounts with only the two items listed above, the author once encountered a bank employee who wanted "something certified so we know who your officers are. Your attorney will know what to draw up." I explained that I was my own attorney and was the president, secretary, and treasurer of the corporation and I would write out and sign and seal whatever they wanted. No, it had to be a nice certificate signed by the secretary of the corporation and sealed. So, I typed out a statement in legalese, put a gold foil seal on it, and the bank opened the account. If you have trouble opening the account, you can use the Banking Resolution (form 4) included with this book, or you can make up a similar form.

LOCAL LICENSES

In some states, counties and municipalities are authorized to levy a license tax on the "privilege" of doing business. (Some would argue that earning a living is a basic human right and not a privilege, but this is not a philosophy book.) Before opening your business, you should obtain a county occupational license, and if you will be working within a city, a city occupational license. Businesses that perform work in several cities, such as builders, must obtain a license from each city in which they work. This does not have to be done until you actually begin a job in a particular city.

County occupational licenses can usually be obtained from the tax collector in the county courthouse. City licenses are usually available at city hall. Be sure to find out if zoning allows your type of business before buying or leasing property because the licensing departments will check the zoning before issuing your license.

HOME BUSINESSES

Problems occasionally arise when persons attempt to start a business in their home. Small new businesses cannot afford to pay rent for commercial space and cities often try to forbid business in residential areas. Getting a county occupational license often gives notice to the city that a business is being conducted in a residential area.

Some people avoid the problem by starting their businesses without occupational licenses, figuring that the penalties are nowhere near the cost of office space. Others get the county license and ignore the city rules. If a person has commercial trucks and equipment parked on his property, there will probably be complaints by neighbors and the city will most likely take legal action. But if a person's business consists merely of making phone calls out of the home and keeping supplies inside the house, the problem may never arise.

If the problem does surface regarding a home business that does not disturb the neighbors, a good argument can be made that the zoning law that prohibits the business is unconstitutional. When zoning laws were first instituted they were not meant to stop people from doing things in a residence that had historically been part of the life in a residence. Consider a painter. Should a zoning law prohibit a person from sitting in his home and painting pictures? If he sells them for a living is there a difference? Can the government force him to rent commercial space?

Similar arguments can be made for many home businesses. (The author is waiting for his city fathers to tell him to stop writing books in his home office.) But court battles with a city are expensive and probably not worth the effort for a small business. The best course of action is to keep a low profile. Using a post office box is sometimes helpful in diverting attention away from the residence. However, the Secretary of State and the occupational license administrator will want a street address. There should be no problem using a residential address and explaining to the city that it is merely the corporate address and that no business is conducted on the premises.

CAPITAL STRUCTURE AND SELLING STOCK 7

CAPITAL STRUCTURE

There is no hard and fast rule as to how much capital you should put into a new corporation or LLC. The more you put in as capital, the more you have at risk in the business, so you would want to put as little as possible. But if you put in too little, a court might some day say you were undercapitalized and find you personally liable for company debts, just as it could for a corporation. Also, there could be tax problems with not counting enough of your contributions as capital or for contributing appreciated property. These matters should be discussed with a tax specialist.

If you are starting a small business which does not need a lot of expensive equipment, a thousand or a few thousand dollars would be a safe amount with which to start. If you do need to buy expensive equipment, and the company can borrow the money from a third party to cover it, you would probably be safe as well. But if you need to purchase expensive equipment and personally loan the money to the company rather than contribute it as capital, you should weigh the risks of a lawsuit and consider consulting an attorney or accountant who specializes in business start-ups.

One thing to keep in mind is that if you do not put in the amount of capital you state in your initial agreement, and are later sued or file bankruptcy, you may be required to come up with any amount unpaid.

For a corporation, the purchaser should submit an "Offer to Purchase Stock" (form 14) before any stock is issued. The offer states that it is made pursuant to IRS Code § 1244. The advantage of this section is that in the event the business fails or the value of the stock drops, the shareholder can write off up to $50,000 ($100,000 for married couples) as ordinary income, rather than as a long term capital loss which would be limited to $3,000 a year.

Some thought should be given to the way in which the ownership of the stock or membership interests will be held. Stock owned in one person's name alone is subject to probate upon death. Making two persons joint owners of the stock (joint tenants with full rights of survivorship) would avoid probate upon the death of one of them. However, taking a joint owner's name off in the event of a disagreement (such as divorce) could be troublesome. Where a couple jointly operates a business, joint ownership would be best. But where one person is the sole party involved in the business, the desire to avoid probate should be weighed against the risk of losing half the business in a divorce. Another way to avoid probate is to put ownership of the stock in a living trust. You are allowed to list your securities as "pay on death" or "transfer on death" in about half of the states. This avoids probate as well.

For living trusts or information on pay on death registration, you should consult an attorney or a book on estate planning such as *Living Trusts and Simple Ways to Avoid Probate* published by Sourcebooks.

PAYMENT FOR INTERESTS

Stock or membership interests may be paid for with money, property, services, or a promissory note. The important thing to remember is that if a person fails to make the specified payment or takes return of the payment, he or she may be liable to the company or its creditors for the full amount that should have been paid. To make this less likely, the board of directors or managers should pass a resolution stating that they have determined that the property is being accepted at its fair market value in the exchange.

LLCs   Some other things for an LLC to consider are:

☞ If a member trades services for an interest in the capital of the company, he must pay income tax on the value of interest at the time the services are exchanged for the interest. (If the interest is only a share of future profits, the tax does not have to be paid until the profits are received.)

☞ When appreciated property is traded to an LLC in exchange for a membership interest, the tax basis of the property carries over to the membership interest. Taxes on the appreciation are paid when the member sells his LLC interest.

☞ If the LLC sells the property, it may have to pay a tax on the amount received over the contributor's basis.

CORPORATIONS   The most important thing to know for a corporation is that § 351 of the IRS Code allows tax-free exchange of property for stock if the persons receiving the stock for the property or for cash *end up owning* at least eighty percent of the voting and other stock in the corporation. If more than twenty percent of the stock is issued in exchange for services instead of property and cash, the transfers of property will be taxable and treated as a sale for cash.

Also, if the stock has par value and the payment is in cash, the payment should not be less than par value but may be more.

Tax rules are complicated and ever-changing. You should consult with a tax expert or a tax guide if you will be doing creative financing.

SECURITIES LAWS

The issuance of securities is subject to both federal and state securities laws. A *security* is equity interest in a company and debt (notes, bonds, etc.). The laws covering securities are so broad that any instrument which represents an investment in an enterprise, such as where the investor is relying on the efforts of others for profit, is considered a security. Even a promissory note has been held to be a security. Once an investment is determined to involve a security, strict rules apply. If the rules are not followed, there can be criminal penalties. Civil damages can also be awarded to purchasers.

The rules are designed to protect people who put up money as an investment in a business. In the stock market crash in 1929, many people lost their life savings in swindles. The government wants to be sure that it doesn't happen again. Unfortunately, the laws can also make it difficult to raise capital for many honest businesses.

The goal if the laws covering sales of securities is that investors be given full disclosure of the risks involved in an investment. To accomplish this goal, the law usually requires that the securities must either be registered with the federal Securities and Exchange Commission or a similar state regulatory body and that lengthy disclosure statements be compiled and distributed.

The law is complicated and strict compliance is required. The penalties are so harsh that most lawyers won't handle securities matters. You most likely would not be able to get through the registration process on your own. But, like your decision to form your business without a lawyer, you may wish to consider some alternatives when attempting to raise capital without a lawyer:

☛ Borrow the money as a personal loan from the friends or relatives. The disadvantage is that you will have to pay them back personally if the business fails. However, you may have to do that anyway if they are close relatives or if you don't follow the securities laws.

☛ Tailor your stock issuance to fall within the exemptions in the securities laws. There are some exemptions in the securities laws for small businesses that may apply to your transaction. (The anti-fraud provisions always apply, even if the transaction is exempt from registration.) Some exemptions are explained in the next section, but you should make at least one appointment with a securities lawyer to be sure you have covered everything and that there have not been any changes in the law. You can often pay for an hour or so of a securities lawyer's time for $100 or $200 and just ask questions about your plans. He or she can tell you what not to do and what your options are. You can then make an informed decision.

FEDERAL EXEMPTIONS FROM SECURITIES LAWS

In most situations where one person, a husband and wife, or a few partners run a business and all parties are active in the enterprise, securities laws do not apply to their issuance of stock to themselves. As a practical matter, if your father or aunt wants to put up some money for some stock in your business, you might not get into trouble. They probably won't seek triple damages and criminal penalties if your business fails. (This can't be said of your father-in-law in the event he becomes your ex-father-in-law some day!)

However, you may wish to obtain money from additional investors to enable your business to grow. This can be done in many circumstances as long as you follow the rules carefully. In some cases, you do not have to file anything with the SEC; but in others, you must file a notice.

FEDERAL PRIVATE PLACEMENT EXEMPTION

If you sell interests in your business to a small group of people without any advertising, you can fall into the private offering exemption if all of the following are true:

- ☛ All persons to whom offers are made are financially astute, are participants in the business, or have a substantial net worth

- ☛ No advertising or general solicitation is used to promote the stock

- ☛ The offer is made to a limited number of persons

- ☛ The shares are purchased for investment and not for immediate resale

- ☛ The persons to whom the stock is offered are given all relevant information (including financial information) regarding the issuance and the corporation. Again, there are numerous court cases explaining each aspect of these rules, including such questions as what is a "financially astute" person

☛ A filing claiming the exemption is made upon the United States Securities and Exchange Commission

FEDERAL
INTRASTATE
OFFERING
EXEMPTION

If you only offer your securities to residents of one state, you may be exempt from federal securities laws. This is because federal laws usually only apply to interstate commerce. Intrastate offerings are covered by SEC Rule 147. If it is followed carefully, your sale will be exempt from federal registration.

FEDERAL SMALL
OFFERINGS
EXEMPTIONS

The SEC has liberalized the rules in recent years in order to make it easier for business to grow. Under Regulation D, adopted by the Securities and Exchange Commission, there are three types of exemptions under rules 504, 505, and 506.

Offering of securities of up to $1,000,000 in a twelve month period can be exempt under SEC Rule 504. Offers can be made to any number of persons, no specific information must be provided, and investors do not have to be sophisticated.

Under Rule 505, offering of up to $5,000,000 can be made in a twelve month period. However, no public advertising may be used and only thirty-five non-accredited investors may purchase stock. Any number of accredited investors may purchase stock.

Accredited investors are sophisticated individuals with high net worth or high income, large trusts or investment companies, or persons involved in the business.

Rule 506 has no limit on the amount of money that may be raised but, like Rule 505, does not allow advertising and limits non-accredited investors to thirty-five.

State Securities Laws

One reason there are exemptions from federal securities laws is that there are so many state laws covering securities that additional registration is not needed. Every state has securities laws, which are called *blue sky laws*. If you wish to offer your stock in all fifty states, you must be registered in all fifty states unless you can fit into one of the exemptions. However, exemptions are very limited.

Typical State Law Private Placement Exemption

The most common one is the private placement exemption. This can apply if all of the following are true:

☛ There are thirty-five or fewer purchasers of shares

☛ No commissions are paid to anyone to promote the stock

☛ No advertising or general solicitation is used to promote the stock

☛ All material information (including financial information) regarding the stock issuance and the company is given to or accessible to all shareholders

☛ A three day right of rescission is given

These rules may sound simple on the surface, but there are many more rules, regulations and court cases explaining each one in more detail. For example, what does "thirty-five persons" mean? Sounds simple, but it can mean more than thirty-five persons. Spouses, persons whose net worth exceeds a million dollars, and founders of the company may not be counted in some circumstances.

As you can see, the exemption doesn't give you much latitude in raising money. Therefore, if you wish to raise money from a wider group of people, you will have to register. You should contact the securities commission of your state to find out more about your state's requirements. The address is in the back of this chapter.

Another good source of information of the securities laws of all fifty states is the *Blue Sky Reporter*, a multi-volume loose leaf service which summarizes the securities laws of the states. A copy should be available in most law libraries.

INTERNET STOCK SALES

With the advent of the Internet, promoters of business interests have a new way of reaching large numbers of people, most of whom are financially able to afford investments in securities. However, all securities laws apply to the Internet and they are being enforced. Recently, state attorneys general have issued cease and desist orders to promoters not registered in their states.

Under current law, you must be registered in a state in order to sell stock to its residents. If you are not registered in a state, you must turn down any residents from that state who want to buy your stock.

You may wonder how the famous Spring Street Brewing raised $1.6 million for its Wit Beer on the Internet. The main reason they were successful was because their president is a securities lawyer and could prepare his own prospectus to file with the SEC and the states. That would have cost anyone else about $100,000. Also, most of their stock sales were inspired by newspaper and magazine articles about them and not from the Internet.

The lawyer who marketed Wit Beer's shares on the Internet has started a business to advise others on raising capital. It is Wit Capital located at 826 Broadway, 6th Floor, New York, NY 10003.

Some Internet sites which may be helpful in raising capital are:

America's Business Funding Directory:
http://www.businessfinance.com

Angel Capital Electronic Network (SBA): http://www.sba.gov

FinanceHub: http://www.financehub.com

NVST: http://www.nvst.com

Private Capital Clearinghouse: http://www.pricap.com

STATE SECURITIES REGISTRATION OFFICES

The following are the addresses of the offices which can provide information on securities registration requirements for each state.

Alabama Securities Commission
770 Washington Street, Suite 570
Montgomery, AL 36130-4700
(205) 242-2984 Phone
(205) 242-0240 Fax

Alaska Department of Commerce
and Economic Development
Division of Banking, Securities,
and Corporations
P.O. Box 110807
Juneau, AK 99811
(907) 465-2521 Phone
(907) 465-2549 Fax
www.state.ak.us/local/akpages/
COMMERCE/bsc.htm

Arizona Corporation Commission
Securities Division
1300 West Washington Street, 3d Floor
Phoenix, AZ 85007
(602) 542-4242 Phone
(602) 542-3583 Fax
http://www.state.az.us/ccsd

Arkansas Securities Department
Heritage West Building
201 East Markham, Suite 300
Little Rock, AR 72201
(501) 324-9260 Phone
(501) 324-9268 Fax

California Department of Corporations
3700 Wilshire Blvd., Suite 600
Los Angeles, California 90010
(213) 736-3482 Phone
(213) 736-3588 Fax
http://www.corp.ca.gov

Colorado Division of Securities
1580 Lincoln Street, Suite 420
Denver, CO 80203
(303) 894-2320 Phone
(303) 861-2126 Fax

Connecticut Securities Division
260 Constitution Plaza
Hartford, CT 06106
(806) 240-8230 Phone
(860) 240-8178 Fax
http://www.state.ct.us/dob/

Delaware Department of Justice
New Castle County
Carvel State Building
820 N. French Street
Wilmington, DE 19801
(302) 577-2515 Phone
(302) 655-0576 Fax

District of Columbia
NASAA Corporate Office
1 Massachusetts Avenue, NW Suite 310
Washington, DC 20001
(202) 737-0900 Phone
(202) 783-3571 Fax

Florida Division of Securities
Plaza Level
Tallahassee, FL 32399-0350
(904) 488-9805 Phone
(904) 681-2428 Fax

Georgia Secretary of State
Suite 802, West Tower
2 Martin Luther King Jr. Drive
Atlanta, GA 30334
(404) 656-3920 Phone
(404) 657-8410 Fax
www.SOS.State.Ga.US/Securities/

Hawaii Department of Commerce
and Consumer Affairs
1010 Richards St.
P. O. Box 40
Honolulu, HI 96810
(808) 586-2744 Phone
(808) 586-2733 Fax

Idaho Department of Finance
700 W. State Street, 2nd Floor,
P.O. Box 83720
Boise, ID 83720-0031
(208) 334-2441 Phone
(208) 332-8099 Fax
www.state.id.us./finance/dof.htm

Illinois Securities Department
Lincoln Tower, Suite 200
520 South Second Street
Springfield, Illinois 62701
Phone: (217) 785-4949
www.sos.state.il.us:80/depts/securities/sec
_home.html

Indiana Securities Division
302 West Washington Street, Room E-111
Indianapolis, IN 46204
(317) 232-6687 Phone
(317) 233-3675 Fax
www.ai.org/sos/securities

Iowa Securities Bureau
Lucas State Office Building, Room 214
Agency Des Moines, IA 50319
(515) 281-4441 Phone
(515) 281-6467 Fax
www.state.ia.us/

Kansas Securities Commissioner
Office of the Securities Commissioner
618 South Kansas Avenue, 2nd Floor
Topeka, KS 66603-3804
(913) 296-3307 Phone
(913) 296-6872 Fax
www.cjnetworks.com/~ksecom

Kentucky Department of
Financial Institutions
477 Versailles Road
Frankfort, KY 40601-3868
(502) 573-3390 Phone
(502) 573-8787 Fax

Louisiana Securities Commission
Energy Center
1100 Poydras Street, Suite 2250
New Orleans, LA 70163
(504) 568-5515 Phone

Maine Securities Division
State House Station 121
Bureau of Banking
Augusta, ME 04333
(207) 624-8551 Phone
(207) 624-8590 Fax
www.state.me.us/pfr/sec/sechome

Maryland Securities Division
200 Saint Paul Place 20th Floor
Baltimore, MD 21202-2020
(410) 576-7045 Phone
(410) 576-6532 Fax

Massachusetts Securities Division
John W. McCormack Building
One Ashburton Place, Room 1701
Boston, MA 02108
(617) 727-3548 phone
www.state.ma.us/sec

Michigan Corporation, Securities
& Land Development Bureau
6546 Mercantile Way
P.O. Box 30222
Lansing, MI 48910
(517) 334-8107 Phone
(517) 334-7813 Fax
www.cis.state.mi.us

Minnesota Department of Commerce
133 East Seventh Street
St. Paul, MN 55101
(612) 296-9431 Phone
(612) 296-4328 Fax
www.commerce.state.mn.us

Mississippi Securities Division
P.O. Box 136
Jackson, MS 39205
(601) 359-6364 Phone
(601) 359-2894 Fax

Missouri Securities Division
Missouri State Information Center
600 West Main St., 2nd Floor
P.O. Box 1276
Jefferson City, MO 65102
http://mosl.sos.state.mo.us

Montana Securities Department
Mitchell Building
P.O. Box 4009
Helena, MT 59604-4009
(406) 444-2040 Phone
(406) 444-5558 Fax
Email: blombardi@mt.gov

Nebraska Bureau of Securities
The Atrium, Suite 311
1200 N Street
Lincoln, NE 68508
(402) 471-3445 Phone
www.ndbf.org

Nevada Securities Division
555 E. Washington Avenue, Suite 5200
Las Vegas, NV 89101
(702) 486-2440 Phone
(702) 486-2452 Fax
www.state.nv.us

New Hampshire Bureau of
Securities Regulation
State House, Room 204
107 North Main St.
Concord, NH 03301-4989
(603) 271-1463 Phone

New Jersey Bureau of Securities
153 Halsey Street, 6th Floor
Newark, NJ 07101
(201) 504-3630 Phone
(201) 504-3631 Fax
Email:
    askConsumerAffairs@oag-lps.state.nj.us

New Mexico Securities Division
725 St. Michaels Drive
Santa Fe, NM 87120
(505) 827-7140 Phone
(505) 884-0617 Fax

New York State Attorney General's Office
120 Broadway, 23rd. Floor
New York, NY 10271
(212) 416-8989 Phone
(212) 416-8816 Fax
www.oag.state.ny.us

North Carolina Securities Division
300 North Salisbury Street, Suite 302
Raleigh, NC 27603-5909
(919) 733-3924 Phone
(919) 733-5172 Fax
www.secstate.state.nc.us/secstate/sos.htm

North Dakota Securities Commission
600 East Boulevard, 5th Floor
Bismarck, ND 58505
(701) 224-2910 Phone
Email: seccom@pioneer.state.nd.us

Ohio Division of Securities
77 South High Street, 22nd. Floor
Columbus, OH 43215
(614) 750-4267 Phone
(614) 466-3316 Fax
www.securities.state.oh.us

Oklahoma Department of Securities
120 North Robinson, Suite 860
Oklahoma City, OK 73102
(405) 280-7706 Phone
(405) 280-7742 Fax
www.oklaosf.state.ok.us/~osc

Oregon Department of Consumer
and Business Services
Division of Finance
and Corporate Securities
350 Winter Street NE, Room 21
Salem, OR 97310
(503) 378-2270 Phone
(503) 378-4178 Fax
www.cbs.state.or.us/external/dfcs

Pennsylvania Division of
Corporation Finance
Pennsylvania Securities Commission
Eastgate Office Building, 2nd Floor,
1010 North 7th Street
Harrisburg, PA 17102-1410
(717)787-8059 Phone
www.state.pa.us/PA_Exec/Securities/

Puerto Rico Commissioner of
Financial Institutions
Centro Europa Building
1492 Ponce de Leon Avenue, Suite 600
San Juan, PR 00907-4127
(787) 723-8445 Phone
(787) 723-3857 Fax

South Carolina Securities Division
P.O. Box 11549
Columbia, SC 29211-1549
(803) 734-1087 Phone

South Dakota Division of Securities
118 West Capital
Pierre, SD 57501-3940
(605) 773-4823 Phone
(605) 773-5953 Fax

Tennessee Securities Division
Volunteer Plaza
500 James Robertson Parkway
Nashville, TN 37243-0485
(615) 741-2947 Phone
(615) 532-8375 Fax
www.state.tn.us/commerce/securdiv.html

Texas State Securities Board
200 E. 10th Street, 5th Floor
Austin, Texas 78701
(512) 305-8300 Phone
(512) 305-8310 Fax
www.ssb.state.tx.us

Utah Division of Securities
160 East 300 South
Salt Lake City, Utah 84111
(801) 530-6600 Phone
(801) 530-6980 Fax
www.commerce.state.ut.us

Vermont Securities Division
89 Main Street
Drawer 20
Montpelier, VT 05620-3101
(802) 828-4857 Phone
(802) 828-2896 Fax
www.state.vt.us/bis

Virginia State Corporation Commission
P.O. Box 1197
Richmond, VA 23218
(804) 371-9671 Phone
(804) 371-9240 Fax

Washington Department of Financial
Institutions, Securities Division
P.O. Box 9033
Olympia, Washington 98507-9033
(206) 753-6928 Phone
(206) 586-5068 Fax
Email: BBeatty@dfi.wa.gov
www.wa.gov/dfi/securities

West Virginia Securities Division
State Capitol Building
Room W100
Charleston, WV 25305
(304) 558-2251 Phone
(304) 558-5200 Fax
www.wvauditor.com
Email: wes@wvauditor

Wisconsin Division of Securities
P.O. Box 1768
Madison, WI 53705
(608) 266-2801 Phone
(608) 256-1259 Fax
http://badger.state.wi.us/agencies/dfi

Wyoming Securities Division
Secretary of the State
24th & State Capital Ave.
Cheyenne, WY 82002-0020
(307) 777-5333 Phone
(307) 777-6217 Fax
Email: securities@missc.state.wy.us

RUNNING A CORPORATION OR AN LLC **8**

DAY TO DAY ACTIVITIES

There are not many differences between running a corporation, LLC, and any other type of business. The most important point to remember is to keep the company affairs separate from your personal affairs. Don't be making frequent loans to yourself from company funds and don't commingle funds.

Another important point to remember is to always refer to the corporation as a corporation or the limited liability company as an LLC. Always use the designation "Inc." or "Corp." or "LLC" on everything. Always sign company documents with your title. If you don't, you may lose your protection from liability. There have been many cases where a person forgot to put the word "pres." after his name and was held personally liable for a corporate debt!

RECORDS

CORPORATIONS   A Nevada corporation is required to keep the following records at its registered office in Nevada:

☛ a copy of its articles of incorporation and any amendments certified by the secretary of state;

☞ a copy of its bylaws and any amendments certified by an officer of the corporation; and

☞ a stock ledger or duplicate stock ledger listing the names of stockholders in alphabetical order, the number of shares owned, and if known, their residences. (However, the corporation can keep this item at another location and just keep the name and address of the custodian in Nevada instead.)

Form of records. The minutes may be in writing or in "another form capable of being converted into written form within a reasonable time." This would mean that they could be kept in a computer or possibly on a videotape. However, it is always best to keep at least one written copy. Accidents can easily erase magnetic media [NRS 78.105 (2)].

Examination of records. Any shareholder of the corporation who has been a shareholder for at least six months or who has written authorization from five percent of the stockholders has the right to examine and copy the corporation's books and records after giving written notice of at least five days [NRS 78.105 (3)].

The shareholder may have his attorney or agent examine the records but the attorney must have a written power of attorney.

LLCs An LLC may provide in its operating agreement that does need not keep any records in the state of Nevada (NRS 86.241), but if it does not so provide, the company must keep the following at a office within the state:

☞ a current alphabetical list of all members and managers;

☞ a copy of the articles of organization and any amendments along with any powers of attorney that apply to them; and

☞ copies of any effective operating agreements.

MEETINGS

CORPORATIONS
The corporation must hold an annual meeting of the directors and shareholders. These meetings may be formal and held in a restaurant or they may be informal and held in the swimming pool. The meetings need not be held in Nevada. The bylaws should specify when and where meetings will be held.

A sole shareholder and director can hold them in his mind without reciting all the verbiage or taking a formal vote. But the important thing is that the meetings are held and that minutes are kept. Regular minutes and meetings are evidence that the corporation is legitimate if the issue ever comes up in court. Minute forms for the annual meetings are included with this book. You can use them as master copies to photocopy each year. Unless you actually change officers or directors or need to take some other corporate action, all that needs to be changed is the date.

When important decisions must be made by the board of shareholders between the annual meetings, the corporation can hold special meetings.

Nevada Statutes sections 78.315 and 78.320 explain the rules for whether there is a quorum, when action can be taken without a meeting, and how to hold meetings telephonically.

Under the procedures of NRS 78.325, action may be taken by the directors without a formal meeting. However, it is best for a small corporation to use formal meetings in case someone later tries to pierce the corporate veil.

LLCs
There is no requirement of regular meeting of the members of a limited liability company. But, once again, since the law is not settled in this area, the more formality you use the greater protection you have against potential liability.

Holding a meeting when major decisions are being made is a good idea. If you are a one-member company, you can hold the meeting in your head. Just remember to fill out a minutes form with the company records. For this purpose you can use form 31 in appendix D.

COMMITTEES

Both corporations and LLCs have the power to appoint committees to carry out their business functions.

CORPORATIONS The committees for a corporation may be authorized by a resolution of the board of directors or by the bylaws. The committees may have the power to act for the board of directors. The committee must have a name as stated in the bylaws or a resolution and must have at least one director as a member (NRS 78.125).

LLCs There are no specific requirements for LLCs. Under the general power to "exercise all powers necessary or convenient to effect any of the purposes for which the company is organized" [NRS 86.281(11)], it could legally form a committee. However, the committee would not have the power to manage the business or to do such acts as incurring debt or acquiring real estate, unless such power was given in the articles of organization (NRS 86.291, 86.301, 86.311).

DISTRIBUTIONS

A corporation or LLC is usually free to make any distributions of money or property to its shareholders or members. The exception is where the distribution would make the company insolvent or unable to pay its debts.

For the specific rules regarding distributions which may make the company insolvent, see NRS 78.288 for corporations and NRS 86.341 and 86.343 for limited liability companies.

ANNUAL REPORTS

Each year every corporation and LLC registered in Nevada must file an annual report.

CORPORATIONS The first report for a corporation is due on or before the first day of the second month after filing the articles of incorporation. Thereafter, the report is due by the last day of the month which is the anniversary of the formation of the corporation. The report is a form provided by the secretary of state and must contain the following information:

☞ the name of the corporation;

☞ the file number of the corporation, if known;

☞ the names and titles of the corporation's required officers (not the permitted officers such as vice-presidents and assistant secretaries);

☞ the names of its directors;

☞ the street or mailing address of each listed officer and director; and

☞ a signature of an officer that certifies the list to be true, complete, and accurate.

The filing fee is currently $85. There is a penalty of $15 for failing to file the report in the time required [NRS 78.150(3) and 78.170].

The charter of any corporation which fails to file is revoked on the first day of the ninth month following the month in which the report was due (NRS 78.175).

A defaulting corporation can be reinstated by paying an additional reinstatement fee of $50 and following the procedures in NRS 78.180 and 78.185.

LLCs An LLC must file an annual report on or before the last day of the month containing the anniversary date of its filing the articles of organization. The report is a form provided by the secretary of state and must contain the following information:

- ☞ the name of the company;

- ☞ the file number of the company, if known;

- ☞ the names, titles, and street or mailing addresses home or business) of the company's managers, or if it does not have managers, then its managing members; and

- ☞ a signature of a manager or managing member certifying that the list is true, complete, and accurate.

The filing fee is currently $85. There is a penalty of $15 for failing to file the report in the time required [NRS 86.263(3) and 86.272].

The charter of any company which fails to file is revoked on the first day of the ninth month following the month in which the report was due (NRS 86.274).

A defaulting corporation can be reinstated by paying an additional reinstatement fee of $50 and following the procedures in NRS 86.276 and 86.278.

EMPLOYMENT REQUIREMENTS

If you will be paying wages to anyone, even just yourself, you will need to comply with all of the employer reporting and withholding laws of both your state and the federal government. Explaining every requirement is beyond the scope of this book, but the following is a summary of most of the requirements.

New hire reporting. To improve the enforcement of child support payments, all employers must report the hiring of each new employee to an agency in the state.

Employment eligibility. To combat the hiring of illegal immigrants, employers must complete the Department of Justice I-9 form for each employee.

Federal tax withholding. Social security and income taxes must be withheld from employees wages and deposited to an authorized bank quarterly, monthly, or more often depending on the amount. The initial step is to obtain a form W-4 from each employee upon hiring. (This same form can also be used to fulfill the previously discussed new hire reporting law.)

State withholding. In states that have income taxes, there is usually a withholding and reporting requirement similar to the federal one.

Local withholding. In cities that have income taxes, there is usually a withholding and reporting requirement similar to the federal one.

Unemployment compensation. There are taxes on employee wages (which employers must pay) that must be paid to the state and federal governments regularly. Employers are also required to send reports quarterly and annually.

Workers' compensation. Depending on the number of employees and type of work, the state may require that workers' compensation insurance be obtained by the employer.

AMENDING A CORPORATION OR AN LLC 9

CORPORATIONS

CORRECTION OF
INSTRUMENTS

Under NRS 78.0295, whenever an instrument which has been filed with the secretary of state is found to be inaccurate or defectively or erroneously executed, attested, sealed, verified or acknowledged, it may be corrected by filing a certificate of correction with the secretary of state which includes:

☛ the name of the corporation;

☛ a description of the document to be corrected, including the filing date;

☛ a description of the incorrect statement or defective execution;

☛ a correction of the incorrect statement or defective execution; and

☛ a signature of an officer of the corporation.

ARTICLES OF
INCORPORATION

Under NRS 78.385, the articles of incorporation may be amended for any reason as long as the provisions are all lawful under NRS 78.035 and 78.037. The statute specifically allows changes:

☛ to modify its name;

☛ to add or subtract corporate powers or purposes;

☛ to substitute powers or purposes;

☛ to increase, decrease or reclassify stock; and

☛ to alter the par value, number, or other rights of its stock.

Before stock is issued. The articles of incorporation may be amended before stock is issued by filing with the secretary of state a certificate of amendment signed by at least two-thirds of the incorporators (NRS 78.380). The certificate must state:

- ☛ the corporation's name;
- ☛ that the signers are two-thirds of the incorporators;
- ☛ the date the original articles were filed; and
- ☛ that no stock has been issued.

After stock is issued. Under NRS 78.390, after stock has been issued, the corporation must follow the following procedures to amend the articles:

- ☛ The board of directors must pass a resolution setting forth the proposed amendment and stating that it is advisable to adopt. It must then call a meeting of stockholders and give notice to each stockholder entitled to vote.

- ☛ If the amendment passes at the stockholders' meeting [NRS 78.390(1.)(b)], the president or vice-president and the secretary or assistant secretary must execute a certificate stating the vote by which the amendment passed, either the amendment or the amended articles, and signed by the president or vice-president and notarized.

Restated articles. After the articles have been amended, the corporation may prepare "Restated Articles of Incorporation" to consolidate all of the changes into one document. These can be filed with the secretary of state accompanied by either a resolution or a form provided by the secretary of state (NRS 78.403). The restated articles can include new changes to the articles, but if they do, they must comply with the rules for amending the articles.

BYLAWS   Nevada has few requirements regarding bylaws of the corporation. Under NRS 78.120, the board of directors may make (and presumably amend) bylaws for the corporation, subject to any bylaws made by the stockholders.

REGISTERED
AGENT OR
REGISTERED
OFFICE

To change the registered agent or registered office, a corporation must file a certificate with the secretary of state signed by an officer, stating:

- ☞ the name of the corporation;
- ☞ the change is authorized by NRS 78.110 and is effective upon filing;
- ☞ the street address of the present registered office;
- ☞ if the address is changing, the address of the new registered office;
- ☞ the name of the present registered agent;
- ☞ if the agent is changing, the name of the new registered agent; and
- ☞ if the agent is changing, an acceptance by the new registered agent.

If the registered agent changes its name or address, it must follow the procedures as outlined in NRS 78.095.

If a registered agent resigns and appoints a successor, it must follow the procedures outlined in NRS 78.097.

LLCs

ARTICLES OF
ORGANIZATION

The articles of organization may be amended either by all of the members or as otherwise provided by the articles or any operating agreement in effect.

The amendment must be filed with the secretary of state and in the form of a certificate which includes:

- ☞ the name of the company;
- ☞ the date of the filing of the original articles;
- ☞ the amendment to the articles; and
- ☞ the signature and acknowledgment by a member or, if manager-managed, by a manager.

Restated articles. After the articles have been amended, the company may prepare "Restated Articles of Organization" to consolidate all of the changes into one document.

REGISTERED
AGENT OR
REGISTERED
OFFICE

To change the registered agent or registered office an LLC must file a certificate with the secretary of state signed by an officer, stating:

- ☞ the name of the company;

- ☞ the change is authorized by NRS 86.235 and is effective upon filing;

- ☞ the street address of the present registered office;

- ☞ if the address is changing, the address of the new registered office;

- ☞ the name of the present registered agent;

- ☞ if the agent is changing, the name of the new registered agent; and

- ☞ if the agent is changing, an acceptance by the new registered agent.

If the registered agent changes its address, it must follow the procedures as outlined in NRS 86.231 (2.).

If a registered agent resigns and appoints a successor, it must follow the procedures outlined in NRS 86.251.

OPERATING
AGREEMENT

The operating agreement of a limited liability company may be amended only by unanimous consent of the member at the time of the amendment (NRS 86.286).

APPENDIX A
SELECTED NEVADA STATUTES
AND FEE SCHEDULES

Included in this appendix are the Nevada corporation statutes that will be most useful in organizing your corporation or limited liability company.

Sections from the following statutes are included in this appendix

Chapter 78 Private Corporations

Chapter 78A Close Corporations

Chapter 86 Limited Liability Companies

The next few pages contain an outline of all corporation and LLC statutes. Those in italics are not included but may be found at your library or law library or on the Internet at:

http://leg.state.nv.us/NRS/index2.htm

CHAPTER 78 PRIVATE CORPORATIONS

General Provisions

78.010 Definitions; construction.CH. 78

78.015 Applicability of chapter; effect on corporations existing before April 1, 1925.

78.020 Limitations on incorporation under chapter; compliance with other laws.

78.025 Reserved power of state to amend or repeal chapter; chapter part of corporation's charter.

78.027 Corporate documents: Microfilming and return.

78.028 Filing of documents written in language other than English.

78.029 Procedure to submit replacement page to secretary of state before filing of document.

78.0295 Incorrect or defective document: Certificate of correction; effective date of correction.

Formation

78.030 Filing of articles of incorporation and certificate of acceptance of appointment of resident agent.

78.035 Articles of incorporation: Required provisions.

78.037 Articles of incorporation: Optional provisions.

78.039 Name of corporation: Distinguishable name required; availability of name of revoked, terminated or merged corporation.

78.040 Name of corporation: Reservation; injunctive relief.

78.045 Articles of incorporation: Approval or certification required before filing of certain articles or amendments.

78.050 Commencement of corporate existence.

78.055 Acceptable evidence of incorporation.

Powers

78.060 General powers.

78.065 Adoption and use of corporate seal or stamp.

78.070 Specific powers.

78.075 Railroad companies: Powers.

78.080 Railroad companies: Rights of way granted by the state, counties and municipalities; limitations; reversion on abandonment; duties of companies.

78.085 Railroad companies: Filing of certified maps and profiles.

Registered Office and Registered Agent

78.090 Resident agent required; address of registered office; powers of bank or corporation who is resident agent; penalty for noncompliance; service of documents on resident agent.

78.095 Change of address of resident agent and registered office.

78.097 Resignation of resident agent; notice to corporation of resignation; appointment of successor.

78.105 Maintenance of records at registered office; inspection and copying of records; civil liability; penalties.

78.107 Denial of request for inspection of records; defense to action for penalties or damages; authority of court to compel production of records.

78.110 Change of resident agent or location of registered office.

Directors and Officers

78.115 Board of directors: Number and qualifications.

78.120 Board of directors: General powers.

78.125 Committees of board of directors: Designation; powers; names; membership.

78.130 Officers of corporation: Selection; qualifications; terms; powers and duties; filling of vacancies.

78.135 Authority of directors and representatives of corporation.

78.138 Directors and officers: Exercise of powers and performance of duties.

78.140 Restrictions on transactions involving interested directors or officers; compensation of directors.

Annual List of Officers and Directors; Defaulting Corporations

78.150 Filing requirements; fee; forms.

78.155 Certificate of authorization to transact business.

78.165 Addresses of officers and directors required; failure to file.

78.170 Defaulting corporations: Identification; penalty.

78.175 Defaulting corporations: Duties of secretary of state; revocation of charter and forfeiture of right to transact business; distribution of assets.

78.180 Defaulting corporations: Conditions and procedure for reinstatement.

78.185 Defaulting corporations: Reinstatement under old or new name.

Stock and Other Securities; Distributions

78.191 "Distribution" defined.

78.195 Issuance of more than one class or series of stock; rights of stockholders.

78.1955 Establishment of matters regarding class or series of stock by resolution of board of directors.

78.196 Required and authorized classes of stock.

78.197 Rights of persons holding obligations of corporation.

78.200 Rights or options to purchase stock.

78.205 Fractions of shares: Issuance; alternatives to issuance.

78.207 Increase or decrease in number of authorized shares of class and series: Resolution by board of directors; vote of stockholders required under certain circumstances.

78.209 Filing certificate of change in number of authorized shares of class and series; contents of certificate; articles of incorporation deemed amended.

78.211 Consideration for shares: Types; adequacy; effect of receipt; actions of corporation pending receipt in future.

78.215 Issuance of shares for consideration or as share dividend.

78.220 Subscription for corporate shares: Payment; collection on default; irrevocability.

78.225 Stockholder's liability: No individual liability except for payment for which shares were authorized to be issued or which was specified in subscription agreement.

78.230 Liability of holder of stock as collateral security; liability of executors, administrators, guardians and trustees.

78.235 Stock certificates: Validation; facsimile signatures; uncertificated shares and informational statements.

78.240 Shares of stock are personal property; transfers.

78.242 Restrictions on transfer of stock.

78.245 Corporate stocks, bonds and securities not taxed when owned by nonresidents or foreign corporations.

78.250 Cancellation of outstanding certificates or change in informational statements: Issuance of new certificates or statements; order for surrender of certificates; penalties for failure to comply.

78.257 Right of stockholders to inspect and audit financial records; exceptions.

78.265 Preemptive rights of stockholders in corporations organized before October 1, 1991.

78.267 Preemptive rights of stockholders in corporations organized on or after October 1, 1991.

78.275 Assessments on stock: Levy and collection; sale after default in payment.

78.280 Purchase by corporation of its own stock at assessment sale when no other available purchaser.

78.283 Treasury shares: Definition; limitations; retirement and disposal.

78.288 Distributions to stockholders.

78.295 Liability of directors for declaration of distributions.

78.300 Liability of directors for unlawful distributions.

78.307 "Investment company" and "open-end investment company" defined; redemption of shares by open-end investment company.

Meetings, Elections, Voting and Notice

78.310 Place of stockholders' and directors' meetings.

78.315 Directors' meetings: Quorum; consent for actions taken without meeting; participation by telephone or similar method.

78.320 Stockholders' meetings: Quorum; consent for actions taken without meeting; participation by telephone or similar method.

78.325 Actions at meetings not regularly called: Ratification and approval.

78.330 Directors: Election; classification; voting power.

78.335 Directors: Removal; filling of vacancies.

78.340 Failure to hold election of directors on regular day does not dissolve corporation.

78.345 Election of directors by order of court upon failure of regular election.

78.347 Application by stockholder for order of court appointing custodian or receiver; authority of custodian.

78.350 Voting rights of stockholders; determination of stockholders entitled to notice of and to vote at meeting.

78.355 Stockholders' proxies.

78.360 Cumulative voting.

78.365 Voting trusts.

78.370 Notice to stockholders.

78.375 Waiver of notice.

Acquisition of Controlling Interest

78.378 Applicability; imposition of stricter requirements; protection of corporation and its stockholders.

78.3781 Definitions.

78.3782 "Acquiring person" defined.

78.3783 "Acquisition" defined.

78.3784 "Control shares" defined.

78.3785 "Controlling interest" defined.

78.3786 "Fair value" defined.

78.3787 "Interested stockholder" defined.

78.3788 "Issuing corporation" defined.

78.3789 Delivery of offeror's statement by acquiring person; contents of statement.

78.379 Voting rights of acquiring person; meeting of stockholders; statements to accompany notice of meeting.

78.3791 Approval of voting rights of acquiring person.

78.3792 Redemption of control shares.

78.3793 Notice to stockholders; purchase of shares by corporation.

Amendment and Restatement of Articles of Incorporation

78.380 Amendment of articles before issuing stock.

86.505 Continuation of company after dissolution for winding up of affairs; limitation on actions by or against dissolved company.

86.521 Distribution of assets after dissolution.

86.531 Articles of dissolution: Preparation and contents; execution.

86.541 Articles of dissolution: Filing; duties of secretary of state; effect of filing.

Miscellaneous Provisions

86.551 Registration of foreign limited-liability company.

86.555 Issuance of occupational or professional license to limited-liability company by board or commission; regulations.

86.561 Secretary of state: Fees.

86.563 Secretary of state: Procedure to submit replacement page before filing of document.

86.566 Secretary of state: Filing of documents written in language other than English.

86.571 Waiver of notice.

CHAPTER 78 PRIVATE CORPORATIONS

General Provisions

78.010 Definitions; construction.

1. As used in this chapter:

(a) "Approval" and "vote" as describing action by the directors or stockholders mean the vote of directors in person or by written consent or of stockholders in person, by proxy or by written consent.

(b) "Articles," "articles of incorporation" and "certificate of incorporation" are synonymous terms and unless the context otherwise requires, include all certificates filed pursuant to 78.030, 78.195, 78.209, 78.380, 78.385 and 78.390 and any articles of merger or exchange filed pursuant to 92A.200 to 92A.240, inclusive. Unless the context otherwise requires, these terms include restated articles and certificates of incorporation.

(c) "Directors" and "trustees" are synonymous terms.

(d) "Receiver" includes receivers and trustees appointed by a court as provided in this chapter or in chapter 32 of NRS.

(e) "Registered office" means the office maintained at the street address of the resident agent.

(f) "Resident agent" means the agent appointed by the corporation upon whom process or a notice or demand authorized by law to be served upon the corporation may be served.

(g) "Stockholder of record" means a person whose name appears on the stock ledger of the corporation.

2. General terms and powers given in this chapter are not restricted by the use of special terms, or by any grant of special powers contained in this chapter.

78.015 Applicability of chapter; effect on corporations existing before April 1, 1925.

1. The provisions of this chapter apply to:

(a) Corporations organized in this state on or after October 1, 1991, except:

(1) Where the provisions of chapters 80, 84 and 89 of are inconsistent with the provisions of this chapter;

(2) Corporations expressly excluded by the provisions of this chapter; and

(3) Corporations governed by the provisions of NRS 81.170 to 81.540, inclusive, and chapter 82 of NRS.

(b) Corporations whose charters are renewed or revived in the manner provided in NRS 78.730.

(c) Corporations organized and still existing under this chapter before October 1, 1991, or any prior act or any amendment thereto.

(d) Close corporations, unless otherwise provided in chapter 78A of NRS.

(e) All insurance companies, mutual fire insurance companies, surety companies, express companies, railroad companies, and public utility companies now existing and formed before October 1, 1991, under any other act or law of this state, subject to any special provisions concerning any class of corporations inconsistent with the provisions of this chapter, in which case the special provisions continue to apply.

2. Neither the existence of corporations formed or existing before April 1, 1925, nor any liability, cause of action, right, privilege or immunity validly existing in favor of or against any such corporation on April 1, 1925, are affected, abridged, taken away or impaired by this chapter, or by any change in the requirements for the formation of corporations provided by this chapter, nor by the amendment or repeal of any laws under which such prior existing corporations were formed or created.

78.020 Limitations on incorporation under chapter; compliance with other laws.

1. Insurance companies, mutual fire insurance companies, surety companies, express companies and railroad companies may be formed under this chapter, but such a corporation may not:

(a) Transact any such business within this state until it has first complied with all laws concerning or affecting the right to engage in such business.

(b) Infringe the laws of any other state or country in which it may intend to engage in business, by so incorporating under this chapter.

2. No trust company, savings and loan association, thrift company or corporation organized for the purpose of conducting a banking business may be organized under this chapter.

78.025 Reserved power of state to amend or repeal chapter; chapter part of corporation's charter. This chapter may be amended or repealed at the pleasure of the legislature, and every corporation created under this chapter, or availing itself of any of the provisions of this chapter, and all stockholders of such corporation shall be bound by such amendment; but such amendment or repeal shall not take away or impair any remedy against any corporation, or its officers, for any liability which shall have been previously incurred. This chapter, and all amendments thereof, shall be a part of the charter of every corporation, except so far as the same are inapplicable and inappropriate to the objects of the corporation.

78.027 Corporate documents: Microfilming and return. The secretary of state may microfilm any document which is filed in his office by a corporation pursuant to this chapter and may return the original document to the corporation.

78.028 Filing of documents written in language other than English. No document which is written in a language other than English may be filed or submitted for filing in the office of the secretary of state pursuant to the provisions of this chapter unless it is accompanied by a verified translation of that document into the English language.

78.029 Procedure to submit replacement page to secretary of state before filing of document. An incorporator or officer of a corporation may authorize the secretary of state in writing to replace any page of a document submitted for filing on an expedited basis, before the actual filing, and to accept the page as if it were part of the originally signed filing. The signed authorization of the incorporator or officer to the secretary of state permits, but does not require, the secretary of state to alter the original document as requested.

78.0295 Incorrect or defective document: Certificate of correction; effective date of correction.

1. A corporation may correct a document filed by the secretary of state if the document contains an incorrect statement or was defectively executed, attested, sealed, verified or acknowledged.

2. To correct a document, the corporation shall:

(a) Prepare a certificate of correction which:

(1) States the name of the corporation;

(2) Describes the document, including, without limitation, its filing date;

(3) Specifies the incorrect statement and the reason it is incorrect or the manner in which the execution or other formal authentication was defective;

(4) Corrects the incorrect statement or defective execution; and

(5) Is signed by an officer of the corporation; and

(b) Deliver the certificate to the secretary of state for filing.

3. A certificate of correction is effective on the effective date of the document it corrects except as to persons relying on the uncorrected document and adversely affected by the correction. As to those persons, the certificate is effective when filed.

Formation

78.030 Filing of articles of incorporation and certificate of acceptance of appointment of resident agent.

1. One or more persons may establish a corporation for the transaction of any lawful business, or to promote or conduct any legitimate object or purpose, pursuant and subject to the requirements of this chapter, by:

(a) Executing, acknowledging and filing in the office of the secretary of state articles of incorporation; and

(b) Filing a certificate of acceptance of appointment, executed by the resident agent of the corporation, in the office of the secretary of state.

2. The articles of incorporation must be as provided in NRS 78.035, and the secretary of state shall require them to be in the form prescribed. If any articles are defective in this respect, the secretary of state shall return them for correction.

78.035 Articles of incorporation: Required provisions. The articles of incorporation must set forth:

1. The name of the corporation. A name appearing to be that of a natural person and containing a given name or initials must not be used as a corporate name except with an additional word or words such as "Incorporated," "Limited," "Inc.," "Ltd.," "Company," "Co.," "Corporation," "Corp.," or other word which identifies it as not being a natural person.

2. The name of the person designated as the corporation's resident agent, the street address of the resident agent where process may be served upon the corporation, and the mailing address of the resident agent if different from the street address.

3. The number of shares the corporation is authorized to issue and, if more than one class or series of stock is authorized, the classes, the series and the number of shares of each class or series which the corporation is authorized to issue, unless the articles authorize the board of directors to fix and determine in a resolution the classes, series and numbers of each class or series as provided in NRS 78.195 and 78.196.

4. Whether the members of the governing board are styled as directors or trustees of the corporation, and the number, names and post office box or street addresses, either residence or business, of the first board of directors or trustees, together with any desired provisions relative to the right to change the number of directors as provided in NRS 78.115.

5. The name and post office box or street address, either residence or business of each of the incorporators executing the articles of incorporation.

78.037 Articles of incorporation: Optional provisions. The articles of incorporation may also contain:

1. A provision eliminating or limiting the personal liability of a director or officer to the corporation or its stockholders for damages for breach of fiduciary duty as a director or officer, but such a provision must not eliminate or limit the liability of a director or officer for:

(a) Acts or omissions which involve intentional misconduct, fraud or a knowing violation of law; or

(b) The payment of distributions in violation of NRS 78.300.

2. Any provision, not contrary to the laws of this state, for the management of the business and for the conduct of the affairs of the corporation, and any provision creating, defining, limiting or regulating the powers of the corporation or the rights, powers or duties of the directors, and the stockholders, or any class of the stockholders, or the holders of bonds or other obligations of the corporation, or governing the distribution or division of the profits of the corporation.

78.039 Name of corporation: Distinguishable name required; availability of name of revoked, terminated or merged corporation.

1. The name proposed for a corporation must be distinguishable from the names of all other artificial persons organized or registered under chapter 78, 78A, 80, 81, 82, 84, 86, 87, 88 or 89 of NRS whose names are on file in the office of the secretary of state. If a proposed name is not so distinguishable, the secretary of state shall return the articles of incorporation containing the proposed name to the incorporator, unless the written acknowledged consent of the holder of the registered or reserved name to use the same name or the requested similar name accompanies the articles of incorporation.

2. For the purposes of this section and NRS 78.040, a proposed name is not distinguished from a registered or reserved name solely because one or the other contains distinctive lettering, a distinctive mark, a trade-mark or a trade name or any combination of these.

3. The name of a corporation whose charter has been revoked, whose existence has terminated, which has merged and is not the surviving corporation, or which for any other reason is no longer in good standing in this state is available for use by any other artificial person.

78.040 Name of corporation: Reservation; injunctive relief.

1. The secretary of state, when requested so to do, shall reserve, for a period of 90 days, the right to use any name available under NRS 78.039, for the use of any proposed corporation. During the period, a name so reserved is not available for use by any corporation, limited partnership or limited-liability company without the consent of the person at whose request the reservation was made.

2. The use by any corporation, limited partnership or limited-liability company of a name in violation of NRS 78.039 or subsection 1 of this section may be enjoined, notwithstanding the fact that the articles of incorporation or organization of the corporation or limited-liability company, or the certificate of limited partnership, may have been filed by the secretary of state.

78.045 Articles of incorporation: Approval or certification required before filing of certain articles or amendments.

1. The secretary of state shall not accept for filing any articles of incorporation or an certificate of amendment of articles of incorporation of any corporation formed pursuant to the laws of this state which provides that the name of the corporation contain the word "bank" or "trust," unless:

(a) It appears from the articles or the certificate of amendment that the corporation proposes to carry on business as a banking or trust company, exclusively or in connection with its business as a bank or savings and loan association; and

(b) The articles or certificate of amendment is first approved by the commissioner of financial institutions.

2. The secretary of state shall not accept for filing any articles of incorporation or any certificate of amendment of articles of incorporation of any corporation formed pursuant to the provisions of this chapter when it appears from the articles or the certificate of amendment that the business to be carried on by the corporation is subject to supervision by the commissioner of insurance or by the commissioner of financial institutions, unless the articles or certificate of amendment is first approved by the commissioner who will be supervising the business of the corporation.

3. Except as otherwise provided in subsection 4, the secretary of state shall not accept for filing any articles of incorporation or any certificate or amendment of articles of incorporation of any corporation formed pursuant to the laws of this state if the name of the corporation contains the words "engineer," "engineered," "engineering," "professional engineer" or "licensed engineer" unless:

(a) The state board of professional engineers and land surveyors certifies that the principals of the corporation are licensed to practice engineering pursuant to the laws of this state; or

(b) The state board of professional engineers and land surveyors certifies that the corporation is exempt from the prohibitions of NRS 625.520.

4. The provisions of subsection 3 do not apply to any corporation, whose securities are publicly traded and regulated by the Securities Exchange Act of 1934, which does not engage in the practice of professional engineering.

5. The commissioner of financial institutions and the commissioner of insurance may approve or disapprove the articles or amendments referred to them pursuant to the provisions of this section.

78.050 Commencement of corporate existence.

1. Upon the filing of the articles of incorporation and the certificate of acceptance pursuant to NRS 78.030, and the payment of the filing fees, the secretary of state shall issue to the corporation a certificate that the articles, containing the required statement of facts, have been filed. From the date the articles are filed, the corporation is a body corporate, by the name set forth in the articles of incorporation, subject to the forfeiture of its charter or dissolution as provided in this chapter.

2. Neither an incorporator nor a director designated in the articles of incorporation thereby becomes a subscriber or stockholder of the corporation.

3. The filing of the articles of incorporation does not, by itself, constitute commencement of business by the corporation.

78.055 Acceptable evidence of incorporation. A copy of any articles of incorporation filed pursuant to this chapter, and certified by the secretary of state under his official seal, or, with respect to a corporation organized before October 1, 1991, a copy of the copy thereof, filed with the county clerk, or microfilmed by the county clerk, under the county seal, certified by the clerk, must be received in all courts and places as prima facie evidence of the facts therein stated, and of the existence and incorporation of the corporation therein named.

Powers

78.060 General powers.

1. Any corporation organized under the provisions of this chapter:

(a) Has all the rights, privileges and powers conferred by this chapter.

(b) Has such rights, privileges and powers as may be conferred upon corporations by any other existing law.

(c) May at any time exercise those rights, privileges and powers, when not inconsistent with the provisions of this chapter, or with the purposes and objects for which the corporation is organized.

(d) Unless otherwise provided in its articles, has perpetual existence.

2. Every corporation, by virtue of its existence as such, is entitled:

(a) To have succession by its corporate name until dissolved and its affairs are wound up according to law.

(b) To sue and be sued in any court of law or equity.

(c) To make contracts.

(d) To hold, purchase and convey real and personal estate and to mortgage or lease any such real and personal estate with its franchises. The power to hold real and personal estate includes the power to take it by devise or bequest in this state, or in any other state, territory or country.

(e) To appoint such officers and agents as the affairs of the corporation require, and to allow them suitable compensation.

(f) To make bylaws not inconsistent with the constitution or laws of the United States, or of this state, for the management, regulation and government of its affairs and property, the transfer of its stock, the transaction of its business, and the calling and holding of meetings of its stockholders.

(g) To wind up and dissolve itself, or be wound up or dissolved, in the manner mentioned in this chapter.

(h) Unless otherwise provided in the articles, to engage in any lawful activity.

78.065 Adoption and use of corporate seal or stamp.

1. Every corporation, by virtue of its existence as such, shall have power to adopt and use a common seal or stamp, and alter the same at pleasure.

2. The use of a seal or stamp by a corporation on any corporate documents is not necessary. The corporation may use a seal or stamp, if it desires, but such use or nonuse shall not in any way affect the legality of the document.

78.070 Specific powers. Subject to such limitations, if any, as may be contained in its articles of incorporation, every corporation has the following powers:

1. To borrow money and contract debts when necessary for the transaction of its business, or for the exercise of its corporate rights, privileges or franchises, or for any other lawful purpose of its incorporation; to issue bonds, promissory notes, bills of exchange, debentures, and other obligations and evidences of indebtedness, payable at a specified time or times, or payable upon the happening of a specified event or events, whether secured by mortgage, pledge or other security, or unsecured, for money borrowed, or in payment for property purchased, or acquired, or for any other lawful object.

2. To guarantee, purchase, hold, take, obtain, receive, subscribe for, own, use, dispose of, sell, exchange, lease, lend, assign, mortgage, pledge, or otherwise acquire, transfer or deal in or with bonds or obligations of, or shares, securities or interests in or issued by, any person, government, governmental agency or political subdivision of government, and to exercise all the rights, powers and privileges of ownership of such an interest, including the right to vote, if any.

3. To purchase, hold, sell, pledge and transfer shares of its own stock, and use therefor its property or money.

4. To conduct business, have one or more offices, and hold, purchase, mortgage and convey real and personal property in this state, and in any of the several states, territories, possessions and dependencies of the United States, the District of Columbia, Puerto Rico and any foreign countries.

5. To do everything necessary and proper for the accomplishment of the objects enumerated in its articles of incorporation or necessary or incidental to the protection and benefit of the corporation, and, in general, to carry on any lawful business necessary or incidental to the attainment of the objects of the corporation, whether or not the business is similar in nature to the objects set forth in the articles of incorporation, except that:

(a) A corporation created under the provisions of this chapter does not possess the power of issuing bills, notes or other evidences of debt for circulation of money; and

(b) This chapter does not authorize the formation of banking corporations to issue or circulate money or currency within this state, or outside of this state, or at all, except the federal currency, or the notes of banks authorized under the laws of the United States.

6. To make donations for the public welfare or for charitable, scientific or educational purposes.

7. To enter into any relationship with another person in connection with any lawful activities.

Registered Office and Registered Agent

78.090 Resident agent required; address of registered office; powers of bank or corporation who is resident agent; penalty for noncompliance; service of documents on resident agent.

1. Except during any period of vacancy described in NRS 78.097, every corporation must have a resident agent who resides or is located in this state. Every resident agent must have a street address for the service of process, and may have a separate mailing address such as a post office box, which may be different from the street address. The street address of the resident agent is the registered office of the corporation in this state.

2. If the resident agent is a bank or corporation, it may:

(a) Act as the fiscal or transfer agent of any state, municipality, body politic or corporation and in that capacity may receive and disburse money.

(b) Transfer, register and countersign certificates of stock, bonds or other evidences of indebtedness and act as agent of any corporation, foreign or domestic, for any purpose required by statute, or otherwise.

(c) Act as trustee under any mortgage or bond issued by any municipality, body politic or corporation, and accept and execute any other municipal or corporate trust not inconsistent with the laws of this state.

(d) Receive and manage any sinking fund of any corporation, upon such terms as may be agreed upon between the corporation and those dealing with it.

3. Every corporation organized pursuant to this chapter which fails or refuses to comply with the requirements of this section is subject to a fine of not less than $100 nor more than $500, to be recovered with costs by the state, before any court of competent jurisdiction, by action at law prosecuted by the attorney general or by the district attorney of the county in which the action or proceeding to recover the fine is prosecuted.

4. All legal process and any demand or notice authorized by law to be served upon a corporation may be served upon the resident agent of the corporation in the manner provided in subsection 2 of NRS 14.020. If any demand, notice or legal process, other than a summons and complaint, cannot be served upon the resident agent, it may be served in the manner provided in NRS 14.030. These manners and modes of service are in addition to any other service authorized by law.

78.095 Change of address of resident agent and registered office.

1. Within 30 days after changing the location of his office from one address to another in this state, a resident agent shall execute a certificate setting forth:

(a) The names of all the corporations represented by the resident agent;

(b) The address at which the resident agent has maintained the registered office for each of such corporations; and

(c) The new address to which the resident agency will be transferred and at which the resident agent will thereafter maintain the registered office for each of the corporations recited in the certificate.

2. Upon the filing of the certificate in the office of the secretary of state the registered office in this state of each of the corporations recited in the certificate is located at the new address of the resident agent thereof as set forth in the certificate.

78.097 Resignation of resident agent; notice to corporation of resignation; appointment of successor.

1. A resident agent who desires to resign shall file with the secretary of state a signed statement for each corporation that he is unwilling to continue to act as the agent of the corporation for the service of process. The execution of the statement must be acknowledged. A resignation is not effective until the signed statement is filed with the secretary of state.

2. The statement of resignation may contain an acknowledged statement of the affected corporation appointing a successor resident agent for that corporation. A certificate of acceptance executed by the new resident agent, stating the full name, complete street address and, if different from the street address, mailing address of the new resident agent, must accompany the statement appointing a successor resident agent.

3. Upon the filing of the statement of resignation with the secretary of state the capacity of the resigning person as resident agent terminates. If the statement of resignation contains no statement by the corporation appointing a successor resident agent, the resigning resident agent shall immediately give written notice, by mail, to the corporation of the filing of the statement and its effect. The notice must be addressed to any officer of the corporation other than the resident agent.

4. If a resident agent dies, resigns or removes from the state, the corporation, within 30 days thereafter, shall file with the secretary of state a certificate of acceptance executed by the new resident agent. The certificate must set forth the full name and complete street address of the new resident agent for the service of process, and may have a separate mailing address, such as post office box, which may be different from the street address.

5. A corporation that fails to file a certificate of acceptance executed by the new resident agent within 30 days after the death, resignation or removal of its former resident agent shall be deemed in default and is subject to the provisions of NRS 78.170 and 78.175.

78.105 Maintenance of records at registered office; inspection and copying of records; civil liability; penalties.

1. A corporation shall keep a copy of the following records at its registered office:

(a) A copy certified by the secretary of state of its articles of incorporation, and all amendments thereto;

(b) A copy certified by an officer of the corporation of its bylaws and all amendments thereto; and

(c) A stock ledger or a duplicate stock ledger, revised annually, containing the names, alphabetically arranged, of all persons who are stockholders of the corporation, showing their places of residence, if known, and the number of shares held by them respectively. In lieu of the stock ledger or duplicate stock ledger, the corporation may keep a statement setting out the name of the custodian of the stock ledger or duplicate stock ledger, and the present and complete post office address, including street and number, if any, where the stock ledger or duplicate stock ledger specified in this section is kept.

2. A corporation shall maintain the records required by subsection 1 in written form or in another form capable of conversion into written form within a reasonable time.

3. Any person who has been a stockholder of record of a corporation for at least 6 months immediately preceding his demand, or any person holding, or thereunto authorized in writing by the holders of, at least 5 percent of all of its outstanding shares, upon at least 5 days' written demand is entitled to inspect in person or by agent or attorney, during usual business hours, the records required by subsection 1 and make copies therefrom. Holders of voting trust certificates representing shares of the corporation must be regarded as stockholders for the purpose of this subsection. Every corporation that neglects or refuses to keep the records required by subsection 1 open for inspection, as required in this subsection, shall forfeit to the state the sum of $25 for every day of such neglect or refusal.

4. If any corporation willfully neglects or refuses to make any proper entry in the stock ledger or duplicate copy thereof, or neglects or refuses to permit an inspection of the records required by subsection 1 upon demand by a person entitled to inspect them, or refuses to permit copies to be made therefrom, as provided in subsection 3, the corporation is liable to the person injured for all damages resulting to him therefrom.

5. When the corporation keeps a statement in the manner provided for in paragraph (c) of subsection 1, the information contained thereon must be given to any stockholder of the corporation demanding the information, when the demand is made during business hours. Every corporation that neglects or refuses to keep a statement available, as in this subsection required, shall forfeit to the state the sum of $25 for every day of such neglect or refusal.

6. In every instance where an attorney or other agent of the stockholder seeks the right of inspection, the demand must be accompanied by a power of attorney executed by the stockholder authorizing the attorney or other agent to inspect on behalf of the stockholder.

7. The right to copy records under subsection 3 includes, if reasonable, the right to make copies by photographic, xerographic or other means.

8. The corporation may impose a reasonable charge to recover the costs of labor and materials and the cost of copies of any documents provided to the stockholder.

78.107 Denial of request for inspection of records; defense to action for penalties or damages; authority of court to compel production of records.

1. An inspection authorized by NRS 78.105 may be denied to a stockholder or other person upon his refusal to furnish to the corporation an affidavit that the inspection is not desired for a purpose which is in the interest of a business or object other than the business of the corporation and that he has not at any time sold or offered for sale any list of stockholders of any domestic or foreign corporation or aided or abetted any person in procuring any such record of stockholders for any such purpose.

2. It is a defense to any action for penalties or damages under NRS 78.105 that the person suing has at any time sold, or offered for sale, any list of stockholders of the corporation, or any other corporation, or has aided or abetted any person in procuring any such stock list for any such purpose, or that the person suing desired inspection for a purpose which is in the interest of a business or object other than the business of the corporation.

3. This section does not impair the power or jurisdiction of any court to compel the production for examination of the books of a corporation in any proper case.

78.110 Change of resident agent or location of registered office.

If a corporation created pursuant to this chapter desires to change the location within this state of its registered office, or change its resident agent, or both, the change may be effected by filing with the secretary of state a certificate of change signed by an officer of the corporation which sets forth:

1. The name of the corporation;

2. That the change authorized by this section is effective upon the filing of the certificate of change;

3. The street address of its present registered office;

4. If the present registered office is to be changed, the street address of the new registered office;

5. The name of its present resident agent; and

6. If the present resident agent is to be changed, the name of the new resident agent. A new resident agent's certificate of acceptance must be a part of or attached to the certificate of change.

Directors and Officers

78.115 Board of directors: Number and qualifications. The business of every corporation must be managed by a board of directors or trustees, all of whom must be natural persons who are at least 18 years of age. A corporation must have at least one director, and may provide in its articles of incorporation or in its bylaws for a fixed number of directors or a variable number of directors within a fixed

minimum and maximum, and for the manner in which the number of directors may be increased or decreased. Unless otherwise provided in the articles of incorporation, directors need not be stockholders.

78.120 Board of directors: General powers.

1. Subject only to such limitations as may be provided by this chapter, or the articles of incorporation of the corporation, the board of directors has full control over the affairs of the corporation.

2. Subject to the bylaws, if any, adopted by the stockholders, the directors may make the bylaws of the corporation.

3. The selection of a period for the achievement of corporate goals is the responsibility of the directors.

78.125 Committees of board of directors: Designation; powers; names; membership.

1. Unless it is otherwise provided in the articles of incorporation, the board of directors may designate one or more committees which, to the extent provided in the resolution or resolutions or in the bylaws of the corporation, have and may exercise the powers of the board of directors in the management of the business and affairs of the corporation, and may have power to authorize the seal of the corporation to be affixed to all papers on which the corporation desires to place a seal.

2. The committee or committees must have such name or names as may be stated in the bylaws of the corporation or as may be determined from time to time by resolution adopted by the board of directors.

3. Each committee must include at least one director. Unless the articles of incorporation or the bylaws provide otherwise, the board of directors may appoint natural persons who are not directors to serve on committees.

78.130 Officers of corporation: Selection; qualifications; terms; powers and duties; filling of vacancies.

1. Every corporation must have a president, a secretary and a treasurer.

2. Every corporation may also have one or more vice presidents, assistant secretaries and assistant treasurers, and such other officers and agents as may be deemed necessary.

3. All officers must be natural persons and must be chosen in such manner, hold their offices for such terms and have such powers and duties as may be prescribed by the bylaws or determined by the board of directors. Any natural person may hold two or more offices.

4. An officer holds office after the expiration of his term until a successor is chosen or until his resignation or removal before the expiration of his term. A failure to elect officers does not require the corporation to be dissolved. Any vacancy occurring in an office of the corporation by

death, resignation, removal or otherwise, must be filled as the bylaws provide, or in the absence of such a provision, by the board of directors.

78.135 Authority of directors and representatives of corporation.

1. The statement in the articles of incorporation of the objects, purposes, powers and authorized business of the corporation constitutes, as between the corporation and its directors, officers or stockholders, an authorization to the directors and a limitation upon the actual authority of the representatives of the corporation. Such limitations may be asserted in a proceeding by a stockholder or the state to enjoin the doing or continuation of unauthorized business by the corporation or its officers, or both, in cases where third parties have not acquired rights thereby, or to dissolve the corporation, or in a proceeding by the corporation or by the stockholders suing in a representative suit against the officers or directors of the corporation for violation of their authority.

2. No limitation upon the business, purposes or powers of the corporation or upon the powers of the stockholders, officers or directors, or the manner of exercise of such powers, contained in or implied by the articles may be asserted as between the corporation or any stockholder and any third person.

3. Any contract or conveyance, otherwise lawful, made in the name of a corporation, which is authorized or ratified by the directors, or is done within the scope of the authority, actual or apparent, given by the directors, binds the corporation, and the corporation acquires rights thereunder, whether the contract is executed or is wholly or in part executory.

78.138 Directors and officers: Exercise of powers and performance of duties.

1. Directors and officers shall exercise their powers in good faith and with a view to the interests of the corporation.

2. In performing their respective duties, directors and officers are entitled to rely on information, opinions, reports, books of account or statements, including financial statements and other financial data, that are prepared or presented by:

(a) One or more directors, officers or employees of the corporation reasonably believed to be reliable and competent in the matters prepared or presented;

(b) Counsel, public accountants, or other persons as to matters reasonably believed to be within the preparer or presenter's professional or expert competence; or

(c) A committee on which the director or officer relying thereon does not serve, established in accordance with NRS 78.125, as to matters within the committee's designated authority and matters on which the committee is

reasonably believed to merit confidence, but a director or officer is not entitled to rely on such information, opinions, reports, books of account or statements if he has knowledge concerning the matter in question that would cause reliance thereon to be unwarranted.

3. Directors and officers, in exercising their respective powers with a view to the interests of the corporation, may consider:

(a) The interests of the corporation's employees, suppliers, creditors and customers;

(b) The economy of the state and nation;

(c) The interests of the community and of society; and

(d) The long-term as well as short-term interests of the corporation and its stockholders, including the possibility that these interests may be best served by the continued independence of the corporation.

This subsection does not create or authorize any causes of action against the corporation or its directors or officers.

4. Directors may resist a change or potential change in control of the corporation if the directors by a majority vote of a quorum determine that the change or potential change is opposed to or not in the best interest of the corporation:

(a) Upon consideration of the interests of the corporation's stockholders and any of the matters set forth in subsection 3; or

(b) Because the amount or nature of the indebtedness and other obligations to which the corporation or any successor to the property of either may become subject in connection with the change or potential change in control provides reasonable grounds to believe that, within a reasonable time:

(1) The assets of the corporation or any successor would be or become less than its liabilities;

(2) The corporation or any successor would be or become insolvent; or

(3) Any voluntary or involuntary proceeding under the federal bankruptcy laws concerning the corporation or any successor would be commenced by any person.

78.140 Restrictions on transactions involving interested directors or officers; compensation of directors.

1. A contract or other transaction is not void or voidable solely because:

(a) The contract or transaction is between a corporation and:

(1) One or more of its directors or officers; or

(2) Another corporation, firm or association in which one or more of its directors or officers are directors or officers or are financially interested;

(b) A common or interested director or officer:

(1) Is present at the meeting of the board of directors or a committee thereof which authorizes or approves the contract or transaction; or

(2) Joins in the execution of a written consent which authorizes or approves the contract or transaction pursuant to subsection 2 of NRS 78.315; or

(c) The vote or votes of a common or interested director are counted for the purpose of authorizing or approving the contract or transaction, if one of the circumstances specified in subsection 2 exists.

2. The circumstances in which a contract or other transaction is not void or voidable pursuant to subsection 1 are:

(a) The fact of the common directorship, office or financial interest is known to the board of directors or committee, and the board or committee authorizes, approves or ratifies the contract or transaction in good faith by a vote sufficient for the purpose without counting the vote or votes of the common or interested director or directors.

(b) The fact of the common directorship, office or financial interest is known to the stockholders, and they approve or ratify the contract or transaction in good faith by a majority vote of stockholders holding a majority of the voting power. The votes of the common or interested directors or officers must be counted in any such vote of stockholders.

(c) The fact of the common directorship, office or financial interest is not known to the director or officer at the time the transaction is brought before the board of directors of the corporation for action.

(d) The contract or transaction is fair as to the corporation at the time it is authorized or approved.

3. Common or interested directors may be counted in determining the presence of a quorum at a meeting of the board of directors or a committee thereof which authorizes, approves or ratifies a contract or transaction, and if the votes of the common or interested directors are not counted at the meeting, then a majority of the disinterested directors may authorize, approve or ratify a contract or transaction.

4. Unless otherwise provided in the articles of incorporation or the bylaws, the board of directors, without regard to personal interest, may establish the compensation of directors for services in any capacity. If the board of directors establishes the compensation of directors pursuant to this subsection, such compensation is presumed to be fair to the corporation unless proven unfair by a preponderance of the evidence.

Annual List of Officers and Directors; Defaulting Corporations

78.150 Filing requirements; fee; forms.

1. A corporation organized under the laws of this state shall, on or before the first day of the second month after the filing of its articles of incorporation with the secretary

of state, file with the secretary of state a list, on a form furnished by him, containing:

(a) The name of the corporation;

(b) The file number of the corporation, if known;

(c) The names and titles of all of its required officers and the names of all of its directors;

(d) The mailing or street address, either residence or business, of each officer and director listed, following the name of the officer or director; and

(e) The signature of an officer of the corporation certifying that the list is true, complete and accurate.

2. The corporation shall annually thereafter, on or before the last day of the month in which the anniversary date of incorporation occurs in each year, file with the secretary of state, on a form furnished by him, an amended list containing all of the information required in subsection 1. If the corporation has had no changes in its required officers and directors since its previous list was filed, no amended list need be filed if an officer of the corporation certifies to the secretary of state as a true and accurate statement that no changes in the required officers or directors has occurred.

3. Upon filing a list of officers and directors, or certifying that no changes have occurred, the corporation shall pay to the secretary of state a fee of $85.

4. The secretary of state shall, 60 days before the last day for filing the annual list required by subsection 2, cause to be mailed to each corporation which is required to comply with the provisions of NRS 78.150 to 78.185, inclusive, and which has not become delinquent, a notice of the fee due pursuant to subsection 3 and a reminder to file a list of officers and directors or a certification of no change. Failure of any corporation to receive a notice or form does not excuse it from the penalty imposed by law.

5. If the list to be filed pursuant to the provisions of subsection 1 or 2 is defective in any respect or the fee required by subsection 3 or 7 is not paid, the secretary of state may return the list for correction or payment.

6. An annual list for a corporation not in default which is received by the secretary of state more than 60 days before its due date shall be deemed an amended list for the previous year.

7. If the corporation is an association as defined in NRS 116.110315, the secretary of state shall not accept the filing required by this section unless it is accompanied by the fee required to be paid pursuant to NRS 116.31155.

78.155 Certificate of authorization to transact business.
When the fee for filing the initial or annual list of officers and directors and designation of resident agent has been paid, the canceled check received by the corporation

constitutes a certificate authorizing it to transact its business within this state until the last day of the month in which the anniversary of its incorporation occurs in the next succeeding calendar year. If the corporation desires a formal certificate upon its payment of the initial or annual fee, its payment must be accompanied by a self-addressed, stamped envelope.

78.165 Addresses of officers and directors required; failure to file.

1. Every list required to be filed under the provisions of NRS 78.150 to 78.185, inclusive, must, after the name of each officer and director listed thereon, set forth the post office box or street address, either residence or business, of each officer and director.

2. If the addresses are not stated for each person on any list offered for filing, the secretary of state may refuse to file the list, and the corporation for which the list has been offered for filing is subject to all the provisions of NRS 78.150 to 78.185, inclusive, relating to failure to file the list within or at the times therein specified, unless a list is subsequently submitted for filing which conforms to the provisions of NRS 78.150 to 78.185, inclusive.

78.170 Defaulting corporations: Identification; penalty.

1. Each corporation required to make a filing and pay the fee prescribed in NRS 78.150 to 78.185, inclusive, which refuses or neglects to do so within the time provided shall be deemed in default.

2. For default there must be added to the amount of the fee a penalty of $15. The fee and penalty must be collected as provided in this chapter.

78.175 Defaulting corporations: Duties of secretary of state; revocation of charter and forfeiture of right to transact business; distribution of assets.

1. The secretary of state shall notify, by letter addressed to its resident agent, each corporation deemed in default pursuant to NRS 78.170. The notice must be accompanied by a statement indicating the amount of the filing fee, penalties and costs remaining unpaid.

2. On the first day of the ninth month following the month in which the filing was required, the charter of the corporation is revoked and its right to transact business is forfeited.

3. The secretary of state shall compile a complete list containing the names of all corporations whose right to do business has been forfeited. The secretary of state shall forthwith notify, by letter addressed to its resident agent, each such corporation of the forfeiture of its charter. The notice must be accompanied by a statement indicating the amount of the filing fee, penalties and costs remaining unpaid.

4. If the charter of a corporation is revoked and the right to transact business is forfeited as provided in subsection 2, all of the property and assets of the defaulting domestic corporation must be held in trust by the directors of the corporation as for insolvent corporations, and the same proceedings may be had with respect thereto as are applicable to insolvent corporations. Any person interested may institute proceedings at any time after a forfeiture has been declared, but if the secretary of state reinstates the charter the proceedings must at once be dismissed and all property restored to the officers of the corporation.

5. Where the assets are distributed they must be applied in the following manner:

(a) To the payment of the filing fee, penalties and costs due to the state;

(b) To the payment of the creditors of the corporation; and

(c) Any balance remaining to distribution among the stockholders.

78.180 Defaulting corporations: Conditions and procedure for reinstatement.

1. Except as otherwise provided in subsections 3 and 4, the secretary of state shall reinstate a corporation which has forfeited its right to transact business under the provisions of this chapter and restore to the corporation its right to carry on business in this state, and to exercise its corporate privileges and immunities, if it:

(a) Files with the secretary of state the list required by NRS 78.150; and

(b) Pays to the secretary of state:

(1) The annual filing fee and penalty set forth in NRS 78.150 and 78.170 for each year or portion thereof during which its charter was revoked; and

(2) A fee of $50 for reinstatement.

2. When the secretary of state reinstates the corporation, he shall:

(a) Immediately issue and deliver to the corporation a certificate of reinstatement authorizing it to transact business as if the filing fee had been paid when due; and

(b) Upon demand, issue to the corporation one or more certified copies of the certificate of reinstatement.

3. The secretary of state shall not order a reinstatement unless all delinquent fees and penalties have been paid, and the revocation of the charter occurred only by reason of failure to pay the fees and penalties.

4. If a corporate charter has been revoked pursuant to the provisions of this chapter and has remained revoked for a period of five consecutive years, the charter must not be reinstated.

78.185 Defaulting corporations: Reinstatement under old or new name.

1. Except as otherwise provided in subsection 2, if a corporation applies to reinstate or revive its charter but its name has been legally acquired by another corporation or other artificial person organized or registered under chapter 78, 78A, 80, 81, 82, 84, 86, 87, 88 or 89 of NRS whose name is on file and in good standing with the secretary of state, the corporation shall in its application for reinstatement submit in writing to the secretary of state some other name under which it desires its corporate existence to be reinstated or revived. If that name is distinguishable from all other names reserved or otherwise on file and in good standing, the secretary of state shall issue to the applying corporation a certificate of reinstatement or revival under that new name.

2. If the applying corporation submits the written acknowledged consent of the artificial person having a name, or the person who has reserved a name, which is not distinguishable from the old name of the applying corporation or a new name it has submitted, it may be reinstated or revived under that name.

3. For the purposes of this section, a proposed name is not distinguished from a name used or reserved solely because one or the other contains distinctive lettering, a distinctive mark, a trade-mark or a trade name or any combination of those.

Stock and Other Securities; Distributions

78.191 "Distribution" defined. As used in NRS 78.195 to 78.307, inclusive, unless the context otherwise requires, the word "distribution" means a direct or indirect transfer of money or other property other than its own shares or the incurrence of indebtedness by a corporation to or for the benefit of its stockholders with respect to any of its shares. A distribution may be in the form of a declaration or payment of a dividend, a purchase, redemption or other acquisition of shares, a distribution of indebtedness, or otherwise.

78.195 Issuance of more than one class or series of stock; rights of stockholders.

1. If a corporation desires to have more than one class or series of stock, the articles of incorporation must prescribe, or vest authority in the board of directors to prescribe, the classes, series and the number of each class or series of stock and the voting powers, designations, preferences, limitations, restrictions and relative rights of each class or series of stock. If more than one class or series of stock is authorized, the articles of incorporation or the resolution of the board of directors passed pursuant to a provision of the articles must prescribe a distinguishing designation for each class and series. The voting powers, designations, preferences, limitations, restrictions, relative rights and distinguishing designation of each class or series of stock must be described in the articles of incorporation or the resolution of the board of directors before the issuance of shares of that class or series.

2. All shares of a series must have voting powers, designations, preferences, limitations, restrictions and relative rights identical with those of other shares of the same series and, except to the extent otherwise provided in the description of the series, with those of other series of the same class.

3. Unless otherwise provided in the articles of incorporation, no stock issued as fully paid up may ever be assessed and the articles of incorporation must not be amended in this particular.

4. Any rate, condition or time for payment of distributions on any class or series of stock may be made dependent upon any fact or event which may be ascertained outside the articles of incorporation or the resolution providing for the distributions adopted by the board of directors if the manner in which a fact or event may operate upon the rate, condition or time of payment for the distributions is stated in the articles of incorporation or the resolution.

5. If the corporation is authorized to issue more than one class of stock or more than one series of any class, the voting powers, designations, preferences, limitations, restrictions and relative rights of the various classes of stock or series thereof and the qualifications, limitations or restrictions of such rights must be set forth in full or summarized on the face or back of each certificate which the corporation issues to represent the stock, or on the informational statement sent pursuant to NRS 78.235, except that, in lieu thereof, the certificate or informational statement may contain a statement setting forth the office or agency of the corporation from which a stockholder may obtain a copy of a statement setting forth in full or summarizing the voting powers, designations, preferences, limitations, restrictions and relative rights of the various classes of stock or series thereof. The corporation shall furnish to its stockholders, upon request and without charge, a copy of any such statement or summary.

6. The provisions of this section do not restrict the directors of a corporation from taking action to protect the interests of the corporation and its stockholders, including, but not limited to, adopting or executing plans, arrangements or instruments that deny rights, privileges, power or authority to a holder of a specified number of shares or percentage of share ownership or voting power.

78.1955 Establishment of matters regarding class or series of stock by resolution of board of directors.

1. If the voting powers, designations, preferences, limitations, restrictions and relative rights of any class or series of stock have been established by a resolution of the board of directors pursuant to a provision in the articles of incorporation, a certificate of designation must be filed with the secretary of state setting forth the resolution. The certificate of designation must be executed by the president or vice president and secretary or assistant secretary and acknowledged by the president or vice president before a person authorized by the laws of Nevada to take acknowledgments of deeds. The certificate of designation so executed and acknowledged must be filed before the issuance of any shares of the class or series.

2. Unless otherwise provided in the articles of incorporation or the certificate of designation being amended, if no shares of a class or series of stock established by a resolution of the board of directors have been issued, the designation of the class or series, the number of the class or series and the voting powers, designations, preferences, limitations, restrictions and relative rights of the class or series may be amended by a resolution of the board of directors pursuant to a certificate of amendment filed in the manner provided in subsection 4.

3. Unless otherwise provided in the articles of incorporation or the certificate of designation, if shares of a class or series of stock established by a resolution of the board of directors have been issued, the designation of the class or series, the number of the class or series and the voting powers, designations, preferences, limitations, restrictions and relative rights of the class or series may be amended by a resolution of the board of directors only if the amendment is approved as provided in this subsection. Unless otherwise provided in the articles of incorporation or the certificate of designation, the proposed amendment adopted by the board of directors must be approved by the vote of stockholders holding shares in the corporation entitling them to exercise a majority of the voting power, or such greater proportion of the voting power as may be required by the articles of incorporation or the certificate of designation, of:

(a) The class or series of stock being amended; and

(b) Each class and each series of stock which, before amendment, is senior to the class or series being amended as to the payment of distributions upon dissolution of the corporation, regardless of any limitations or restrictions on the voting power of that class or series.

4. A certificate of amendment to a certificate of designation must be filed with the secretary of state and must:

(a) Set forth the original designation and the new designation, if the designation of the class or series is being amended;

(b) State that no shares of the class or series have been issued or state that the approval of the stockholders required pursuant to subsection 3 has been obtained; and

(c) Set forth the amendment to the class or series or set forth the designation of the class or series, the number of the class or series and the voting powers, designations, preferences, limitations, restrictions and relative rights of the class or series, as amended.

The certificate of amendment must be executed by the president or vice president and secretary or assistant secretary and acknowledged by the president or vice president before a person authorized by the laws of Nevada to take acknowledgments of deeds. NRS 78.380, 78.385 and 78.390 do not apply to certificates of amendment filed pursuant to this section.

78.196 Required and authorized classes of stock.

1. Each corporation must have:

(a) One or more classes of shares that together have unlimited voting rights; and

(b) One or more classes of shares that together are entitled to receive the net assets of the corporation upon dissolution.

If the articles of incorporation provide for only one class of stock, that class of stock has unlimited voting rights and is entitled to receive the net assets of the corporation upon dissolution.

2. The articles of incorporation, or a resolution of the board of directors pursuant thereto, may authorize one or more classes of stock that:

(a) Have special, conditional or limited voting powers, or no right to vote, except to the extent otherwise prohibited by this chapter;

(b) Are redeemable or convertible:

(1) At the option of the corporation, the stockholders or another person, or upon the occurrence of a designated event;

(2) For cash, indebtedness, securities or other property; or

(3) In a designated amount or in an amount determined in accordance with a designated formula or by reference to extrinsic data or events;

(c) Entitle the stockholders to distributions calculated in any manner, including dividends that may be cumulative, noncumulative or partially cumulative;

(d) Have preference over any other class of shares with respect to distributions, including dividends and distributions upon the dissolution of the corporation;

(e) Have par value; or

(f) Have powers, designations, preferences, limitations, restrictions and relative rights dependent upon any fact or event which may be ascertained outside of the articles of incorporation or the resolution if the manner in which the fact or event may operate on such class or series of stock is stated in the articles of incorporation or the resolution.

3. The description of voting powers, designations, preferences, limitations, restrictions and relative rights of the share classes contained in this section is not exclusive.

78.197 Rights of persons holding obligations of corporation. A corporation may provide in its articles of incorporation that the holder of a bond, debenture or other obligation of the corporation may have any of the rights of a stockholder in the corporation.

78.200 Rights or options to purchase stock. A corporation may create and issue, whether in connection with the issue and sale of any shares of stock or other securities of the corporation, rights or options entitling the holders thereof to purchase from the corporation any shares of its stock of any class or classes, to be evidenced by or in such instrument or instruments as are approved by the board of directors. The terms upon which, the time or times, which may be limited or unlimited in duration, at or within which, and the price or prices at which any such shares may be purchased from the corporation upon the exercise of any such a right or option must be fixed and stated in the articles of incorporation or in a resolution or resolutions adopted by the board of directors providing for the creation and issue of the rights or options, and, in every case, set forth or incorporated by reference in the instrument or instruments evidencing the rights or options.

78.205 Fractions of shares: Issuance; alternatives to issuance.

1. A corporation is not obliged to but may execute and deliver a certificate for or including a fraction of a share.

2. In lieu of executing and delivering a certificate for a fraction of a share, a corporation may:

(a) Pay to any person otherwise entitled to become a holder of a fraction of a share:

(1) The appraised value of that share if the appraisal was properly demanded; or

(2) If no appraisal was demanded or an appraisal was not properly demanded, an amount in cash specified for that purpose as the value of the fraction in the articles, plan of reorganization, plan of merger or exchange, resolution of the board of directors, or other instrument pursuant to which the fractional share would otherwise be issued, or, if not specified, then as may be determined for that purpose by the board of directors of the issuing corporation;

(b) Issue such additional fraction of a share as is necessary to increase the fractional share to a full share; or

(c) Execute and deliver registered or bearer scrip over the manual or facsimile signature of an officer of the corporation or of its agent for that purpose, exchangeable as provided on the scrip for full share certificates, but the scrip does not entitle the holder to any rights as a stockholder except as provided on the scrip. The scrip may provide that it becomes void unless the rights of the holders are exercised within a specified period and may contain any other provisions or conditions that the corporation deems advisable. Whenever any scrip ceases to be exchangeable for full share certificates, the shares that would otherwise have been issuable as provided on the scrip are deemed to be treasury shares unless the scrip contains other provisions for their disposition.

78.207 Increase or decrease in number of authorized shares of class and series: Resolution by board of directors; vote of stockholders required under certain circumstances.

1. Unless otherwise provided in the articles of incorporation, a corporation organized and existing under the laws of this state that desires to change the number of shares of a class and series, if any, of its authorized stock by increasing or decreasing the number of authorized shares of the class and series and correspondingly increasing or decreasing the number of issued and outstanding shares of the same class and series held by each stockholder of record at the effective date and time of the change, may, except as otherwise provided in subsections 2 and 3, do so by a resolution adopted by the board of directors, without obtaining the approval of the stockholders. The resolution may also provide for a change of the par value, if any, of the same class and series of the shares increased or decreased. After the effective date and time of the change, the corporation may issue its stock in accordance therewith.

2. A proposal to increase or decrease the number of authorized shares of any class and series, if any, that includes provisions pursuant to which only money will be paid or scrip will be issued to stockholders who:

(a) Before the increase or decrease in the number of shares becomes effective, in the aggregate hold 10 percent or more of the outstanding shares of the affected class and series; and

(b) Would otherwise be entitled to receive fractions of shares in exchange for the cancellation of all of their outstanding shares, must be approved by the vote of stockholders holding a majority of the voting power of the affected class and series, or such greater proportion as may be provided in the articles of incorporation, regardless of limitations or restrictions on the voting power thereof.

3. If a proposed increase or decrease in the number of authorized shares of any class or series would alter or change any preference or any relative or other right given to any other class or series of outstanding shares, then the increase or decrease must be approved by the vote, in addition to any vote otherwise required, of the holders of shares representing a majority of the voting power of each

class or series whose preference or rights are affected by the increase or decrease, regardless of limitations or restrictions on the voting power thereof.

4. Any proposal to increase or decrease the number of authorized shares of any class and series, if any, that includes provisions pursuant to which only money will be paid or scrip will be issued to stockholders who:

(a) Before the increase or decrease in the number of shares becomes effective, hold 1 percent or more of the outstanding shares of the affected class and series; and

(b) Would otherwise be entitled to receive a fraction of a share in exchange for the cancellation of all of their outstanding shares, is subject to the provisions of NRS 92A.300 to 92A.500, inclusive. If the proposal is subject to those provisions, any stockholder who is obligated to accept money or scrip rather than receive a fraction of a share resulting from the action taken pursuant to this section may dissent in accordance with those provisions and obtain payment of the fair value of the fraction of a share to which the stockholder would otherwise be entitled.

78.209 Filing certificate of change in number of authorized shares of class and series; contents of certificate; articles of incorporation deemed amended.

1. A change pursuant to NRS 78.207 is not effective until after the filing in the office of the secretary of state of a certificate, signed by the corporation's president, or a vice president, and its secretary, or an assistant secretary, and acknowledged by the president or vice president before a person authorized by the laws of this state to take acknowledgments of deeds, setting forth:

(a) The current number of authorized shares and the par value, if any, of each class and series, if any, of shares before the change;

(b) The number of authorized shares and the par value, if any, of each class and series, if any, of shares after the change;

(c) The number of shares of each affected class and series, if any, to be issued after the change in exchange for each issued share of the same class or series;

(d) The provisions, if any, for the issuance of fractional shares, or for the payment of money or the issuance of scrip to stockholders otherwise entitled to a fraction of a share and the percentage of outstanding shares affected thereby;

(e) That any required approval of the stockholders has been obtained; and

(f) Whether the change is effective on filing the certificate or, if not, the date and time at which the change will be effective, which must not be more than 90 days after the certificate is filed.

The provisions in the articles of incorporation of the corporation regarding the authorized number and par

value, if any, of the changed class and series, if any, of shares shall be deemed amended as provided in the certificate at the effective date and time of the change.

2. Unless an increase or decrease of the number of authorized shares pursuant to NRS 78.207 is accomplished by an action that otherwise requires an amendment to the corporation's articles of incorporation, such an amendment is not required by that section.

78.211 Consideration for shares: Types; adequacy; effect of receipt; actions of corporation pending receipt in future.

1. The board of directors may authorize shares to be issued for consideration consisting of any tangible or intangible property or benefit to the corporation, including, but not limited to, cash, promissory notes, services performed, contracts for services to be performed or other securities of the corporation.

2. Before the corporation issues shares, the board of directors must determine that the consideration received or to be received for the shares to be issued is adequate. The judgment of the board of directors as to the adequacy of the consideration received for the shares issued is conclusive in the absence of actual fraud in the transaction.

3. When the corporation receives the consideration for which the board of directors authorized the issuance of shares, the shares issued therefor are fully paid.

4. The corporation may place in escrow shares issued for a contract for future services or benefits or a promissory note, or make any other arrangements to restrict the transfer of the shares. The corporation may credit distributions made for the shares against their purchase price, until the services are performed, the benefits are received or the promissory note is paid. If the services are not performed, the benefits are not received or the promissory note is not paid, the shares escrowed or restricted and the distributions credited may be canceled in whole or in part.

78.215 Issuance of shares for consideration or as share dividend.

1. A corporation may issue and dispose of its authorized shares for such consideration as may be prescribed in the articles of incorporation or, if no consideration is so prescribed, then for such consideration as may be fixed by the board of directors.

2. If a consideration is prescribed for shares without par value, that consideration must not be used to determine the fees required for filing articles of incorporation pursuant to NRS 78.760.

3. Unless the articles of incorporation provide otherwise, shares may be issued pro rata and without consideration to the corporation's stockholders or to the stockholders of one

or more classes or series. An issuance of shares under this subsection is a share dividend.

4. Shares of one class or series may not be issued as a share dividend in respect of shares of another class or series unless:

(a) The articles of incorporation so authorize;

(b) A majority of the votes entitled to be cast by the class or series to be issued approve the issue; or

(c) There are no outstanding shares of the class or series to be issued.

5. If the board of directors does not fix the record date for determining stockholders entitled to a share dividend, it is the date the board of directors authorizes the share dividend.

78.220 Subscription for corporate shares: Payment; collection on default; irrevocability.

1. Subscriptions to the shares of a corporation, whether made before or after its organization, shall be paid in full at such time or in such installments at such times as determined by the board of directors. Any call made by the board of directors for payment on subscriptions shall be uniform as to all shares of the same class or series.

2. If default is made in the payment of any installment or call, the corporation may proceed to collect the amount due in the same manner as any debt due the corporation. In addition, the corporation may sell a sufficient number of the subscriber's shares at public auction to pay for the installment or call and any incidental charges incurred as a result of the sale. No penalty causing a forfeiture of a subscription, of stock for which a subscription has been executed, or of amounts paid thereon, may be declared against any subscriber unless the amount due remains unpaid for 30 days after written demand. Such written demand shall be deemed made when it is mailed by registered or certified mail, return receipt requested, to the subscriber's last known address. If any of the subscriber's shares are sold at public auction, any excess of the proceeds over the total of the amount due plus any incidental charges of the sale shall be paid to the subscriber or his legal representative. If an action is brought to recover the amount due on a subscription or call, any judgment in favor of the corporation shall be reduced by the amount of the net proceeds of any sale by the corporation of the subscriber's stock.

3. If a receiver of a corporation has been appointed, all unpaid subscriptions shall be paid at such times and in such installments as the receiver or the court may direct, subject, however, to the provisions of the subscription contract.

4. A subscription for shares of a corporation to be organized is irrevocable for 6 months unless otherwise provided by the subscription agreement or unless all of the subscribers consent to the revocation of the subscription.

78.225 Stockholder's liability: No individual liability except for payment for which shares were authorized to be issued or which was specified in subscription agreement.

Unless otherwise provided in the articles of incorporation, no stockholder of any corporation formed under the laws of this state is individually liable for the debts or liabilities of the corporation. A purchaser of shares of stock from the corporation is not liable to the corporation or its creditors with respect to the shares, except to pay the consideration for which the shares were authorized to be issued or which was specified in the written subscription agreement.

78.230 Liability of holder of stock as collateral security; liability of executors, administrators, guardians and trustees.

1. No person holding shares in any corporation as collateral security shall be personally liable as a stockholder.

2. No executor, administrator, guardian or trustee, unless he, without authorization, shall have voluntarily invested the trust funds in such shares, shall be personally liable as a stockholder, but the estate and funds in the hands of such executor, administrator, guardian or trustee shall be liable.

78.235 Stock certificates: Validation; facsimile signatures; uncertificated shares and informational statements.

1. Except as otherwise provided in subsection 4, every stockholder is entitled to have a certificate, signed by officers or agents designated by the corporation for the purpose, certifying the number of shares owned by him in the corporation.

2. Whenever any certificate is countersigned or otherwise authenticated by a transfer agent or transfer clerk, and by a registrar, then a facsimile of the signatures of the officers or agents, the transfer agent or transfer clerk or the registrar of the corporation may be printed or lithographed upon the certificate in lieu of the actual signatures. If a corporation uses facsimile signatures of its officers and agents on its stock certificates, it cannot act as registrar of its own stock, but its transfer agent and registrar may be identical if the institution acting in those dual capacities countersigns or otherwise authenticates any stock certificates in both capacities.

3. If any officer or officers who have signed, or whose facsimile signature or signatures have been used on, any certificate or certificates for stock cease to be an officer or officers of the corporation, whether because of death, resignation or other reason, before the certificate or certificates have been delivered by the corporation, the certificate or certificates may nevertheless be adopted by the corporation and be issued and delivered as though the person or persons who signed the certificate or certificates, or whose facsimile signature or signatures have been used thereon, had not ceased to be an officer or officers of the corporation.

4. A corporation may provide in its articles of incorporation or in its bylaws for the issuance of uncertificated shares of some or all of the shares of any or all of its classes or series. The issuance of uncertificated shares has no effect on existing certificates for shares until surrendered to the corporation, or on the respective rights and obligations of the stockholders. Unless otherwise provided by a specific statute, the rights and obligations of stockholders are identical whether or not their shares of stock are represented by certificates.

5. Within a reasonable time after the issuance or transfer of shares without certificates, the corporation shall send the stockholder a written statement containing the information required on the certificates pursuant to subsection 1. At least annually thereafter, the corporation shall provide to its stockholders of record, a written statement confirming the information contained in the informational statement previously sent pursuant to this subsection.

78.240 Shares of stock are personal property; transfers. The shares of stock in every corporation shall be personal property and shall be transferable on the books of the corporation, in such manner and under such regulations as may be provided in the bylaws, and as provided in chapter 104 of NRS.

78.242 Restrictions on transfer of stock.

1. Subject to the limitation imposed by NRS 104.8204, a written restriction on the transfer or registration of transfer of the stock of a corporation, if permitted by this section, may be enforced against the holder of the restricted stock or any successor or transferee of the holder, including an executor, administrator, trustee, guardian or other fiduciary entrusted with like responsibility for the person or estate of the holder.

2. A restriction on the transfer or registration of transfer of the stock of a corporation may be imposed by the articles of incorporation or by the bylaws or by an agreement among any number of stockholders or between one or more stockholders and the corporation. No restriction so imposed is binding with respect to stocks issued before the adoption of the restriction unless the stockholders are parties to an agreement or voted in favor of the restriction.

3. A restriction on the transfer or the registration of transfer of shares is valid and enforceable against the transferee of the stockholder if the restriction is not prohibited by other law and its existence is noted conspicuously on the front or back of the stock certificate or is contained in the statement of information required by NRS 78.235. Unless so noted, a restriction is not enforceable against a person without knowledge of the restriction.

4. A restriction on the transfer or registration of transfer of stock of a corporation is permitted, without limitation by this enumeration, if it:

(a) Obligates the stockholder first to offer to the corporation or to any other stockholder or stockholders of the corporation or to any other person or persons or to any combination of the foregoing a prior opportunity, to be exercised within a reasonable time, to acquire the stock;

(b) Obligates the corporation or any holder of stock of the corporation or any other person or any combination of the foregoing to purchase stock which is the subject of an agreement respecting the purchase and sale of the stock;

(c) Requires the corporation or any stockholder or stockholders to consent to any proposed transfer of the stock or to approve the proposed transferee of stock;

(d) Prohibits the transfer of the stock to designated persons or classes of persons, and such designation is not manifestly unreasonable; or

(e) Prohibits the transfer of stock:

(1) To maintain the corporation's status when it is dependent on the number or identity of its stockholders;

(2) To preserve exemptions under federal or state laws governing taxes or securities; or

(3) For any other reasonable purpose.

5. For the purposes of this section, "stock" includes a security convertible into or carrying a right to subscribe for or to acquire stock.

78.245 Corporate stocks, bonds and securities not taxed when owned by nonresidents or foreign corporations. No stocks, bonds or other securities issued by any corporation organized under this chapter, nor the income or profits therefrom, nor the transfer thereof by assignment, descent, testamentary disposition or otherwise, shall be taxed by this state when such stocks, bonds or other securities shall be owned by nonresidents of this state or by foreign corporations.

78.250 Cancellation of outstanding certificates or change in informational statements: Issuance of new certificates or statements; order for surrender of certificates; penalties for failure to comply.

1. When the articles of incorporation are amended in any way affecting the statements contained in certificates for outstanding shares or informational statements sent pursuant to NRS 78.235, or it becomes desirable for any reason, in the discretion of the board of directors, to cancel any outstanding certificate for shares and issue a new certificate therefor conforming to the rights of the holder, the board of directors may send additional informational statements as provided in NRS 78.235 and order any holders of outstanding certificates for shares to surrender and exchange them for new certificates within a reasonable time to be fixed by the board of directors.

2. Such an order may provide that the holder of any certificate so ordered to be surrendered is not entitled to vote or to receive distributions or exercise any of the other rights of stockholders of record until he has complied with the order, but the order operates to suspend such rights only after notice and until compliance.

3. The duty to surrender any outstanding certificates may also be enforced by action at law.

78.257 Right of stockholders to inspect and audit financial records; exceptions.

1. Any person who has been a stockholder of record of any corporation and owns not less than 15 percent of all of the issued and outstanding shares of the stock of such corporation or has been authorized in writing by the holders of at least 15 percent of all its issued and outstanding shares, upon at least 5 days' written demand, is entitled to inspect in person or by agent or attorney, during normal business hours, the books of account and all financial records of the corporation, to make extracts therefrom, and to conduct an audit of such records. Holders of voting trust certificates representing 15 percent of the issued and outstanding shares of the corporation shall be regarded as stockholders for the purpose of this subsection. The right of stockholders to inspect the corporate records may not be limited in the articles or bylaws of any corporation.

2. All costs for making extracts of records or conducting an audit must be borne by the person exercising his rights under subsection 1.

3. The rights authorized by subsection 1 may be denied to any stockholder upon his refusal to furnish the corporation an affidavit that such inspection, extracts or audit is not desired for any purpose not related to his interest in the corporation as a stockholder. Any stockholder or other person, exercising rights under subsection 1, who uses or attempts to use information, documents, records or other data obtained from the corporation, for any purpose not related to the stockholder's interest in the corporation as a stockholder, is guilty of a gross misdemeanor.

4. If any officer or agent of any corporation keeping records in this state willfully neglects or refuses to permit an inspection of the books of account and financial records upon demand by a person entitled to inspect them, or refuses to permit an audit to be conducted, as provided in subsection 1, the corporation shall forfeit to the state the sum of $100 for every day of such neglect or refusal, and the corporation, officer or agent thereof is jointly and severally liable to the person injured for all damages resulting to him.

5. A stockholder who brings an action or proceeding to enforce any right under this section or to recover damages resulting from its denial:

(a) Is entitled to costs and reasonable attorney's fees, if he prevails; or

(b) Is liable for such costs and fees, if he does not prevail, in the action or proceeding.

6. Except as otherwise provided in this subsection, the provisions of this section do not apply to any corporation listed and traded on any recognized stock exchange nor do they apply to any corporation that furnishes to its stockholders a detailed, annual financial statement. A person who owns, or is authorized in writing by the owners of, at least 15 percent of the issued and outstanding shares of the stock of a corporation that has elected to be governed by subchapter S of the Internal Revenue Code and whose shares are not listed or traded on any recognized stock exchange is entitled to inspect the books of the corporation pursuant to subsection 1 and has the rights, duties and liabilities provided in subsections 2 to 5, inclusive.

78.265 Preemptive rights of stockholders in corporations organized before October 1, 1991.

1. The provisions of this section apply to corporations organized in this state before October 1, 1991.

2. Except to the extent limited or denied by this section or the articles of incorporation, shareholders have a preemptive right to acquire unissued shares, treasury shares or securities convertible into such shares.

3. Unless otherwise provided in the articles of incorporation:

(a) A preemptive right does not exist:

(1) To acquire any shares issued to directors, officers or employees pursuant to approval by the affirmative vote of the holders of a majority of the shares entitled to vote or when authorized by a plan approved by such a vote of shareholders;

(2) To acquire any shares sold for a consideration other than cash;

(3) To acquire any shares issued at the same time that the shareholder who claims a preemptive right acquired his shares;

(4) To acquire any shares issued as part of the same offering in which the shareholder who claims a preemptive right acquired his shares; or

(5) To acquire any shares, treasury shares or securities convertible into such shares, if the shares or the shares into which the convertible securities may be converted are upon issuance registered pursuant to section 12 of the Securities Exchange Act of 1934 (15 U.S.C. § 78l).

(b) Holders of shares of any class that is preferred or limited as to dividends or assets are not entitled to any preemptive right.

(c) Holders of common stock are not entitled to any preemptive right to shares of any class that is preferred or limited as to dividends or assets or to any obligations, unless convertible into shares of common stock or carrying a right to subscribe to or acquire shares of common stock.

(d) Holders of common stock without voting power have no preemptive right to shares of common stock with voting power.

(e) The preemptive right is only an opportunity to acquire shares or other securities upon such terms as the board of directors fixes for the purpose of providing a fair and reasonable opportunity for the exercise of such right.

78.267 Preemptive rights of stockholders in corporations organized on or after October 1, 1991.

1. The provisions of this section apply to corporations organized in this state on or after October 1, 1991.

2. The stockholders of a corporation do not have a preemptive right to acquire the corporation's unissued shares except to the extent the articles of incorporation so provide.

3. A statement included in the articles of incorporation that "the corporation elects to have preemptive rights" or words of similar import have the following effects unless the articles of incorporation otherwise provide:

(a) The stockholders of the corporation have a preemptive right, granted on uniform terms and conditions prescribed by the board of directors to provide a fair and reasonable opportunity to exercise the right, to acquire proportional amounts of the corporation's unissued shares upon the decision of the board of directors to issue them.

(b) A stockholder may waive his preemptive right. A waiver evidenced by a writing is irrevocable even though it is not supported by consideration.

(c) There is no preemptive right with respect to:

(1) Shares issued as compensation to directors, officers, agents or employees of the corporation, its subsidiaries or affiliates;

(2) Shares issued to satisfy rights of conversion or options created to provide compensation to directors, officers, agents or employees of the corporation, its subsidiaries or affiliates;

(3) Shares authorized in articles of incorporation which are issued within 6 months from the effective date of incorporation; or

(4) Shares sold otherwise than for money.

(d) Holders of shares of any class without general voting rights but with preferential rights to distributions or assets have no preemptive rights with respect to shares of any class.

(e) Holders of shares of any class with general voting rights but without preferential rights to distributions or assets have no preemptive rights with respect to shares of any class with preferential rights to distributions or assets unless the shares with preferential rights are convertible into or carry a right to subscribe for or acquire shares without preferential rights.

(f) Shares subject to preemptive rights that are not acquired by stockholders may be issued to any person for 1 year after being offered to stockholders at a consideration set by the board of directors that is not lower than the consideration set for the exercise of preemptive rights. An offer at a lower consideration or after the expiration of one year is subject to the stockholders' preemptive rights.

4. As used in this section, "shares" includes a security convertible into or carrying a right to subscribe for or acquire shares.

78.275 Assessments on stock: Levy and collection; sale after default in payment.

1. The directors may at such times and in such amount, as they may from time to time deem the interest of the corporation to require, levy and collect assessments upon the assessable stock of the corporation in the manner provided in this section.

2. Notice of each assessment must be given to the stockholders personally, or by publication once a week for at least 4 weeks, in some newspaper published in the county in which the registered office or place of business of the corporation is located, and in a newspaper published in the county wherein the property of the corporation is situated if in this state, and if no paper is published in either of those counties, then the newspaper published nearest to the registered office in the state.

3. If after the notice has been given, any stockholder defaults in the payment of the assessment upon the shares held by him, so many of those shares may be sold as will be necessary for the payment of the assessment upon all the shares held by him, together with all costs of advertising and expenses of sale. The sale of the shares must be made at the office of the corporation at public auction to the highest bidder, after a notice thereof published for 4 weeks as directed in this section, and a copy of the notice mailed to each delinquent stockholder if his address is known 4 weeks before the sale. At the sale the person who offers to pay the assessment so due, together with the expenses of advertising and sale, for the smallest number of shares, or portion of a share, as the case may be, shall be deemed the highest bidder.

78.280 Purchase by corporation of its own stock at assessment sale when no other available purchaser.

1. Every corporation in this state may, whenever at any assessment sale of the stock of the corporation no person will take the stock and pay the assessment, or amount unpaid and due thereon and costs, purchase such stock and hold the stock for the benefit of the corporation.

2. All purchases of its own stock by any corporation in this state which have been previously made at assessment sales

whereas outside persons have failed to bid, and which purchases were for the amount of assessments due, and costs or otherwise, are valid, and vest the legal title to the stock in the corporation.

3. The stock so purchased is subject to the control of the remaining stockholders, who may dispose of the stock as they may deem fit.

4. Whenever any portion of the stock of any corporation is held by the corporation by purchase or otherwise, a majority of the remaining shares of stock in the corporation is a majority of the shares of the stock in the incorporated company, for all purposes of election or voting on any question before a stockholders' meeting.

78.283 Treasury shares: Definition; limitations; retirement and disposal.

1. As used in this section, "treasury shares" means shares of a corporation issued and thereafter acquired by the corporation or another entity, the majority of whose outstanding voting power to elect its general partner, directors, managers or members of the governing body is beneficially held, directly or indirectly, by the corporation, which have not been retired or restored to the status of unissued shares.

2. Treasury shares do not carry voting rights or participate in distributions, may not be counted as outstanding shares for any purpose and may not be counted as assets of the corporation for the purpose of computing the amount available for distributions. Unless the articles of incorporation provide otherwise, treasury shares may be retired and restored to the status of authorized and unissued shares without an amendment to the articles of incorporation or may be disposed of for such consideration as the board of directors may determine.

3. This section does not limit the right of a corporation to vote its shares held by it in a fiduciary capacity.

78.288 Distributions to stockholders.

1. Except as otherwise provided in subsection 2 and the articles of incorporation, a board of directors may authorize and the corporation may make distributions to its stockholders.

2. No distribution may be made if, after giving it effect:

(a) The corporation would not be able to pay its debts as they become due in the usual course of business; or

(b) Except as otherwise specifically allowed by the articles of incorporation, the corporation's total assets would be less than the sum of its total liabilities plus the amount that would be needed, if the corporation were to be dissolved at the time of distribution, to satisfy the preferential rights upon dissolution of stockholders whose preferential rights are superior to those receiving the distribution.

3. The board of directors may base a determination that a distribution is not prohibited under subsection 2 on:

(a) Financial statements prepared on the basis of accounting practices that are reasonable in the circumstances;

(b) A fair valuation, including, but not limited to, unrealized appreciation and depreciation; or

(c) Any other method that is reasonable in the circumstances.

4. The effect of a distribution under subsection 2 must be measured:

(a) In the case of a distribution by purchase, redemption or other acquisition of the corporation's shares, as of the earlier of:

(1) The date money or other property is transferred or debt incurred by the corporation; or

(2) The date upon which the stockholder ceases to be a stockholder with respect to the acquired shares.

(b) In the case of any other distribution of indebtedness, as of the date the indebtedness is distributed.

(c) In all other cases, as of:

(1) The date the distribution is authorized if the payment occurs within 120 days after the date of authorization; or

(2) The date the payment is made if it occurs more than 120 days after the date of authorization.

5. A corporation's indebtedness to a stockholder incurred by reason of a distribution made in accordance with this section is at parity with the corporation's indebtedness to its general unsecured creditors except to the extent subordinated by agreement.

6. Indebtedness of a corporation, including indebtedness issued as a distribution, is not considered a liability for purposes of determinations under subsection 2 if its terms provide that payment of principal and interest are made only if and to the extent that payment of a distribution to stockholders could then be made pursuant to this section. If the indebtedness is issued as a distribution, each payment of principal or interest must be treated as a distribution, the effect of which must be measured on the date the payment is actually made.

78.295 Liability of directors for declaration of distributions. A director is fully protected in relying in good faith upon the books of account of the corporation or statements prepared by any of its officials as to the value and amount of the assets, liabilities or net profits of the corporation, or any other facts pertinent to the existence and amount of money from which distributions may properly be declared.

78.300 Liability of directors for unlawful distributions.

1. The directors of a corporation shall not make distributions to stockholders except as provided by this chapter.

2. In case of any willful or grossly negligent violation of the provisions of this section, the directors under whose administration the violation occurred, except those who caused their dissent to be entered upon the minutes of the meeting of the directors at the time, or who not then being present caused their dissent to be entered on learning of such action, are jointly and severally liable, at any time within 3 years after each violation, to the corporation, and, in the event of its dissolution or insolvency, to its creditors at the time of the violation, or any of them, to the lesser of the full amount of the distribution made or of any loss sustained by the corporation by reason of the distribution to stockholders.

78.307 "Investment company" and "open-end investment company" defined; redemption of shares by open-end investment company.

1. As used in this section, unless the context requires otherwise:

(a) "Investment company" means any corporation, trust, association or fund which is engaged or proposes to engage in the business of investing, reinvesting, owning, holding or trading in securities, and whose assets are invested principally in cash or in securities of other issuers.

(b) "Open-end investment company" means any investment company which issues one or more series or classes of securities under the terms of which the holder of the security, upon presentation thereof to the issuer, is entitled to receive approximately his proportionate share of the current net assets of the issuer applicable to such series or class, or the cash equivalent thereof.

2. An open-end investment company may, from time to time, redeem its shares, in accordance with their terms, at approximately the proportionate share of the current net assets of the issuer applicable to such shares, or the cash equivalent thereof.

Meetings, Elections, Voting and Notice

78.310 Place of stockholders' and directors' meetings. Meetings of stockholders and directors of any corporation organized under the provisions of this chapter may be held within or without this state, in the manner provided by the bylaws of the corporation. The articles of incorporation may designate any place or places where such stockholders' or directors' meetings may be held, but in the absence of any provision therefor in the articles of incorporation, then the meetings must be held within or without this state, as directed from time to time by the bylaws of the corporation.

78.315 Directors' meetings: Quorum; consent for actions taken without meeting; participation by telephone or similar method.

1. Unless the articles of incorporation or the bylaws provide for a different proportion, a majority of the board of directors of the corporation then in office, at a meeting duly assembled, is necessary to constitute a quorum for the transaction of business, and the act of directors holding a majority of the voting power of the directors, present at a meeting at which a quorum is present, is the act of the board of directors.

2. Unless otherwise restricted by the articles of incorporation or bylaws, any action required or permitted to be taken at a meeting of the board of directors or of a committee thereof may be taken without a meeting if, before or after the action, a written consent thereto is signed by all the members of the board or of the committee.

3. Unless otherwise restricted by the articles of incorporation or bylaws, members of the board of directors or the governing body of any corporation, or of any committee designated by such board or body, may participate in a meeting of the board, body or committee by means of a telephone conference or similar method of communication by which all persons participating in the meeting can hear each other. Participation in a meeting pursuant to this subsection constitutes presence in person at the meeting.

78.320 Stockholders' meetings: Quorum; consent for actions taken without meeting; participation by telephone or similar method.

1. Unless this chapter, the articles of incorporation or the bylaws provide for different proportions:

(a) A majority of the voting power, which includes the voting power that is present in person or by proxy, regardless of whether the proxy has authority to vote on all matters, constitutes a quorum for the transaction of business; and

(b) Action by the stockholders on a matter other than the election of directors is approved if the number of votes cast in favor of the action exceeds the number of votes cast in opposition to the action.

2. Unless otherwise provided in the articles of incorporation or the bylaws, any action required or permitted to be taken at a meeting of the stockholders may be taken without a meeting if a written consent thereto is signed by stockholders holding at least a majority of the voting power, except that if a different proportion of voting power is required for such an action at a meeting, then that proportion of written consents is required.

3. In no instance where action is authorized by written consent need a meeting of stockholders be called or notice given.

4. Unless otherwise restricted by the articles of incorporation or bylaws, stockholders may participate in a meeting of stockholders by means of a telephone

conference or similar method of communication by which all persons participating in the meeting can hear each other. Participation in a meeting pursuant to this subsection constitutes presence in person at the meeting.

78.325 Actions at meetings not regularly called: Ratification and approval.

1. Whenever all persons entitled to vote at any meeting, whether of directors, trustees or stockholders, consent, either by:

(a) A writing on the records of the meeting or filed with the secretary; or

(b) Presence at such meeting and oral consent entered on the minutes; or

(c) Taking part in the deliberations at such meeting without objection; the doings of such meeting shall be as valid as if had at a meeting regularly called and noticed.

2. At such meeting any business may be transacted which is not excepted from the written consent or to the consideration of which no objection for want of notice is made at the time.

3. If any meeting be irregular for want of notice or of such consent, provided a quorum was present at such meeting, the proceedings of the meeting may be ratified and approved and rendered likewise valid and the irregularity or defect therein waived by a writing signed by all parties having the right to vote at such meeting.

4. Such consent or approval of stockholders or creditors may be by proxy or attorney, but all such proxies and powers of attorney must be in writing.

78.330 Directors: Election; classification; voting power.

1. Unless elected pursuant to NRS 78.320, directors of every corporation must be elected at the annual meeting of the stockholders by a plurality of the votes cast at the election. Unless otherwise provided in the bylaws, the board of directors have the authority to set the date, time and place for the annual meeting of the stockholders. If for any reason directors are not elected pursuant to NRS 78.320 or at the annual meeting of the stockholders, they may be elected at any special meeting of the stockholders which is called and held for that purpose.

2. The articles of incorporation or the bylaws may provide for the classification of directors as to the duration of their respective terms of office or as to their election by one or more authorized classes or series of shares, but at least one-fourth in number of the directors of every corporation must be elected annually.

3. The articles of incorporation may provide that the voting power of individual directors or classes of directors may be greater than or less than that of any other individual directors or classes of directors, and the different voting powers may be stated in the articles of incorporation or may be dependent upon any fact or event that may be ascertained outside the articles of incorporation if the manner in which the fact or event may operate on those voting powers is stated in the articles of incorporation. If the articles of incorporation provide that any directors may have voting power greater than or less than other directors, every reference in this chapter to a majority or other proportion of directors shall be deemed to refer to a majority or other proportion of the voting power of all of the directors or classes of directors, as may be required by the articles of incorporation.

78.335 Directors: Removal; filling of vacancies.

1. Any director may be removed from office by the vote of stockholders representing not less than two-thirds of the voting power of the issued and outstanding stock entitled to voting power, except that:

(a) In the case of corporations which have provided in their articles of incorporation for the election of directors by cumulative voting, no director may be removed from office under the provisions of this section except upon the vote of stockholders owning sufficient shares to have prevented his election to office in the first instance; and

(b) The articles of incorporation may require the concurrence of a larger percentage of the stock entitled to voting power in order to remove a director.

2. Whenever the holders of any class or series of shares are entitled to elect one or more directors, unless otherwise provided in the articles of incorporation, removal of any such director requires only the proportion of votes, specified in subsection 1, of the holders of that class or series, and not the votes of the outstanding shares as a whole.

3. All vacancies, including those caused by an increase in the number of directors, may be filled by a majority of the remaining directors, though less than a quorum, unless it is otherwise provided in the articles of incorporation.

4. Unless otherwise provided in the articles of incorporation, when one or more directors give notice of his or their resignation to the board, effective at a future date, the board may fill the vacancy or vacancies to take effect when the resignation or resignations become effective, each director so appointed to hold office during the remainder of the term of office of the resigning director or directors.

78.340 Failure to hold election of directors on regular day does not dissolve corporation. If the directors shall not be elected on the day designated for the purpose, the corporation shall not for that reason be dissolved; but every director shall continue to hold his office and discharge his duties until his successor has been elected.

78.345 Election of directors by order of court upon failure of regular election.

1. If any corporation fails to elect directors within 18 months after the last election of directors required by NRS 78.330, the district court has jurisdiction in equity, upon application of any one or more stockholders holding stock entitling them to exercise at least 15 percent of the voting power, to order the election of directors in the manner required by NRS 78.330.

2. The application must be made by petition filed in the county where the registered office of the corporation is located and must be brought on behalf of all stockholders desiring to be joined therein. Such notice must be given to the corporation and the stockholders as the court may direct.

3. The directors elected pursuant to this section have the same rights, powers and duties and the same tenure of office as directors elected by the stockholders at the annual meeting held at the time prescribed therefor, next before the date of the election pursuant to this section, would have had.

78.347 Application by stockholder for order of court appointing custodian or receiver; authority of custodian.

1. Any stockholder may apply to the district court to appoint one or more persons to be custodians of the corporation, and, if the corporation is insolvent, to be receivers of the corporation when:

(a) The business of the corporation is suffering or is threatened with irreparable injury because the directors are so divided respecting the management of the affairs of the corporation that a required vote for action by the board of directors cannot be obtained and the stockholders are unable to terminate this division; or

(b) The corporation has abandoned its business and has failed within a reasonable time to take steps to dissolve, liquidate or distribute its assets in accordance with this chapter.

2. A custodian appointed pursuant to this section has all the powers and title of a trustee appointed under NRS 78.590, 78.635 and 78.650, but the authority of the custodian is to continue the business of the corporation and not to liquidate its affairs or distribute its assets, except when the district court so orders and except in cases arising pursuant to paragraph (b) of subsection 1.

78.350 Voting rights of stockholders; determination of stockholders entitled to notice of and to vote at meeting.

1. Unless otherwise provided in the articles of incorporation, or in the resolution providing for the issuance of the stock adopted by the board of directors pursuant to authority expressly vested in it by the provisions of the articles of incorporation, every stockholder of record of a corporation is entitled at each meeting of stockholders thereof to one vote for each share of stock standing in his name on the records of the corporation. If the articles of incorporation, or the resolution providing for the issuance of the stock adopted by the board of directors pursuant to authority expressly vested in it by the articles of incorporation, provides for more or less than one vote per share for any class or series of shares on any matter, every reference in this chapter to a majority or other proportion of stock shall be deemed to refer to a majority or other proportion of the voting power of all of the shares or those classes or series of shares, as may be required by the articles of incorporation, or in the resolution providing for the issuance of the stock adopted by the board of directors pursuant to authority expressly vested in it by the provisions of the articles of incorporation, or the provisions of this chapter.

2. Unless contrary provisions are contained in the articles of incorporation, the directors may prescribe a period not exceeding 60 days before any meeting of the stockholders during which no transfer of stock on the books of the corporation may be made, or may fix a day not more than 60 days before the holding of any such meeting as the day as of which stockholders entitled to notice of and to vote at such meetings must be determined. Only stockholders of record on that day are entitled to notice or to vote at such meeting.

3. The provisions of this section do not restrict the directors from taking action to protect the interests of the corporation and its stockholders, including, but not limited to, adopting or executing plans, arrangements or instruments that deny rights, privileges, power or authority to a holder or holders of a specified number of shares or percentage of share ownership or voting power.

78.355 Stockholders' proxies.

1. At any meeting of the stockholders of any corporation any stockholder may designate another person or persons to act as a proxy or proxies. If any stockholder designates two or more persons to act as proxies, a majority of those persons present at the meeting, or, if only one is present, then that one has and may exercise all of the powers conferred by the stockholder upon all of the persons so designated unless the stockholder provides otherwise.

2. Without limiting the manner in which a stockholder may authorize another person or persons to act for him as proxy pursuant to subsection 1, the following constitute valid means by which a stockholder may grant such authority:

(a) A stockholder may execute a writing authorizing another person or persons to act for him as proxy. The proxy may be limited to action on designated matters. Execution may be accomplished by the signing of the writing by the stockholder or his authorized officer, director, employee or agent or by causing the signature of the stockholder to be affixed to the writing by any reasonable means, including, but not limited to, a facsimile signature.

(b) A stockholder may authorize another person or persons to act for him as proxy by transmitting or authorizing the transmission of a telegram, cablegram or other means of electronic transmission to the person who will be the holder of the proxy or to a firm which solicits proxies or like agent who is authorized by the person who will be the holder of the proxy to receive the transmission. Any such telegram, cablegram or other means of electronic transmission must either set forth or be submitted with information from which it can be determined that the telegram, cablegram or other electronic transmission was authorized by the stockholder. If it is determined that the telegram, cablegram or other electronic transmission is valid, the persons appointed by the corporation to count the votes of stockholders and determine the validity of proxies and ballots or other persons making those determinations must specify the information upon which they relied.

3. Any copy, communication by telecopier, or other reliable reproduction of the writing or transmission created pursuant to subsection 2, may be substituted for the original writing or transmission for any purpose for which the original writing or transmission could be used, if the copy, communication by telecopier, or other reproduction is a complete reproduction of the entire original writing or transmission.

4. No such proxy is valid after the expiration of 6 months from the date of its creation, unless it is coupled with an interest, or unless the stockholder specifies in it the length of time for which it is to continue in force, which may not exceed 7 years from the date of its creation. Subject to these restrictions, any proxy properly created is not revoked and continues in full force and effect until another instrument or transmission revoking it or a properly created proxy bearing a later date is filed with or transmitted to the secretary of the corporation or another person or persons appointed by the corporation to count the votes of stockholders and determine the validity of proxies and ballots.

78.360 Cumulative voting.

1. The articles of incorporation of any corporation may provide that at all elections of directors of the corporation each holder of stock possessing voting power is entitled to as many votes as equal the number of his shares of stock multiplied by the number of directors to be elected, and that he may cast all of his votes for a single director or may distribute them among the number to be voted for or any two or more of them, as he may see fit. To exercise the right of cumulative voting, one or more of the stockholders requesting cumulative voting must give written notice to the president or secretary of the corporation that the

stockholder desires that the voting for the election of directors be cumulative.

2. The notice must be given not less than 48 hours before the time fixed for holding the meeting, if notice of the meeting has been given at least 10 days before the date of the meeting, and otherwise not less than 24 hours before the meeting. At the meeting, before the commencement of voting for the election of directors, an announcement of the giving of the notice must be made by the chairman or the secretary of the meeting or by or on behalf of the stockholder giving the notice. Notice to stockholders of the requirement of this subsection must be contained in the notice calling the meeting or in the proxy material accompanying the notice.

78.365 Voting trusts.

1. A stockholder, by agreement in writing, may transfer his stock to a voting trustee or trustees for the purpose of conferring the right to vote the stock for a period not exceeding 15 years upon the terms and conditions therein stated. Any certificates of stock so transferred must be surrendered and canceled and new certificates for the stock issued to the trustee or trustees in which it must appear that they are issued pursuant to the agreement, and in the entry of ownership in the proper books of the corporation that fact must also be noted, and thereupon the trustee or trustees may vote the stock so transferred during the terms of the agreement. A duplicate of every such agreement must be filed in the registered office of the corporation and at all times during its terms be open to inspection by any stockholder or his attorney.

2. At any time within the 2 years next preceding the expiration of an agreement entered into pursuant to the provisions of subsection 1, or the expiration of an extension of that agreement, any beneficiary of the trust may, by written agreement with the trustee or trustees, extend the duration of the trust for a time not to exceed 15 years after the scheduled expiration date of the original agreement or the latest extension. An extension is not effective unless the trustee, before the expiration date of the original agreement or the latest extension, files a duplicate of the agreement providing for the extension in the registered office of the corporation. An agreement providing for an extension does not affect the rights or obligations of any person not a party to that agreement.

3. An agreement between two or more stockholders, if in writing and signed by them, may provide that in exercising any voting rights the stock held by them must be voted:

(a) Pursuant to the provisions of the agreement;

(b) As they may subsequently agree; or

(c) In accordance with a procedure agreed upon.

4. An agreement entered into pursuant to the provisions of subsection 3 is not effective for a term of more than 15 years, but at any time within the 2 years next preceding the expiration of the agreement the parties thereto may extend its duration for as many additional periods, each not to exceed 15 years, as they wish.

5. An agreement entered into pursuant to the provisions of subsection 1 or 3 is not invalidated by the fact that by its terms its duration is more than 15 years, but its duration shall be deemed amended to conform with the provisions of this section.

78.370 Notice to stockholders.

1. Whenever under the provisions of this chapter stockholders are required or authorized to take any action at a meeting, the notice of the meeting must be in writing and signed by the president or a vice president, or the secretary, or an assistant secretary, or by such other natural person or persons as the bylaws may prescribe or permit or the directors may designate.

2. The notice must state the purpose or purposes for which the meeting is called and the time when, and the place, which may be within or without this state, where it is to be held.

3. A copy of the notice must be delivered personally or mailed postage prepaid to each stockholder of record entitled to vote at the meeting not less than 10 nor more than 60 days before the meeting. If mailed, it must be directed to the stockholder at his address as it appears upon the records of the corporation, and upon the mailing of any such notice the service thereof is complete, and the time of the notice begins to run from the date upon which the notice is deposited in the mail for transmission to the stockholder. Personal delivery of any such notice to any officer of a corporation or association, or to any member of a partnership, constitutes delivery of the notice to the corporation, association or partnership.

4. The articles of incorporation or the bylaws may require that the notice be also published in one or more newspapers.

5. Notice delivered or mailed to a stockholder in accordance with the provisions of this section and the provisions, if any, of the articles of incorporation or the bylaws is sufficient, and in the event of the transfer of his stock after such delivery or mailing and before the holding of the meeting it is not necessary to deliver or mail notice of the meeting to the transferee.

6. Any stockholder may waive notice of any meeting by a writing signed by him, or his duly authorized attorney, either before or after the meeting.

7. Unless otherwise provided in the articles of incorporation or the bylaws, whenever notice is required to be given, under any provision of this chapter or the articles of incorporation or bylaws of any corporation, to any stockholder to whom:

(a) Notice of two consecutive annual meetings, and all notices of meetings or of the taking of action by written consent without a meeting to him during the period between those two consecutive annual meetings; or

(b) All, and at least two, payments sent by first-class mail of dividends or interest on securities during a 12-month period, have been mailed addressed to him at his address as shown on the records of the corporation and have been returned undeliverable, the giving of further notices to him is not required. Any action or meeting taken or held without notice to such a stockholder has the same effect as if the notice had been given. If any such stockholder delivers to the corporation a written notice setting forth his current address, the requirement that notice be given to him is reinstated. If the action taken by the corporation is such as to require the filing of a certificate under any of the other sections of this chapter, the certificate need not state that notice was not given to persons to whom notice was not required to be given pursuant to this subsection.

78.375 Waiver of notice.
Whenever any notice whatever is required to be given under the provisions of this chapter, a waiver thereof in writing, signed by the person or persons entitled to the notice, whether before or after the time stated therein, shall be deemed equivalent thereto.

Acquisition of Controlling Interest

78.378 Applicability; imposition of stricter requirements; protection of corporation and its stockholders.

1. The provisions of NRS 78.378 to 78.3793, inclusive, are applicable to any acquisition of a controlling interest in an issuing corporation unless the articles of incorporation or bylaws of the corporation in effect on the 10th day following the acquisition of a controlling interest by an acquiring person provide that the provisions of those sections do not apply.

2. The articles of incorporation, the bylaws or a resolution adopted by the directors of the issuing corporation may impose stricter requirements on the acquisition of a controlling interest in the corporation than the provisions of NRS 78.378 to 78.3793, inclusive.

3. The provisions of NRS 78.378 to 78.3793, inclusive, do not restrict the directors of an issuing corporation from taking action to protect the interests of the corporation and its stockholders, including, but not limited to, adopting or executing plans, arrangements or instruments that deny rights, privileges, power or authority to a holder of a specified number of shares or percentage of share ownership or voting power.

78.3781 Definitions. As used in NRS 78.378 to 78.3793, inclusive, unless the context otherwise requires, the words and terms defined in NRS 78.3782 to 78.3788, inclusive, have the meanings ascribed to them in those sections.

78.3782 "Acquiring person" defined. "Acquiring person" means any person who, individually or in association with others, acquires or offers to acquire, directly or indirectly, a controlling interest in an issuing corporation. The term does not include any person who, in the ordinary course of business and without an intent to avoid the requirements of NRS 78.378 to 78.3793, inclusive, acquires voting shares for the benefit of others, in respect of which he is not specifically authorized to exercise or direct the exercise of voting rights.

78.3783 "Acquisition" defined.

1. Except as otherwise provided in subsection 2, "acquisition" means the direct or indirect acquisition of a controlling interest.

2. "Acquisition" does not include any acquisition of shares in good faith, and without an intent to avoid the requirements of NRS 78.378 to 78.3793, inclusive:

(a) By an acquiring person authorized pursuant to NRS 78.378 to 78.3793, inclusive, to exercise voting rights, to the extent that the new acquisition does not result in the acquiring person obtaining a controlling interest greater than that previously authorized; or

(b) Pursuant to:

(1) The laws of descent and distribution;

(2) The enforcement of a judgment;

(3) The satisfaction of a pledge or other security interest; or

(4) A merger or reorganization effected in compliance with the provisions of NRS 78.622 or 92A.200 to 92A.240, inclusive, to which the issuing corporation is a party.

78.3784 "Control shares" defined. "Control shares" means those outstanding voting shares of an issuing corporation which an acquiring person and those persons acting in association with an acquiring person:

1. Acquire in an acquisition or offer to acquire in an acquisition; and

2. Acquire within 90 days immediately preceding the date when the acquiring person became an acquiring person.

78.3785 "Controlling interest" defined. "Controlling interest" means the ownership of outstanding voting shares of an issuing corporation sufficient, but for the provisions of NRS 78.378 to 78.3793, inclusive, to enable the acquiring person, directly or indirectly and individually or in association with others, to exercise:

1. One-fifth or more but less than one-third;

2. One-third or more but less than a majority; or

3. A majority or more, of all the voting power of the corporation in the election of directors.

78.3786 "Fair value" defined. "Fair value" means a value not less than the highest price per share paid by the acquiring person in an acquisition.

78.3787 "Interested stockholder" defined. "Interested stockholder" means a person who directly or indirectly exercises the voting power of an issuing corporation and who is:

1. An acquiring person;

2. An officer of the corporation; or

3. An employee and director of the corporation.

78.3788 "Issuing corporation" defined. "Issuing corporation" means a corporation which is organized in this state and which:

1. Has 200 or more stockholders, at least 100 of whom are stockholders of record and residents of this state; and

2. Does business in this state directly or through an affiliated corporation.

78.3789 Delivery of offeror's statement by acquiring person; contents of statement. An acquiring person who has made or offered to make an acquisition of a controlling interest in an issuing corporation may deliver an offeror's statement to the registered office of the corporation. The acquiring person may request in the statement that the directors of the corporation call a special meeting of the stockholders of the corporation, as provided in NRS 78.379. The statement must set forth:

1. A recital that the statement is given pursuant to this section;

2. The name of the acquiring person and of every person associated with him in the acquisition;

3. The number of shares in any class of voting securities owned, as of the date of the statement, by the acquiring person and each person with whom he is associated, or which the acquiring person intends to acquire;

4. The percentage of the voting securities of the corporation owned, as of the date of the statement, by the acquiring person and each person with whom he is associated, or which the acquiring person intends to acquire; and

5. If the acquiring person has not yet acquired the securities of the corporation, a detailed description of:

(a) The terms and conditions of the proposed acquisition; and

(b) The means by which any required consideration, and any indebtedness incurred to consummate the transaction, are to be paid.

78.379 Voting rights of acquiring person; meeting of stockholders; statements to accompany notice of meeting.

1. An acquiring person and those acting in association with an acquiring person obtain only such voting rights in the control shares as are conferred by a resolution of the stockholders of the corporation, approved at a special or annual meeting of the stockholders.

2. If an acquiring person so requests in an offeror's statement delivered pursuant to NRS 78.3789, and if he gives an undertaking to pay the expenses of the meeting, the directors of the corporation shall, within 10 days after delivery of the statement, call a special meeting of the stockholders to determine the voting rights to be accorded the control shares.

3. A notice of any meeting of stockholders at which the question of voting rights is to be determined must be accompanied by:

(a) A complete copy of the offeror's statement; and

(b) A statement of the board of directors of the corporation setting forth the position of the board with respect to the acquisition or, if it is the case, stating that the board makes no recommendation concerning the matter.

4. A special meeting of stockholders called pursuant to this section:

(a) Must not be held before the expiration of 30 days after the delivery of the offeror's statement, unless the statement contains a request that the meeting be held sooner.

(b) Must be held within 50 days after the delivery of the statement, unless the acquiring person otherwise agrees in writing that the meeting may be held after that time.

5. If the offeror's statement does not include a request that a special meeting be called, the question of voting rights must be presented to the next special or annual meeting of the stockholders.

78.3791 Approval of voting rights of acquiring person.
Except as otherwise provided by the articles of incorporation of the issuing corporation, a resolution of the stockholders granting voting rights to the control shares acquired by an acquiring person must be approved by:

1. The holders of a majority of the voting power of the corporation; and

2. If the acquisition will result in any change of the kind described in subsection 3 of NRS 78.390, the holders of a majority of each class or series affected, excluding those shares held by any interested stockholder.

78.3792 Redemption of control shares.

1. If so provided in the articles of incorporation or the bylaws of the issuing corporation in effect on the 10th day following the acquisition of a controlling interest by an acquiring person, the issuing corporation may call for redemption of not less than all the control shares at the average price paid for the control shares, if:

(a) An offeror's statement is not delivered with respect to the acquisition as provided in NRS 78.3789 on or before the 10th day after the acquisition of the control shares; or

(b) An offeror's statement is delivered, but the control shares are not accorded full voting rights by the stockholders.

2. The issuing corporation shall call for redemption within 30 days after the occurrence of the event prescribed in paragraph (a) or (b) of subsection 1, and the shares must be redeemed within 60 days after the call.

78.3793 Notice to stockholders; purchase of shares by corporation.

1. Unless otherwise provided in the articles of incorporation or the bylaws of the issuing corporation in effect on the 10th day following the acquisition of a controlling interest by an acquiring person, if the control shares are accorded full voting rights pursuant to NRS 78.378 to 78.3793, inclusive, and the acquiring person has acquired control shares with a majority or more of all the voting power, any stockholder of record, other than the acquiring person, who has not voted in favor of authorizing voting rights for the control shares is entitled to demand payment for the fair value of his shares.

2. The board of directors of the issuing corporation shall, within 20 days after the vote of the stockholders authorizing voting rights for the control shares, cause a notice to be sent to any stockholder, other than the acquiring person, who has not voted in favor of authorizing voting rights for the control shares, advising him of the fact and of his right to receive fair value for his shares as provided in subsection 3.

3. Within 20 days after the mailing of the notice described in subsection 2, any stockholder of the corporation, other than the acquiring person, who has not voted in favor of authorizing voting rights for the control shares, may deliver to the registered office of the corporation a written demand that the corporation purchase, for fair value, all or any portion of his shares. The corporation shall comply with the demand within 30 days after its delivery.

Amendment and Restatement of Articles of Incorporation

78.380 Amendment of articles before issuing stock.

1. At least two-thirds of the incorporators or of the board of directors of any corporation, before issuing any stock, may amend the original articles of incorporation thereof as may be desired by executing and acknowledging or proving in the manner required for original articles of incorporation, and filing with the secretary of state a

certificate amending, modifying, changing or altering the original articles, in whole or in part. The certificate must:

(a) Declare that the signers thereof are at least two-thirds of the incorporators or of the board of directors of the corporation, and state the corporation's name.

(b) State the date upon which the original articles thereof were filed with the secretary of state.

(c) Affirmatively declare that to the date of the certificate, no stock of the corporation has been issued.

2. The amendment is effective upon the filing of the certificate with the secretary of state.

3. This section does not permit the insertion of any matter not in conformity with this chapter.

78.385 Amendment of articles after issuing stock: Scope of amendments.

1. Any corporation having stock may amend its articles of incorporation in any of the following respects:

(a) By addition to its corporate powers and purposes, or diminution thereof, or both.

(b) By substitution of other powers and purposes, in whole or in part, for those prescribed by its articles of incorporation.

(c) By increasing, decreasing or reclassifying its authorized stock, by changing the number, par value, preferences, or relative, participating, optional or other rights, or the qualifications, limitations or restrictions of such rights, of its shares, or of any class or series of any class thereof whether or not the shares are outstanding at the time of the amendment, or by changing shares with par value, whether or not the shares are outstanding at the time of the amendment, into shares without par value or by changing shares without par value, whether or not the shares are outstanding at the time of the amendment, into shares with par value, either with or without increasing or decreasing the number of shares, and upon such basis as may be set forth in the certificate of amendment.

(d) By changing the name of the corporation.

(e) By making any other change or alteration in its articles of incorporation that may be desired.

2. All such changes or alterations may be effected by one certificate of amendment; but any articles of incorporation so amended, changed or altered, may contain only such provisions as it would be lawful and proper to insert in original articles of incorporation, pursuant to NRS 78.035 and 78.037, if the original articles were executed, acknowledged and filed at the time of making the amendment.

78.390 Amendment of articles after issuing stock: Procedure.

1. Every amendment adopted pursuant to the provisions of NRS 78.385 must be made in the following manner:

(a) The board of directors must adopt a resolution setting forth the amendment proposed and declaring its advisability, and call a meeting, either annual or special, of the stockholders entitled to vote for the consideration thereof.

(b) At the meeting, of which notice must be given to each stockholder entitled to vote pursuant to the provisions of this section, a vote of the stockholders entitled to vote in person or by proxy must be taken for and against the proposed amendment. If it appears upon the canvassing of the votes that stockholders holding shares in the corporation entitling them to exercise at least a majority of the voting power, or such greater proportion of the voting power as may be required in the case of a vote by classes or series, as provided in subsections 3 and 5, or as may be required by the provisions of the articles of incorporation, have voted in favor of the amendment, the president, or vice president, and secretary, or assistant secretary, shall execute a certificate setting forth the amendment, or setting forth the articles of incorporation as amended, and the vote by which the amendment was adopted, and the president or vice president shall acknowledge the certificate before a person authorized by the laws of the place where the acknowledgment is taken to take acknowledgments of deeds.

(c) The certificate so executed and acknowledged must be filed in the office of the secretary of state.

2. Upon filing the certificate the articles of incorporation are amended accordingly.

3. If any proposed amendment would alter or change any preference or any relative or other right given to any class or series of outstanding shares, then the amendment must be approved by the vote, in addition to the affirmative vote otherwise required, of the holders of shares representing a majority of the voting power of each class or series affected by the amendment regardless of limitations or restrictions on the voting power thereof.

4. Provision may be made in the articles of incorporation requiring, in the case of any specified amendments, a larger proportion of the voting power of stockholders than that required by this section.

5. Different series of the same class of shares do not constitute different classes of shares for the purpose of voting by classes except when the series is adversely affected by an amendment in a different manner than other series of the same class.

78.403 Restatement of articles.

1. A corporation may restate, or amend and restate, in a single certificate the entire text of its articles of incorporation as amended by filing with the secretary of state a certificate entitled "Restated Articles of Incorporation of ....," which must set forth the articles as amended to the date of the certificate. If the certificate alters or amends the articles

in any manner, it must comply with the provisions of this chapter governing such amendments and must be accompanied by:

(a) A resolution; or

(b) A form prescribed by the secretary of state, setting forth which provisions of the articles of incorporation on file with the secretary of state are being altered or amended.

2. If the certificate does not alter or amend the articles, it must be signed by the president or vice president and the secretary or assistant secretary of the corporation and state that they have been authorized to execute the certificate by resolution of the board of directors adopted on the date stated, and that the certificate correctly sets forth the text of the articles of incorporation as amended to the date of the certificate.

3. The following may be omitted from the restated articles:

(a) The names, addresses, signatures and acknowledgments of the incorporators;

(b) The names and addresses of the members of the past and present boards of directors; and

(c) The name and address of the resident agent.

4. Whenever a corporation is required to file a certified copy of its articles, in lieu thereof it may file a certified copy of the most recent certificate restating its articles as amended, subject to the provisions of subsection 2, together with certified copies of all certificates of amendment filed subsequent to the restated articles and certified copies of all certificates supplementary to the original articles.

Secretary of State: Duties and Fees

78.755 Duties: Collection of fees; employment of new technology to aid in performance.

1. The secretary of state, for services relating to his official duties and the records of his office, shall charge and collect the fees designated in NRS 78.760 to 78.785, inclusive.

2. The secretary of state may accept the filing of documents by facsimile machine and employ new technology, as it is developed, to aid in the performance of all duties required by law. The secretary of state may establish rules, fee schedules and regulations not inconsistent with law, for filing documents by facsimile machine and for the adoption, employment and use of new technology in the performance of his duties.

78.760 Filing fees: Articles of incorporation.

1. The fee for filing articles of incorporation is prescribed in the following schedule:

If the amount represented by the total number of shares provided for in the articles or agreement is:

$25,000 or less $125

Over $25,000 and not over $75,000 $175

Over $75,000 and not over $200,000 $225

Over $200,000 and not over $500,000 $325

Over $500,000 and not over $1,000,000 $425

Over $1,000,000: For the first $1,000,000 $425

For each additional $500,000 or fraction thereof $225

2. The maximum fee which may be charged under this section is $25,000 for:

(a) The original filing of articles of incorporation.

(b) A subsequent filing of any instrument which authorizes an increase in stock.

3. For the purposes of computing the filing fees according to the schedule in subsection 1, the amount represented by the total number of shares provided for in the articles of incorporation is:

(a) The aggregate par value of the shares, if only shares with a par value are therein provided for;

(b) The product of the number of shares multiplied by $1, regardless of any lesser amount prescribed as the value or consideration for which shares may be issued and disposed of, if only shares without par value are therein provided for; or

(c) The aggregate par value of the shares with a par value plus the product of the number of shares without par value multiplied by $1, regardless of any lesser amount prescribed as the value or consideration for which the shares without par value may be issued and disposed of, if shares with and without par value are therein provided for.

For the purposes of this subsection, shares with no prescribed par value shall be deemed shares without par value.

4. The secretary of state shall calculate filing fees pursuant to this section with respect to shares with a par value of less than one-tenth of a cent as if the par value were one-tenth of a cent.

78.765 Filing fees: Certificate changing number of authorized shares; amendment of articles; certificate of correction.

1. The fee for filing a certificate changing the number of authorized shares pursuant to NRS 78.209 or a certificate of amendment to articles of incorporation that increases the corporation's authorized stock or a certificate of correction that increases the corporation's authorized stock is the difference between the fee computed at the rates specified in NRS 78.760 upon the total authorized stock of the corporation, including the proposed increase, and the fee computed at the rates specified in NRS 78.760 upon the total authorized capital, excluding the proposed increase. In no case may the amount be less than $75.

2. The fee for filing a certificate of amendment to articles of incorporation that does not increase the corporation's

authorized stock or a certificate of correction that does not increase the corporation's authorized stock is $75.

3. The fee for filing a certificate pursuant to NRS 78.195 or an amended certificate pursuant to NRS 78.1955 is $75.

78.767 Filing fees: Certificates of restated articles of incorporation.

1. The fee for filing a certificate of restated articles of incorporation that does not increase the corporation's authorized stock is $75.

2. The fee for filing a certificate of restated articles of incorporation that increases the corporation's authorized stock is the difference between the fee computed pursuant to NRS 78.760 based upon the total authorized stock of the corporation, including the proposed increase, and the fee computed pursuant to NRS 78.760 based upon the total authorized stock of the corporation, excluding the proposed increase. In no case may the amount be less than $75.

78.770 Filing fees: Articles of merger; articles of exchange.

1. The fee for filing articles of merger of two or more domestic corporations is the difference between the fee computed at the rates specified in NRS 78.760 upon the aggregate authorized stock of the corporation created by the merger and the fee so computed upon the aggregate amount of the total authorized stock of the constituent corporations.

2. The fee for filing articles of merger of one or more domestic corporations with one or more foreign corporations is the difference between the fee computed at the rates specified in NRS 78.760 upon the aggregate authorized stock of the corporation created by the merger and the fee so computed upon the aggregate amount of the total authorized stock of the constituent corporations which have paid fees as required by NRS 78.760 and 80.050.

3. In no case may the amount paid be less than $75, and in no case may the amount paid pursuant to subsection 2 exceed $25,000.

4. The fee for filing articles of exchange is $125.

78.780 Filing fees: Certificates of extension and dissolution.

1. The fee for filing a certificate of extension of corporate existence of any corporation is an amount equal to one-fourth of the fee computed at the rates specified in NRS 78.760 for filing articles of incorporation.

2. The fee for filing a certificate of dissolution whether it occurs before or after payment of capital and beginning of business is $30.

78.785 Miscellaneous fees.

1. The fee for filing a certificate of change of location of a corporation's registered office and resident agent, or a new designation of resident agent, is $15.

2. The fee for certifying articles of incorporation where a copy is provided is $10.

3. The fee for certifying a copy of an amendment to articles of incorporation, or to a copy of the articles as amended, where a copy is furnished, is $10.

4. The fee for certifying an authorized printed copy of the general corporation law as compiled by the secretary of state is $10.

5. The fee for reserving a corporate name is $20.

6. The fee for executing a certificate of corporate existence which does not list the previous documents relating to the corporation, or a certificate of change in a corporate name, is $15.

7. The fee for executing a certificate of corporate existence which lists the previous documents relating to the corporation is $20.

8. The fee for executing, certifying or filing any certificate or document not provided for in NRS 78.760 to 78.785, inclusive, is $20.

9. The fee for copies made at the office of the secretary of state is $1 per page.

10. The fee for filing articles of incorporation, articles of merger, or certificates of amendment increasing the basic surplus of a mutual or reciprocal insurer must be computed pursuant to NRS 78.760, 78.765 and 78.770, on the basis of the amount of basic surplus of the insurer.

11. The fee for examining and provisionally approving any document at any time before the document is presented for filing is $100.

78.795 Registration of natural person or corporation willing to serve as resident agent for corporation, limited-liability company or limited partnership.

1. Any natural person or corporation residing or located in this state may, on or after January 1 of any year but before January 31 of that year, register his willingness to serve as the resident agent of a domestic or foreign corporation, limited-liability company or limited partnership with the secretary of state. The registration must be accompanied by a fee of $250.

2. The secretary of state shall maintain a list of those persons who are registered pursuant to subsection 1 and make the list available to persons seeking to do business in this state.

CHAPTER 78A CLOSE CORPORATIONS

General Provisions

78A.010 Applicability of chapter. The provisions of this chapter apply to all close corporations formed pursuant to NRS 78A.020. Unless otherwise provided by this chapter, the provisions of chapter 78 of NRS are applicable to all close corporations.

78A.015 Filing of documents written in language other than English.

No document which is written in a language other than English may be filed or submitted for filing in the office of the secretary of state pursuant to the provisions of this chapter unless it is accompanied by a verified translation of that document into the English language.

78A.020 Procedure; requirements concerning stock; contents of articles of incorporation.

1. A close corporation must be formed in accordance with NRS 78.030 to 78.055, inclusive, subject to the following requirements:

(a) All of the issued stock of the corporation of all classes, exclusive of treasury shares, must be represented by certificates and must be held of record by a specified number of persons, not to exceed 30.

(b) All of the issued stock of all classes must be subject to one or more of the restrictions on transfer pursuant to NRS 78A.050.

(c) The corporation shall not offer any of its stock of any class that would constitute a public offering within the meaning of the Securities Act of 1933, 15 U.S.C. §§ 77 et seq.

2. The articles of incorporation of a close corporation must:

(a) Set forth the matters required by NRS 78.035 except that the articles must state that there will be no board of directors if so agreed pursuant to NRS 78A.070.

(b) Contain a heading stating the name of the corporation and that it is a close corporation.

3. The articles of incorporation of a close corporation may set forth the qualifications of stockholders by specifying the classes of persons who are entitled to be holders of record of stock of any class, the classes of persons who are not entitled to be holders of record of stock of any class, or both.

4. To determine the number of holders of record of the stock of a close corporation, stock that is held in joint or common tenancy or by community property must be treated as held by one stockholder.

78A.030 Procedure for existing corporation to become close corporation.

1. Any corporation organized under chapter 78 of NRS may become a close corporation pursuant to this chapter by executing, acknowledging, filing and recording, in accordance with NRS 78.390, a certificate of amendment of the certificate of incorporation which must:

(a) Contain a statement that the corporation elects to become a close corporation; and

(b) Meet the requirements of subsection 2 of NRS 78A.020.

2. Except as otherwise provided in subsection 3, the amendment must be adopted in accordance with the requirements of NRS 78.390.

3. The amendment must be approved by a vote of the holders of record of at least two-thirds of the shares of each class of stock of the corporation that are outstanding and entitled to vote, unless the articles of incorporation or bylaws require approval by a greater proportion.

Shares of Stock

78A.040 Notice required on share certificates; effect of notice and restrictions on transfer of shares; shareholders to be provided with copies of provisions restricting rights.

1. The following statement must appear conspicuously on each share certificate issued by a close corporation:

The rights of stockholders in a close corporation may differ materially from the rights of shareholders in other corporations. Copies of the certificate of incorporation, bylaws, shareholders' agreements and other documents, any of which may restrict transfers of stock and affect voting and other rights, may be obtained by a shareholder on written request to the corporation.

2. A person claiming an interest in the shares of a close corporation that has complied with the requirement of subsection 1 is bound by the documents referred to in the notice. A person claiming an interest in the shares of a close corporation that has not complied with the requirement of subsection 1 is bound by any document that he or a person through whom he claims has knowledge or notice.

3. A close corporation shall provide to any shareholder upon his written request and without charge, copies of the provisions that restrict transfer or affect voting or other rights of shareholders appearing in the articles of incorporation, bylaws, shareholders' agreements or voting trust agreements filed with the corporations.

4. Except as otherwise provided in subsection 5, the close corporation may refuse to register the transfer of stock into the name of a person to whom the stock of a close corporation has been transferred if the person has, or is presumed to have, notice that the transfer of the stock is in violation of a restriction on the transfer of stock. If the close corporation refuses to register the transfer of stock into the name of the transferee, the close corporation must notify the transferee of its refusal and state the reasons therefor.

5. Subsection 4 does not apply if:

(a) The transfer of stock, even if contrary to the restrictions on transfer of stock, has been consented to by all the stockholders of the close corporation; or

(b) The close corporation has amended its certificate of incorporation in accordance with NRS 78A.180.

6. The provisions of this section do not impair any rights of a transferee to:

(a) Rescind the transaction by which he acquired the stock; or

(b) Recover under any applicable warranty.

7. As used in this section, "transfer" is not limited to a transfer for value.

78A.050 Transfer of shares prohibited; exceptions.

1. An interest in the shares of a close corporation may not be transferred, except to the extent permitted by the certificate of incorporation, the bylaws, a shareholders' agreement or a voting trust agreement.

2. Except as otherwise provided by the certificate of incorporation, the provisions of this section do not apply to a transfer:

(a) To the corporation or to any other shareholder of the same class or series of shares.

(b) To heirs at law.

(c) That has been approved in writing by all of the holders of the shares of the corporation having voting rights.

(d) To an executor or administrator upon the death of a shareholder or to a trustee or receiver as a result of a bankruptcy, insolvency, dissolution or similar proceeding brought by or against a shareholder.

(e) By merger or share exchange or an exchange of existing shares for other shares of a different class or series in the corporation.

(f) By a pledge as collateral for a loan that does not grant the pledgee any voting rights possessed by the pledgor.

(g) Made after the termination of the status of the corporation as a close corporation.

78A.060 Effect of attempt to transfer shares in violation of prohibition.

1. An attempt to transfer shares in a close corporation in violation of a prohibition against such a transfer is ineffective.

2. An attempt to transfer shares in a close corporation in violation of a prohibition against transfer that is not binding on the transferee because:

(a) The notice required by NRS 78A.040 was not given; or

(b) The prohibition is held unenforceable by a court of competent jurisdiction, gives the corporation an option to purchase the shares from the transferee for the same price and on the same terms that he purchased them. To exercise the option, the corporation must give the transferee written notice within 30 days after they receive a share certificate for registration in the name of the transferee.

Powers and Duties

78A.070 Shareholders' agreements: Authority to enter; effect; amendment.

1. All shareholders of a close corporation who are entitled to vote may agree in writing to regulate the exercise of the corporate powers and the management of the business and affairs of the corporation or the relationship among the shareholders of the corporation.

2. An agreement authorized by this section is effective even if the agreement:

(a) Eliminates a board of directors.

(b) Restricts the discretion or powers of the board of directors or authorizes director proxies or weighted voting rights.

(c) Treats the corporation as a partnership.

(d) Creates a relationship among the shareholders or between the shareholders and the corporation that would otherwise be appropriate among partners.

3. If the corporation has a board of directors, an agreement authorized by this section that restricts the discretion or powers of the board of directors:

(a) Relieves directors of liability imposed by law; and

(b) Imposes that liability on each person in whom the discretion or power of the board is vested, to the extent that the discretion or power of the board of directors is governed by the agreement.

4. A provision eliminating a board of directors in an agreement authorized by this section is not effective unless the articles of incorporation contain a statement to that effect.

5. A provision entitling one or more shareholders to dissolve the corporation under NRS 78A.160 is effective if a statement of this right is contained in the articles of incorporation.

6. To amend an agreement authorized by this section, all shareholders entitled to vote must approve the amendment in writing, unless the agreement provides otherwise.

7. Subscribers for shares may act as shareholders with respect to an agreement authorized by this section if shares are not issued when the agreement was made.

8. This section does not prohibit any other agreement between or among shareholders in a close corporation.

78A.080 Shareholders' agreements: Validity.
A written agreement among stockholders of a close corporation or any provision of the certificate of incorporation or of the bylaws of the corporation that relates to any phase of the affairs of the corporation, including, but not limited to, the management of its business, the declaration and payment of dividends or other division of profits, the election of directors or officers, the employment of stockholders by the corporation or the arbitration of disputes is not invalid on the ground that it is an attempt by the parties to the

agreement or by the stockholders of the corporation to treat the corporation as if it were a partnership or to arrange relations among the stockholders or between the stockholders and the corporation in a manner that would be appropriate only among partners.

78A.090 Operation without board of directors; elimination and reinstatement of board.

1. A close corporation may operate without a board of directors if the certificate of incorporation contains a statement to that effect.

2. An amendment to the certificate of incorporation eliminating a board of directors must be approved:

(a) By all the shareholders of the corporation, whether or not otherwise entitled to vote on amendments; or

(b) If no shares have been issued, by all subscribers for shares, if any, or if none, by the incorporators.

3. While a corporation is operating without a board of directors as authorized by subsection 1:

(a) All corporate powers must be exercised by or under the authority of, and the business and affairs of the corporation managed under the direction of, the shareholders.

(b) Unless the articles of incorporation provide otherwise:

(1) Action requiring the approval of the board of directors or of both the board of directors and the shareholders is authorized if approved by the shareholders; and

(2) Action requiring a majority or greater percentage vote of the board of directors is authorized if approved by the majority or greater percentage of votes of the shareholders entitled to vote on the action.

(c) A requirement by a state or the United States that a document delivered for filing contain a statement that specified action has been taken by the board of directors is satisfied by a statement that the corporation is a close corporation without a board of directors and that the action was approved by the shareholders.

(d) The shareholders by resolution may appoint one or more shareholders to sign documents as designated directors.

4. An amendment to the articles of incorporation that deletes the provision which eliminates a board of directors must be approved by the holders of at least two-thirds of the votes of each class or series of shares of the corporation, voting as separate voting groups, whether or not otherwise entitled to vote on amendments. The amendment must specify the number, names and mailing addresses of the directors of the corporation or describe who will perform the duties of the board of directors.

78A.100 Annual meeting. A close corporation shall hold an annual meeting if one or more shareholders delivers a written notice to the corporation requesting a meeting.

Upon receipt of a notice, the close corporation must hold a meeting within 30 days.

78A.110 Execution of documents by person acting in more than one capacity. Notwithstanding any law to the contrary, a person who holds more than one office in a close corporation may execute, acknowledge or verify in more than one capacity any document required to be executed, acknowledged or verified by the holders of two or more offices.

78A.120 Limitation on liability of shareholders. Personal liability may not be imposed upon shareholders of a close corporation solely as a result of the failure of the close corporation to observe the usual corporate formalities or requirements relating to the exercise of corporate powers or management of its business and affairs, where such failure results from the distinct nature and permissible functioning of a close corporation.

78A.130 Merger or share exchange; sale, lease or exchange of assets.

1. A plan of merger or share exchange that if effected would:

(a) Terminate the close corporation status must be approved by the holders of at least two-thirds of the votes of each class or series of shares of the close corporation, voting as separate voting groups, whether or not the holders are entitled to vote on the plan.

(b) Create the surviving corporation as a close corporation must be approved by the holders of at least two-thirds of the votes of each class or series of shares of the surviving corporation, voting as separate voting groups, whether or not the holders are entitled to vote on the plan.

2. If not made in the usual and regular course of business, a sale, lease, exchange or other disposition of all or substantially all of the property of a close corporation must be approved by the holders of at least two-thirds of the votes of each class or series of shares of the corporation, voting as separate voting groups, whether or not the holders are entitled to vote on the transaction.

78A.140 Appointment of custodian, receiver or provisional director.

1. Upon application of a stockholder, the court may appoint one or more persons to be custodians and, if the corporation is insolvent, to be receivers of any close corporation when:

(a) The business and affairs of the close corporation are managed by the stockholders who are so divided that the business of the corporation is suffering or is threatened with irreparable injury and any remedy with respect to such a deadlock provided in the certificate of incorporation or bylaws or in any written agreement of the stockholders has failed; or

(b) The petitioning stockholder has the right to the dissolution of the corporation under a provision of the certificate of incorporation permitted by NRS 78A.160.

2. If the court determines that it would be in the best interest of the corporation, the court may appoint a provisional director in lieu of appointing a custodian or receiver for a close corporation. Such an appointment does not preclude any subsequent order of the court appointing a custodian or receiver for the corporation.

78A.150 Provisional director: Requirements for appointment; qualifications, rights and powers; compensation.

1. Notwithstanding any contrary provision of the certificate of incorporation, the bylaws or an agreement of the stockholders, the court may appoint a provisional director for a close corporation if the shareholders or directors, if any, are so divided concerning the management of the business and affairs of the corporation that the votes required for action by the board of directors cannot be obtained, with the consequence that the business and affairs of the corporation cannot be conducted to the advantage of the stockholders generally.

2. An application for relief pursuant to this section must be filed:

(a) By at least one-half of the number of directors then in office;

(b) By the holders of at least one-third of all stock then entitled to elect directors; or

(c) If there is more than one class of stock then entitled to elect one or more directors, by the holders of two-thirds of the stock of each class.

The certificate of incorporation of a close corporation may provide that a lesser proportion of the directors, the stockholders or a class of stockholders may apply for relief under this section.

3. A provisional director:

(a) Must be an impartial person who is not a stockholder or a creditor of the corporation or of any subsidiary or affiliate of the corporation and whose further qualifications, if any, may be determined by the court.

(b) Is not a custodian or receiver of the corporation and does not have the title and powers of a custodian or receiver appointed under NRS 78A.140.

(c) Has the rights and powers of an elected director of the corporation, including the right to notice of and to vote at meetings of directors, until such time as he may be removed by order of the court.

4. The compensation of a provisional director must be determined by agreement between the provisional director and the corporation subject to the approval of the court, which may fix his compensation in the absence of

agreement or in the event of disagreement between the provisional director and the corporation.

78A.160 Option of stockholder to dissolve corporation: Inclusion in certificate of incorporation; exercise of option; notice on stock certificate.

1. The certificate of incorporation of any close corporation may include a provision granting to any stockholder or to the holder of any specified number or percentage of shares of any class of stock an option to have the corporation dissolved at will or upon the occurrence of any specified event or contingency. Whenever any option to dissolve is exercised, the stockholders who exercise the option shall give written notice thereof to all other stockholders. Thirty days after the notice is sent, the dissolution of the corporation must proceed as if the required number of stockholders having voting power consented in writing to dissolution of the corporation as provided by NRS 78.320.

2. If the certificate of incorporation as originally filed does not contain a provision authorized by subsection 1, the certificate may be amended to include such a provision if adopted by the affirmative vote of the holders of all the outstanding stock, whether or not otherwise entitled to vote, unless the certificate of incorporation specifically authorizes such an amendment by a vote which is not less than two-thirds of all the outstanding stock, whether or not otherwise entitled to vote.

3. Each stock certificate in any corporation whose certificate of incorporation authorizes dissolution as permitted by this section must conspicuously note on the face of the certificate the existence of the provision or the provision is ineffective.

Termination of Status as Close Corporation

78A.170 Time of termination of status. A close corporation is subject to the provisions of this chapter until:

1. The corporation files with the secretary of state a certificate of amendment deleting from the certificate of incorporation the provisions required or permitted by NRS 78A.020, to be stated in the certificate of incorporation; or

2. A provision or condition required or permitted by NRS 78A.020 to be stated in a certificate of incorporation has been breached and the corporation or any stockholder has not acted pursuant to NRS 78A.190 to prevent the loss of status or remedy the breach.

78A.180 Voluntary termination of status.

1. A corporation may voluntarily terminate its status as a close corporation, and cease to be subject to the provisions of this chapter, by amending the certificate of incorporation to delete therefrom the additional provisions required or permitted by NRS 78A.020 to be stated in the certificate of incorporation of a close corporation. An amendment

must be adopted and become effective in accordance with NRS 78.390, except that it must be approved by a vote of the holders of record of at least two-thirds of the voting shares of each class of stock of the corporation that are outstanding.

2. The certificate of incorporation of a close corporation may provide that on any amendment to terminate the status as a close corporation, a vote greater than two-thirds or a vote of all shares of any class may be required. If the certificate of incorporation contains such a provision, that provision may not be amended, repealed or modified by any vote less than that required to terminate the status of the corporation as a close corporation.

78A.190 Involuntary termination of status; intervention by court.

1. The status of a corporation as a close corporation terminates if one or more of the provisions or conditions of this chapter cease to exist or be fulfilled unless:

(a) Within 30 days after the occurrence of the event, or within 30 days after the event has been discovered by the corporation, whichever is later, the corporation files with the secretary of state a certificate, executed and acknowledged, stating that a specified provision or condition included in the certificate of incorporation to qualify the corporation as a close corporation has ceased to be applicable and furnishes a copy of the certificate to each stockholder; and

(b) The corporation, concurrently with the filing of a certificate, takes such steps as are necessary to correct the situation that threatens the status as a close corporation, including the refusal to register the transfer of stock which has been wrongfully transferred as provided by NRS 78A.050 or commencing a proceeding under subsection 2.

2. Upon the suit of the close corporation or any stockholder, the court has jurisdiction to:

(a) Issue all orders necessary to prevent the corporation from losing its status as a close corporation.

(b) Restore the status of the corporation as a close corporation by enjoining or setting aside any act or threatened act on the part of the corporation or a stockholder that would be inconsistent with any of the provisions or conditions required or permitted by this chapter to be stated in the certificate of incorporation of a close corporation, unless it is an act approved in accordance with NRS 78A.050.

(c) Enjoin or set aside any transfer or threatened transfer of stock of a close corporation that is contrary to the terms of the certificate of incorporation or of any permitted restriction on transfer.

(d) Enjoin any public offering or threatened public offering of stock of the close corporation.

78A.200 Effect of termination of status.

1. A corporation that terminates its status as a close corporation is subject to the provisions of chapter 78 of NRS.

2. Termination of the status of a close corporation does not affect any right of a shareholder or of the corporation under an agreement or the articles of incorporation unless invalidated by law.

CHAPTER 86 LIMITED-LIABILITY COMPANIES

General Provisions

86.011 Definitions. As used in this chapter, unless the context otherwise requires, the words and terms defined in NRS 86.021 to 86.125, inclusive, have the meanings ascribed to them in those sections.

86.021 "Articles of organization" defined. "Articles of organization" means the articles of organization filed with the secretary of state for the purpose of forming a limited-liability company pursuant to this chapter.

86.031 "Bankrupt" defined. "Bankrupt" is limited to the effect of the federal statutes codified as Title 11 of the United States Code.

86.041 "Contribution" defined. Repealed.

86.051 "Foreign limited-liability company" defined. "Foreign limited-liability company" means a limited-liability company formed under the laws of any jurisdiction other than this state.

86.061 "Limited-liability company" and "company" defined. "Limited-liability company" or "company" means a limited-liability company organized and existing under this chapter.

86.065 "Majority in interest" defined. "Majority in interest" means a majority of the interests in the current profits of a limited-liability company.

86.071 "Manager" defined. "Manager" means a person, or one of several persons, designated in or selected pursuant to the articles of organization or operating agreement of a limited-liability company to manage the company.

86.081 "Member" defined. "Member" means the owner of an interest in a limited-liability company.

86.091 "Member's interest" defined. "Member's interest" means his share of the economic interests in a limited-liability company, including profits, losses and distributions of assets.

86.101 "Operating agreement" defined. "Operating agreement" means any valid written agreement of the members as to the affairs of a limited-liability company and the conduct of its business.

86.106 "Participating member" defined. Repealed.

86.111 "Real property" defined. "Real property" includes land, any interest, leasehold or estate in land, and any improvements on it.

86.121 "Registered office" defined. "Registered office" of a limited-liability company means the office maintained at the street address of its resident agent.

86.125 "Resident agent" defined. "Resident agent" means the agent appointed by the company upon whom process or a notice or demand authorized by law to be served upon the company may be served.

86.131 Applicability of chapter to foreign and interstate commerce.

The provisions of this chapter apply to commerce with foreign nations and among the several states. It is the intention of the legislature by enactment of this chapter that the legal existence of limited-liability companies formed under this chapter be recognized beyond the limits of this state and that, subject to any reasonable requirement of registration, any such company transacting business outside this state be granted protection of full faith and credit under Section 1 of Article IV of the Constitution of the United States.

Organization

86.141 Purpose for organization. A limited-liability company may be organized under this chapter for any lawful purpose, except insurance.

86.151 Method of formation; issuance of certificate by secretary of state; membership.

1. One or more persons may form a limited-liability company by:

(a) Executing, acknowledging and filing with the secretary of state articles of organization for the company; and

(b) Filing with the secretary of state a certificate of acceptance of appointment, executed by the resident agent of the company.

2. Upon the filing of the articles of organization and the certificate of acceptance with the secretary of state, and the payment to him of the required filing fees, the secretary of state shall issue to the company a certificate that the articles, containing the required statement of facts, have been filed.

3. A signer of the articles of organization or a manager designated in the articles does not thereby become a member of the company. At all times after commencement of business by the company, the company must have one or more members. The filing of the articles does not, by itself, constitute commencement of business by the company.

86.155 Perpetual existence of company. Unless otherwise provided in its articles of organization or operating agreement, a limited-liability company has perpetual existence.

86.161 Articles of organization: Contents.

1. The articles of organization must set forth:

(a) The name of the limited-liability company;

(b) The name and complete street address of its resident agent, and the mailing address of the resident agent if different from the street address;

(c) The name and post office or street address, either residence or business, of each of the organizers executing the articles;

(d) If the company is to be managed by one or more managers, the name and post office or street address, either residence or business, of each manager; and

(e) If the company is to be managed by the members, the name and post office or street address, either residence or business, of each member.

2. The articles may set forth any other provision, not inconsistent with law, which the members elect to set out in the articles of organization for the regulation of the internal affairs of the company, including any provisions which under this chapter are required or permitted to be set out in the operating agreement of the company.

3. It is not necessary to set out in the articles of organization:

(a) The rights, if any, of the members to contract debts on behalf of the limited-liability company; or (b) Any of the powers enumerated in this chapter.

86.171 Name of company: Distinguishable name required; availability of name of revoked, terminated or merged company.

1. The name of a limited-liability company formed under the provisions of this chapter must contain the words "Limited-Liability Company," "Limited Company," or "Limited" or the abbreviations "Ltd.," "L.L.C.," "L.C.," "LLC," or "LC." The word "Company" may be abbreviated as "Co."

2. The name proposed for a limited-liability company must be distinguishable from the names of all other artificial persons organized or registered under chapter 78, 78A, 80, 81, 82, 84, 86, 87, 88 or 89 of NRS whose names are on file in the office of the secretary of state. If a proposed name is not so distinguishable, the secretary of state shall return the articles of organization to the organizer, unless the written acknowledged consent of the holder of the registered name to use the same name or the requested similar name accompanies the articles of organization.

3. For the purposes of this section and NRS 86.176, a proposed name is not distinguished from a registered or reserved name solely because one or the other contains distinctive lettering, a distinctive mark, a trade-mark or a trade name, or any combination of these.

4. The name of a limited-liability company whose charter has been revoked, whose existence has terminated, which has merged and is not the surviving company, or which for any other reason is no longer in good standing is available for use by any other artificial person.

86.176 Name of company: Reservation; injunctive relief.

1. The secretary of state, when requested so to do, shall reserve, for a period of 90 days, the right to use any name available under NRS 86.171, for the use of any proposed limited-liability company. During the period, a name so reserved is not available for use by any corporation, limited partnership or limited-liability company without the consent of the person at whose request the reservation was made.

2. The use by any corporation, limited partnership or limited-liability company of a name in violation of NRS 86.171 or subsection 1 of this section may be enjoined, notwithstanding the fact that the articles of incorporation or organization of the corporation or limited-liability company or the certificate of limited partnership may have been filed by the secretary of state.

86.201 Articles of organization: Filing.

1. Upon filing the articles of organization and the certificate of acceptance of the resident agent, and the payment of filing fees, the limited-liability company is considered legally organized pursuant to this chapter.

2. A limited-liability company must not transact business or incur indebtedness, except that which is incidental to its organization or to obtaining subscriptions for or payment of contributions, until the secretary of state has filed the articles of organization and the certificate of acceptance.

(Added to NRS by 1991, 1294; A 1993, 1014; 1995, 1127, 2108)

86.211 Articles of organization: Notice imparted by filing.
The fact that the articles of organization are on file in the office of the secretary of state is notice that the limited-liability company is a limited-liability company and is notice of all other facts sets forth therein which are required to be set forth in the articles of organization, unless the existence and facts set forth have been rebutted and made a part of a record of any court of competent jurisdiction.

86.221 Amendment of articles of organization; restated articles of organization.

1. The articles of organization of a limited-liability company may be amended for any purpose, not inconsistent with law, as determined by all of the members or permitted by the articles or an operating agreement.

2. An amendment must be made in the form of a certificate setting forth:

(a) The name of the limited-liability company;

(b) The date of filing of the articles of organization; and

(c) The amendment to the articles of organization.

3. The certificate of amendment must be signed and acknowledged by a manager of the company, or if management is not vested in a manager, by a member.

4. Restated articles of organization may be executed and filed in the same manner as a certificate of amendment.

86.226 Filing of certificate of amendment or judicial decree of amendment.

1. A signed and acknowledged certificate of amendment, or a certified copy of a judicial decree of amendment, must be filed with the secretary of state. A person who executes a certificate as an agent, officer or fiduciary of the limited-liability company need not exhibit evidence of his authority as a prerequisite to filing. Unless the secretary of state finds that a certificate does not conform to law, upon his receipt of all required filing fees he shall file the certificate.

2. Upon the filing of a certificate of amendment or judicial decree of amendment in the office of the secretary of state, the articles of organization are amended as set forth therein.

Operation

86.231 Resident agent and registered office: Maintenance; change of address.

1. Except during any period of vacancy described in NRS 86.251, a limited-liability company shall have a resident agent who must have a street address for the service of process. The street address of the resident agent is the registered office of the limited-liability company in this state.

2. Within 30 days after changing the location of his office from one address to another in this state, a resident agent shall file a certificate with the secretary of state setting forth the names of the limited-liability companies represented by him, the address at which he has maintained the office for each of the limited-liability companies, and the new address to which the office is transferred.

86.235 Change of resident agent or location of registered office. If a limited-liability company created pursuant to this chapter desires to change the location within this state of its registered office, or change its resident agent, or both, the change may be effected by filing with the secretary of state a certificate of change that sets forth:

1. The name of the limited-liability company;

2. That the change authorized by this section is effective upon the filing of the certificate of change;

3. The street address of its present registered office;

4. If the present registered office is to be changed, the street address of the new registered office;

5. The name of its present resident agent; and

6. If the present resident agent is to be changed, the name of the new resident agent. The new resident agent's certificate of acceptance must be a part of or attached to the certificate of change.

The certificate of change must be signed by a manager of the limited-liability company or, if no manager has been elected, by a member of the company.

86.241 Records: Maintenance at office in state; inspection and copying.

1. Each limited-liability company shall continuously maintain in this state an office, which may but need not be a place of its business in this state, at which it shall keep, unless otherwise provided by an operating agreement:

(a) A current list of the full name and last known business address of each member and manager, separately identifying the members in alphabetical order and the managers, if any, in alphabetical order;

(b) A copy of the filed articles of organization and all amendments thereto, together with executed copies of any powers of attorney pursuant to which any document has been executed; and

(c) Copies of any then effective operating agreement of the company.

2. Records kept pursuant to this section are subject to inspection and copying at the reasonable request, and at the expense, of any member during ordinary business hours, unless otherwise provided in an operating agreement.

86.251 Resident agent: Resignation; designation of successor after death, resignation or movement from state.

1. A resident agent who desires to resign shall file with the secretary of state a signed statement for each limited-liability company that he is unwilling to continue to act as the agent of the limited-liability company for the service of process. The execution of the statement must be acknowledged. A resignation is not effective until the signed statement is filed with the secretary of state.

2. The statement of resignation may contain an acknowledged statement of the affected limited-liability company appointing a successor resident agent for that limited-liability company, giving the agent's full name, street address for the service of process, and mailing address if different from the street address. A certificate of acceptance

executed by the new resident agent must accompany the statement appointing a successor resident agent.

3. Upon the filing of the statement of resignation with the secretary of state the capacity of the resigning person as resident agent terminates. If the statement of resignation contains no statement by the limited-liability company appointing a successor resident agent, the resigning agent shall immediately give written notice, by mail, to the limited-liability company of the filing of the statement and its effect. The notice must be addressed to any manager or, if none, to any member, of the limited-liability company other than the resident agent.

4. If a resident agent dies, resigns or moves from the state, the limited-liability company, within 30 days thereafter, shall file with the secretary of state a certificate of acceptance executed by the new resident agent. The certificate must set forth the name, complete street address and mailing address, if different from the street address, of the new resident agent.

5. Each limited-liability company which fails to file a certificate of acceptance executed by the new resident agent within 30 days after the death, resignation or removal of its resident agent as provided in subsection 4, shall be deemed in default and is subject to the provisions of NRS 86.272 and 86.274.

86.261 Service of process, notice or demand upon resident agent.

1. The resident agent appointed by a limited-liability company is an agent of the company upon whom any process, notice or demand required or permitted by law to be served upon the company may be served.

2. This section does not limit or affect the right to serve any process, notice or demand required or permitted by law to be served upon a limited-liability company in any other manner permitted by law.

86.263 Annual filing of list of managers or managing members; fee; notice.

1. A limited-liability company shall, on or before the last day of the month in which the anniversary date of its formation occurs, file with the secretary of state, on a form furnished by him, a list containing:

(a) The name of the limited-liability company;

(b) The file number of the limited-liability company, if known;

(c) The names and titles of all of its managers or, if there is no manager, all of its managing members;

(d) The mailing or street address, either residence or business, of each manager or managing member listed, following the name of the manager or managing member; and

(e) The signature of a manager or managing member of the limited-liability company certifying that the list is true, complete and accurate.

2. The limited-liability company shall annually thereafter, on or before the last day of the month in which the anniversary date of organization occurs, file with the secretary of state, on a form furnished by him, an amended list containing all of the information required in subsection 1. If the limited-liability company has had no changes in its managers or, if there is no manager, its managing members, since its previous list was filed, no amended list need be filed if a manager or managing member of the limited-liability company certifies to the secretary of state as a true and accurate statement that no changes in the managers or managing members have occurred.

3. Upon filing the list of managers or managing members, or certifying that no changes have occurred, the limited-liability company shall pay to the secretary of state a fee of $85.

4. The secretary of state shall, 60 days before the last day for filing the list required by subsection 1, cause to be mailed to each limited-liability company required to comply with the provisions of this section, which has not become delinquent, a notice of the fee due under subsection 3 and a reminder to file a list of managers or managing members or a certification of no change. Failure of any company to receive a notice or form does not excuse it from the penalty imposed by law.

5. If the list to be filed pursuant to the provisions of subsection 1 or 2 is defective or the fee required by subsection 3 is not paid, the secretary of state may return the list for correction or payment.

6. An annual list for a limited-liability company not in default received by the secretary of state more than 60 days before its due date shall be deemed an amended list for the previous year.

86.266 Certificate authorizing company to transact business.
When the fee for filing the annual list of managers or members and designation of a resident agent has been paid, the canceled check received by the limited-liability company constitutes a certificate authorizing it to transact its business within this state until the last day of the month in which the anniversary of its formation occurs in the next succeeding calendar year. If the company desires a formal certificate upon its payment of the annual fee, its payment must be accompanied by a self-addressed, stamped envelope.

86.269 Contents of annual list: Names and addresses; penalties.
1. Every list required to be filed under the provisions of NRS 86.263 must, after the name of each manager and member listed thereon, set forth the post office box or street address, either residence or business, of each manager or member.

2. If the addresses are not stated for each person on any list offered for filing, the secretary of state may refuse to file the list, and the limited-liability company for which the list has been offered for filing is subject to the provisions of NRS 86.272 and 86.274 relating to failure to file the list within or at the times therein specified, unless a list is subsequently submitted for filing which conforms to the provisions of this section.

86.272 Defaulting companies: Identification; penalty.
1. Each limited-liability company required to make a filing and pay the fee prescribed in NRS 86.263 which refuses or neglects to do so within the time provided is in default.

2. For default there must be added to the amount of the fee a penalty of $15. The fee and penalty must be collected as provided in this chapter.

86.274 Defaulting companies: Duties of secretary of state; forfeiture; distribution of assets.
1. The secretary of state shall notify, by letter addressed to its resident agent, each limited-liability company deemed in default pursuant to the provisions of this chapter. The notice must be accompanied by a statement indicating the amount of the filing fee, penalties and costs remaining unpaid.

2. On the first day of the ninth month following the month in which the filing was required, the charter of the company is revoked and its right to transact business is forfeited.

3. The secretary of state shall compile a complete list containing the names of all limited-liability companies whose right to do business has been forfeited. The secretary of state shall forthwith notify each limited-liability company by letter addressed to its resident agent of the forfeiture of its charter. The notice must be accompanied by a statement indicating the amount of the filing fee, penalties and costs remaining unpaid.

4. If the charter of a limited-liability company is revoked and the right to transact business is forfeited, all of the property and assets of the defaulting company must be held in trust by the managers or, if none, by the members of the company, and the same proceedings may be had with respect to its property and assets as apply to the dissolution of a limited-liability company. Any person interested may institute proceedings at any time after a forfeiture has been declared, but if the secretary of state reinstates the charter the proceedings must be dismissed and all property restored to the company.

5. If the assets are distributed they must be applied in the following manner:

(a) To the payment of the filing fee, penalties and costs due to the state; and

(b) To the payment of the creditors of the company.

Any balance remaining must be distributed among the members as provided in subsection 1 of NRS 86.521.

86.276 Defaulting companies: Procedure and conditions for reinstatement.

1. Except as otherwise provided in subsections 3 and 4, the secretary of state shall reinstate any limited-liability company which has forfeited its right to transact business under the provisions of this chapter and restore to the company its right to carry on business in this state, and to exercise its privileges and immunities, if it:

(a) Files with the secretary of state the list required by NRS 86.263; and

(b) Pays to the secretary of state:

(1) The annual filing fee and penalty set forth in NRS 86.263 and 86.272 for each year or portion thereof during which its charter has been revoked; and

(2) A fee of $50 for reinstatement.

2. When the secretary of state reinstates the limited-liability company, he shall:

(a) Immediately issue and deliver to the company a certificate of reinstatement authorizing it to transact business as if the filing fee had been paid when due; and

(b) Upon demand, issue to the company one or more certified copies of the certificate of reinstatement.

3. The secretary of state shall not order a reinstatement unless all delinquent fees and penalties have been paid, and the revocation of the charter occurred only by reason of failure to pay the fees and penalties.

4. If a company's charter has been revoked pursuant to the provisions of this chapter and has remained revoked for a period of 5 consecutive years, the charter must not be reinstated.

86.278 Defaulting companies: Reinstatement under old or new name.

1. Except as otherwise provided in subsection 2, if a limited-liability company applies to reinstate its charter but its name has been legally acquired or reserved by another limited-liability company or other artificial person organized or registered under chapter 78, 78A, 80, 81, 82, 84, 86, 87, 88 or 89 of NRS whose name is on file and in good standing with the secretary of state, the company shall submit in writing to the secretary of state some other name under which it desires its existence to be reinstated. If that name is distinguishable from all other names reserved or otherwise on file and in good standing, the secretary of state shall issue to the applying limited-liability company a certificate of reinstatement under that new name.

2. If the applying limited-liability company submits the written acknowledged consent of the artificial person having the name, or the person reserving the name, which is not distinguishable from the old name of the applying company or a new name it has submitted, it may be reinstated under that name.

3. For the purposes of this section, a proposed name is not distinguished from a name used or reserved solely because one or the other contains distinctive lettering, a distinctive mark, a trade-mark or a trade name or any combination of those.

86.281 General powers. A limited-liability company organized and existing under this chapter may:

1. Sue and be sued, complain and defend, in its name;

2. Purchase, take, receive, lease or otherwise acquire, own, hold, improve, use and otherwise deal in and with real or personal property, or an interest in it, wherever situated;

3. Sell, convey, mortgage, pledge, lease, exchange, transfer and otherwise dispose of all or any part of its property and assets;

4. Lend money to and otherwise assist its members;

5. Purchase, take, receive, subscribe for or otherwise acquire, own, hold, vote, use, employ, sell, mortgage, lend, pledge or otherwise dispose of, and otherwise use and deal in and with shares, member's interests or other interests in or obligations of domestic or foreign limited-liability companies, domestic or foreign corporations, joint ventures or similar associations, general or limited partnerships or natural persons, or direct or indirect obligations of the United States or of any government, state, territory, governmental district or municipality or of any instrumentality of it;

6. Make contracts and guarantees and incur liabilities, borrow money at such rates of interest as the company may determine, issue its notes, bonds and other obligations and secure any of its obligations by mortgage or pledge of all or any part of its property, franchises and income;

7. Lend, invest and reinvest its money and take and hold real property and personal property for the payment of money so loaned or invested;

8. Conduct its business, carry on its operations and have and exercise the powers granted by this chapter in any state, territory, district or possession of the United States, or in any foreign country;

9. Appoint managers and agents, define their duties and fix their compensation;

10. Cease its activities and surrender its articles of organization;

11. Exercise all powers necessary or convenient to effect any of the purposes for which the company is organized; and

12. Hold a license issued pursuant to the provisions of chapter 463 of NRS.

86.286 Operating agreement. A limited-liability company may, but is not required to, adopt an operating agreement. An operating agreement may be adopted only by the unanimous vote or unanimous written consent of the members, and the operating agreement must be in writing. Unless otherwise provided in the operating agreement, amendments to the agreement may be adopted only by the unanimous vote or unanimous written consent of the persons who are members at the time of amendment.

86.291 Management. Except as otherwise provided in this section, the articles of organization or the operating agreement, management of a limited-liability company is vested in its members in proportion to their contribution to its capital, as adjusted from time to time to reflect properly any additional contributions or withdrawals by the members. If provision is made in the articles of organization, management of the company may be vested in a manager or managers, who may but need not be members, in the manner prescribed by the operating agreement of the company. The manager or managers also hold the offices and have the responsibilities accorded to them by the members and set out in the operating agreement.

86.301 Limitation on authority to contract debt or incur liability.

Except as otherwise provided in this chapter or in its articles of organization, no debt may be contracted or liability incurred by or on behalf of a limited-liability company, except by one or more of its managers if management of the limited-liability company has been vested by the members in a manager or managers or, if management of the limited-liability company is retained by the members, then as provided in the articles of organization.

86.311 Acquisition, ownership and disposition of property. Real and personal property owned or purchased by a limited-liability company must be held and owned, and conveyance made, in the name of the company. Except as otherwise provided in the articles of organization, instruments and documents providing for the acquisition, mortgage or disposition of property of the company are valid and binding upon the company if executed by one or more managers of a company which has a manager or managers or as provided by the articles of organization of a company in which management has been retained by the members.

86.321 Contributions to capital: Form. The contributions to capital of a member to a limited-liability company may be in cash, property or services rendered, or a promissory note or other binding obligation to contribute cash or property or to perform services.

86.331 Resignation or withdrawal of member: Limitation; payment to member who rightfully resigns or withdraws.

1. Except as otherwise provided in chapter 463 of NRS, other applicable law, the articles of organization or the operating agreement, a member may not resign or withdraw as a member from a limited-liability company before the dissolution and winding up of the company.

2. If a member has a right to resign or withdraw, the amount that a resigning or withdrawing member is entitled to receive from the company for his interest must be determined pursuant to the provisions of this chapter, chapter 463 of NRS, the articles of organization or the operating agreement. If not otherwise provided therein, a resigning or withdrawing member is entitled to receive, within a reasonable time after resignation or withdrawal, the fair market value of his interest on the date of resignation or withdrawal.

86.335 Resignation or withdrawal of member in violation of operating agreement; loss of rights to participate upon resignation or withdrawal.

Except as otherwise provided in this chapter, chapter 463 of NRS, the articles of organization or the operating agreement:

1. If the resignation or withdrawal of a member violates the operating agreement:

(a) The amount payable to the member who has resigned or withdrawn is the fair market value of his interest reduced by the amount of all damages sustained by the company or its other members as a result of the violation; and

(b) The company may defer the payment for so long as necessary to prevent unreasonable hardship to the company.

2. Except as otherwise provided in chapter 463 of NRS, the articles of organization or the operating agreement, a member who resigns or withdraws ceases to be a member, has no voting rights and has no right to participate in the management of the company, even if under this section a payment due him from the company is deferred.

86.341 Distribution of profits. A limited-liability company may, from time to time, divide the profits of its business and distribute them to its members, and any transferee as his interest may appear, upon the basis stipulated in the operating agreement. If the operating agreement does not otherwise provide, profits and losses must be allocated proportionately to the value, as shown in the records of the company, of the contributions made by each member and not returned.

86.343 Prohibition on distribution of profits.

1. A distribution of the profits of a limited-liability company must not be made if, after giving it effect:

(a) The company would not be able to pay its debts as they become due in the usual course of business; or

(b) Except as otherwise specifically permitted by the articles of organization, the total assets of the company would be less than the sum of its total liabilities.

2. The manager or, if management of the company is not vested in a manager or managers, the members may base a determination that a distribution is not prohibited under this section on:

(a) Financial statements prepared on the basis of accounting practices that are reasonable in the circumstances;

(b) A fair valuation, including unrealized appreciation and depreciation; or

(c) Any other method that is reasonable in the circumstances.

3. The effect of a distribution under this section must be measured:

(a) In the case of a distribution by purchase, redemption or other acquisition by the company of member's interests, as of the earlier of:

(1) The date on which money or other property is transferred or debt incurred by the company; or

(2) The date on which the member ceases to be a member with respect to his acquired interest.

(b) In the case of any other distribution of indebtedness, as of the date on which the indebtedness is distributed.

(c) In all other cases, as of:

(1) The date on which the distribution is authorized if the payment occurs within 120 days after the date of authorization; or

(2) The date on which the payment is made if it occurs more than 120 days after the date of authorization.

4. Indebtedness of the company, including indebtedness issued as a distribution, is not considered a liability for purposes of determinations under this section if its terms provide that payment of principal and interest are to be made only if and to the extent that payment of a distribution to the members could then be made pursuant to this section. If the indebtedness is issued as a distribution, each payment of principal or interest must be treated as a distribution, the effect of which must be measured as of the date of payment.

86.346 Distributions: Form; status of member or transferee.

1.1. Unless otherwise provided in the operating agreement, a member, regardless of the nature of his contributions, or a transferee, regardless of the nature of his predecessor's contributions, has no right to demand or receive any distribution from a limited-liability company in any form other than cash.

1.2. Except as otherwise provided in NRS 86.391 and 86.521, and unless otherwise provided in the operating agreement, at the time a member or transferee becomes entitled to receive a distribution he has the status of and is entitled to all remedies available to a creditor of the company with respect to the distribution.

86.351 Transfer or assignment of member's interest; rights of transferee; substituted members.

1. The interest of each member of a limited-liability company is personal property. The articles of organization or operating agreement may prohibit or regulate the transfer of a member's interest. Unless otherwise provided in the articles or agreement, a transferee of a member's interest has no right to participate in the management of the business and affairs of the company or to become a member unless a majority in interest of the other members approve the transfer. If so approved, the transferee becomes a substituted member. The transferee is only entitled to receive the share of profits or other compensation by way of income, and the return of contributions, to which his transferor would otherwise be entitled.

2. A substituted member has all the rights and powers and is subject to all the restrictions and liabilities of his transferor, except that the substitution of the transferee does not release the transferor from any liability to the company.

Liability, Indemnification and Insurance

86.361 Liability of persons assuming to act as company without authority. All persons who assume to act as a limited-liability company without authority to do so are jointly and severally liable for all debts and liabilities of the company.

86.371 Liability of member or manager for debts or liabilities of company. Unless otherwise provided in the articles of organization or an agreement signed by the member or manager to be charged, no member or manager of any limited-liability company formed under the laws of this state is individually liable for the debts or liabilities of the company.

86.381 Member of company is not proper party in proceeding by or against company; exception. A member of a limited-liability company is not a proper party to proceedings by or against the company, except where the object is to enforce the member's right against or liability to the company.

86.391 Liability to company of member or contributor to capital.

1. A member is liable to a limited-liability company:

(a) For a difference between his contributions to capital as actually made and as stated in the articles of organization or operating agreement as having been made; and

(b) For any unpaid contribution to capital which he agreed in the articles of organization or operating agreement to make in the future at the time and on the conditions stated in the articles of organization or operating agreement.

2. A member holds as trustee for the company:

(a) Specific property stated in the articles of organization or operating agreement as contributed by him, but which was not contributed or which has been wrongfully or erroneously returned; and

(b) Money or other property wrongfully paid or conveyed to him on account of his contribution or the contribution of a predecessor with respect to his member's interest.

3. The liabilities of a member as set out in this section can be waived or compromised only by the consent of all of the members, but a waiver or compromise does not affect the right of a creditor of the company to enforce the liabilities if he extended credit or his claim arose before the effective date of an amendment of the articles of organization or operating agreement effecting the waiver or compromise.

4. When a contributor has rightfully received the return in whole or in part of his contribution to capital, the contributor is liable to the company for any sum, not in excess of the return with interest, necessary to discharge its liability to all of its creditors who extended credit or whose claims arose before the return.

86.401 Rights of judgment creditor of member. On application to a court of competent jurisdiction by a judgment creditor of a member, the court may charge the member's interest with payment of the unsatisfied amount of the judgment with interest. To the extent so charged, the judgment creditor has only the rights of an assignee of the member's interest. This section does not deprive any member of the benefit of any exemption applicable to his interest.

86.411 Indemnification of manager, member, employee or agent: Proceeding other than by company. A limited-liability company may indemnify any person who was or is a party or is threatened to be made a party to any threatened, pending or completed action, suit or proceeding, whether civil, criminal, administrative or investigative, except an action by or in the right of the company, by reason of the fact that he is or was a manager, member, employee or agent of the company, or is or was serving at the request of the company as a manager, member, employee or agent of another limited-liability company, corporation, partnership, joint venture, trust or other enterprise, against expenses, including attorney's fees, judgments, fines and amounts paid in settlement actually and reasonably incurred by him in connection with the

action, suit or proceeding if he acted in good faith and in a manner which he reasonably believed to be in or not opposed to the best interests of the company, and, with respect to any criminal action or proceeding, had no reasonable cause to believe his conduct was unlawful. The termination of any action, suit or proceeding by judgment, order, settlement or conviction, or upon a plea of nolo contendere or its equivalent, does not, of itself, create a presumption that the person did not act in good faith and in a manner which he reasonably believed to be in or not opposed to the best interests of the limited-liability company, and that, with respect to any criminal action or proceeding, he had reasonable cause to believe that his conduct was unlawful.

86.421 Indemnification of manager, member, employee or agent: Proceeding by company. A limited-liability company may indemnify any person who was or is a party or is threatened to be made a party to any threatened, pending or completed action or suit by or in the right of the company to procure a judgment in its favor by reason of the fact that he is or was a manager, member, employee or agent of the company, or is or was serving at the request of the company as a manager, member, employee or agent of another limited-liability company, corporation, partnership, joint venture, trust or other enterprise against expenses, including amounts paid in settlement and attorneys' fees actually and reasonably incurred by him in connection with the defense or settlement of the action or suit if he acted in good faith and in a manner in which he reasonably believed to be in or not opposed to the best interests of the company. Indemnification may not be made for any claim, issue or matter as to which such a person has been adjudged by a court of competent jurisdiction, after exhaustion of all appeals therefrom, to be liable to the company or for amounts paid in settlement to the company, unless and only to the extent that the court in which the action or suit was brought or other court of competent jurisdiction determines upon application that in view of all the circumstances of the case, he is fairly and reasonably entitled to indemnity for such expenses as the court deems proper.

86.431 Indemnification of manager, member, employee or agent: Scope; authorization.

1. To the extent that a manager, member, employee or agent of a limited-liability company has been successful on the merits or otherwise in defense of any action, suit or proceeding described in NRS 86.411 and 86.421, or in defense of any claim, issue or matter therein, the company shall indemnify him against expenses, including attorney's fees, actually and reasonably incurred by him in connection with the defense.

2. Any indemnification under NRS 86.411 and 86.421, unless ordered by a court or advanced pursuant to NRS 86.441, may be made by the limited-liability company only as authorized in the specific case upon a determination that indemnification of the manager, member, employee or agent is proper in the circumstances. The determination must be made:

(a) By the members or managers as provided in the articles of organization or the operating agreement;

(b) If there is no provision in the articles of organization or the operating agreement, by a majority in interest of the members who are not parties to the action, suit or proceeding;

(c) If a majority in interest of the members who are not parties to the action, suit or proceeding so order, by independent legal counsel in a written opinion; or

(d) If members who are not parties to the action, suit or proceeding cannot be obtained, by independent legal counsel in a written opinion.

86.441 Indemnification of member or manager: Advancement of expenses. The articles of organization, the operating agreement or a separate agreement made by a limited-liability company may provide that the expenses of members and managers incurred in defending a civil or criminal action, suit or proceeding must be paid by the company as they are incurred and in advance of the final disposition of the action, suit or proceeding, upon receipt of an undertaking by or on behalf of the manager or member to repay the amount if it is ultimately determined by a court of competent jurisdiction that he is not entitled to be indemnified by the company. The provisions of this section do not affect any rights to advancement of expenses to which personnel of the company other than managers or members may be entitled under any contract or otherwise by law.

86.451 Indemnification of manager, member, employee or agent: Effect of provisions on other rights; continuation after cessation of status. Indemnification or advancement of expenses authorized in or ordered by a court pursuant to NRS 86.411 to 86.441, inclusive:

1. Does not exclude any other rights to which a person seeking indemnification or advancement of expenses may be entitled under the articles of organization or any operating agreement, vote of members or disinterested managers, if any, or otherwise, for an action in his official capacity or an action in another capacity while holding his office, except that indemnification, unless ordered by a court pursuant to NRS 86.421 or for the advancement of expenses made pursuant to NRS 86.441, may not be made to or on behalf of any member or manager if a final adjudication establishes that his acts or omissions involved

intentional misconduct, fraud or a knowing violation of the law and was material to the cause of action.

2. Continues for a person who has ceased to be a member, manager, employee or agent and inures to the benefit of his heirs, executors and administrators.

86.461 Maintenance of insurance or other financial arrangements against liability of member, manager, employee or agent.

1. A limited-liability company may purchase and maintain insurance or make other financial arrangements on behalf of any person who is or was a member, manager, employee or agent of the company, or is or was serving at the request of the company as a manager, member, employee or agent of another corporation, limited-liability company, partnership, joint venture, trust or other enterprise for any liability asserted against him and liability and expenses incurred by him in his capacity as a manager, member, employee or agent, or arising out of his status as such, whether or not the company has the authority to indemnify him against such liability and expenses.

2. The other financial arrangements made by the company pursuant to subsection 1 may include:

(a) The creation of a trust fund.

(b) The establishment of a program of self-insurance.

(c) The securing of its obligation of indemnification by granting a security interest or other lien on any assets of the company.

(d) The establishment of a letter of credit, guaranty or surety.

No financial arrangement made pursuant to this subsection may provide protection for a person adjudged by a court of competent jurisdiction, after exhaustion of all appeals therefrom, to be liable for intentional misconduct, fraud or a knowing violation of law, except with respect to the advancement of expenses or indemnification ordered by a court.

3. Any insurance or other financial arrangement made on behalf of a person pursuant to this section may be provided by the company or any other person approved by the managers, if any, or by the members, if no managers exist, even if all or part of the other person's member's interest in the company is owned by the company.

86.471 Effect of providing insurance or other financial arrangements against liability of member, manager, employee or agent. In the absence of fraud:

1. The decision of a limited-liability company as to the propriety of the terms and conditions of any insurance or other financial arrangement made pursuant to NRS 86.461 and the choice of the person to provide the insurance or other financial arrangement is conclusive; and

2. The insurance or other financial arrangement:

(a) Is not void or voidable; and

(b) Does not subject any manager or member approving it to personal liability for his action,

even if a manager or member approving the insurance or other financial arrangement is a beneficiary of the insurance or other financial arrangement.

86.481 Exclusion of company which provides self-insurance from Title 57 of NRS. A limited-liability company or its subsidiary which provides self-insurance for itself or for an affiliated limited-liability company pursuant to NRS 86.461 is not subject to the provisions of Title 57 of NRS.
Nevada Insurance Code, NRS Title 57

Dissolution

86.491 Events requiring dissolution and winding up of affairs. A limited-liability company organized under this chapter must be dissolved and its affairs wound up:

1. At the time, if any, specified in the articles of organization;

2. Upon the occurrence of an event specified in an operating agreement; or

3. By the unanimous written agreement of all members.

86.505 Continuation of company after dissolution for winding up of affairs; limitation on actions by or against dissolved company. The dissolution of a limited-liability company does not impair any remedy or cause of action available to or against it or its managers or members arising before its dissolution and commenced within 2 years after the date of the dissolution. A dissolved company continues as a company for the purpose of prosecuting and defending suits, actions, proceedings and claims of any kind or nature by or against it and of enabling it gradually to settle and close its business, to collect and discharge its obligations, to dispose of and convey its property, and to distribute its assets, but not for the purpose of continuing the business for which it was established.

86.521 Distribution of assets after dissolution.

1. In settling accounts after dissolution, the liabilities of a limited-liability company are entitled to payment in the following order:

(a) Those to creditors, including members who are creditors, in the order of priority as provided and to the extent otherwise permitted by law, except those to members of the limited-liability company on account of their contributions;

(b) Those to members of the limited-liability company in respect of their share of the profits and other compensation by way of income on their contributions; and

(c) Those to members of the limited-liability company in respect of their contributions to capital.

2. Subject to any statement in the operating agreement, members share in the company's assets in respect to their claims for capital and in respect to their claims for profits or for compensation by way of income on their contributions, respectively, in proportion to the respective amounts of the claims.

86.531 Articles of dissolution: Preparation and contents; execution.

1. When all debts, liabilities and obligations have been paid and discharged or adequate provision has been made therefor and all of the remaining property and assets have been distributed to the members, articles of dissolution must be prepared, signed and acknowledged, setting forth:

(a) The name of the limited-liability company;

(b) That all debts, obligations and liabilities have been paid and discharged or that adequate provision has been made therefor;

(c) That all the remaining property and assets have been distributed among its members in accordance with their respective rights and interests; and

(d) That there are no suits pending against the company in any court or that adequate provision has been made for the satisfaction of any judgment, order or decree which may be entered against it in any pending suit.

2. The articles must be signed by a manager, or if there is no manager by a member, of the company.

86.541 Articles of dissolution: Filing; duties of secretary of state; effect of filing.

1. The signed and acknowledged articles of dissolution must be filed with the secretary of state. Unless the secretary of state finds that the articles of dissolution do not conform to law, he shall when all fees and license taxes prescribed by law have been paid issue a certificate that the limited-liability company is dissolved.

2. Upon the filing of the articles of dissolution the existence of the company ceases, except for the purpose of suits, other proceedings and appropriate action as provided in this chapter. The manager or managers in office at the time of dissolution, or the survivors of them, are thereafter trustees for the members and creditors of the dissolved company and as such have authority to distribute any property of the company discovered after dissolution, convey real estate and take such other action as may be necessary on behalf of and in the name of the dissolved company.

Miscellaneous Provisions

86.551 Registration of foreign limited-liability company. A foreign limited-liability company may register with the secretary of state by complying with the provisions of NRS

88.570 to 88.605, inclusive, which provide for registration of foreign limited partnerships, except that:

1. The provisions of subsection 7 of NRS 88.575 do not apply; and

2. Cancellation is accomplished by filing articles of dissolution signed by all managers, if any, or by all members, if there are no managers.

86.555 Issuance of occupational or professional license to limited-liability company by board or commission; regulations.

1. Except as otherwise provided by statute, an agency, board or commission that regulates an occupation or profession pursuant to Title 54, 55 or 56 of NRS may grant a license to a limited-liability company or a foreign limited-liability company if the agency, board or commission is authorized to grant a license to a corporation formed pursuant to chapter 78 of NRS.

2. An agency, board or commission that makes a license available to a limited-liability company or foreign limited-liability company pursuant to subsection 1 shall adopt regulations:

(a) Listing the persons in the limited-liability company or foreign limited-liability company who must qualify for the license or indicating that the agency, board or commission will use other means to determine whether the limited-liability company or foreign limited-liability company qualifies for a license;

(b) Listing the persons who may engage in the activity for which the license is required on behalf of the limited-liability company or foreign limited-liability company;

(c) Indicating whether the limited-liability company or foreign limited-liability company may engage in a business other than the business for which the license is required;

(d) Listing the changes, if any, in the management or control of the limited-liability company or foreign limited-liability company that require notice, review, approval or other action by the agency, board or commission; and

(e) Setting forth the conditions under which a limited-liability company or foreign limited-liability company may obtain a license.

3. An agency, board or commission that adopts regulations pursuant to subsection 2 shall not impose a restriction or requirement on a limited-liability company or foreign limited-liability company which is significantly different from or more burdensome than the restrictions or requirements imposed on a partnership or corporation.

86.561 Secretary of state: Fees.

1. The secretary of state shall charge and collect for:

(a) Filing the original articles of organization, or for registration of a foreign company, $125;

(b) Amending or restating the articles of organization, or amending the registration of a foreign company, $75;

(c) Filing the articles of dissolution of a domestic or foreign company, $30;

(d) Filing a statement of change of address of a records or registered office, or change of the resident agent, $15;

(e) Certifying articles of organization or an amendment to the articles, in both cases where a copy is provided, $10;

(f) Certifying an authorized printed copy of this chapter, $10;

(g) Reserving a name for a limited-liability company, $20;

(h) Executing, filing or certifying any other document, $20; and

(i) Copies made at the office of the secretary of state, $1 per page.

2. The secretary of state shall charge and collect at the time of any service of process on him as agent for service of process of a limited-liability company, $10 which may be recovered as taxable costs by the party to the action causing the service to be made if the party prevails in the action.

3. Except as otherwise provided in this section, the fees set forth in NRS 78.785 apply to this chapter.

86.563 Secretary of state: Procedure to submit replacement page before filing of document. An organizer, manager or managing member of a limited-liability company may authorize the secretary of state in writing to replace any page of a document submitted for filing on an expedited basis, before the actual filing, and to accept the page as if it were part of the originally signed filing. The signed authorization of the organizer, manager or managing member to the secretary of state permits, but does not require, the secretary of state to alter the original document as requested.

86.566 Secretary of state: Filing of documents written in language other than English. No document which is written in a language other than English may be filed or submitted for filing in the office of the secretary of state pursuant to the provisions of this chapter unless it is accompanied by a verified translation of that document into the English language.

86.571 Waiver of notice. When, under the provisions of this chapter or under the provisions of the articles of organization or operating agreement of a limited-liability company, notice is required to be given to a member or to a manager of the company, if it has a manager or managers, a waiver in writing signed by the person or persons entitled to the notice, whether before or after the time stated in it, is equivalent to the giving of notice.

DEAN HELLER
Secretary of State

101 North Carson Street, Suite 3
Carson City, Nevada 89701-4786
Phone: (775) 684 5708

FEE SCHEDULE
(Effective 10/1/95)

INITIAL FILING FEE FOR PROFIT CORPORATIONS:
(Fee based on the value of the total number of authorized shares stated in the Articles of Incorporation)

$25,000 or less..	$125.00
$25,001 and not over $75,000..	$175.00
$75,001 and not over $200,000..	$225.00
$200,001 and not over $500,000..	$325.00
$500,001 and not over $1,000,000...	$425.00
For the first $1,000,000..	$425.00
For each additional $500,000..	$225.00
Maximum fee..	$25,000.00

For the purpose of computing the filing fee, the value (capital) represented by the total number of shares authorized in the Articles of Incorporation is determined by computing the:

(a) total authorized shares multiplied by their par value or;
(b) total authorized shares without par value multiplied by $1.00 or;
(c) the sum of (a) and (b) above if both par and no par shares.

Filing fees are calculated on a minimum par value of one-tenth of a cent (.001), regardless if the stated par value is less.

INITIAL FILING FEE FOR NON PROFIT CORPORATIONS WITHOUT STOCK: $25.00

INITIAL FILING FEE FOR LIMITED LIABILITY COMPANIES: $125.00

INITIAL FILING FEE FOR LIMITED PARTNERSHIPS: $125.00

INITIAL FILING FEE FOR LIMITED LIABILITY PARTNERSHIPS: $125.00

MISCELLANEOUS FOR PROFIT FEES:			
Certificate of Amendment, minimum fee	$75.00	Certification of documents – per certification	$10.00
Certificate pursuant to NRS 78.209, minimum fee	$75.00	Preclearance of any document	$100.00
Certificate pursuant to NRS 78.1955	$75.00	Miscellaneous filings	$20.00
Restated Articles , minimum fee	$75.00		
Certificate of Correction, minimum fee	$75.00		
Mergers/Articles of Exchange	$125.00	*MISCELLANEOUS NON PROFIT FEES:*	
Notice of Cancellation	$30.00	Non profit – Certificate of Amendment/Correction	$25.00
Certificate/Articles of Dissolution	$30.00	Non profit – List of Officers and Directors	$15.00
Notice of Withdrawal	$30.00	Non profit – Late fee on Annual List	$ 5.00
List of Officers, Directors and Resident Agent	$85.00	Non profit – Certificate of Dissolution	$25.00
Late fee on List	$15.00	Non profit – Reinstatement	$25.00
Change of Resident Agent/address/records office	$15.00		
Resignation of Resident Agent	$20.00	All other fees, unless otherwise denoted by statute, are the	
Reinstatement	$50.00	same as those for profit business entities.	
Name reservation	$20.00		

NOTICE: Filings not accompanied by adequate fees for services requested will be returned unfiled.

Nevada Secretary of State Form FEE1999.01
Revised on: 02/16/99

State of Nevada
Secretary of State
101 North Carson Street, Suite 3
Carson City, Nevada 89701-4786

Phone: (775) 684 5708

COPIES AND CERTIFICATION SERVICES FEE SCHEDULE

The following is a list of copies and certification services and the associated fees. Fees are per document unless otherwise noted.

SERVICE REQUESTED:

Copies..	$1.00 per page
Certification of Document...	$10.00

Certificates:

Certificate of Existence (evidence of good standing – short form)...............	$15.00
Certificate of Existence (listing amendments – long form)........................	$20.00
Certificate Evidencing Name Change..	$15.00
Certificate of Fact of Merger...	$20.00
Certificate of Default...	$20.00
Certificate of Revocation...	$20.00
Certificate of Dissolution..	$20.00
Certificate of Withdrawal..	$20.00
Certificate of Cancellation...	$20.00
Certificate of Non-Existence...	$20.00
Miscellaneous Certificates...	$20.00
Apostille (Hague Treaty Nations)/Certification (Non-Hague Treaty Nations)...	$20.00
Exemplification..	$20.00

EXPEDITE SERVICE:

Expedite service is available for copies, certificate and certification services. Fees for expedite service are in addition to the fees as listed above.

24 Hour Expedite Service: Order may be picked up or mailed out within 24-hours.

Copies:

1 to 10 pages..	$25.00
11 to 100 pages...	$50.00
100 or more pages..	$75.00

Certificates (per entity name):

1 to 10 certificates...	$25.00
11 to 20 certificates..	$50.00
21 to 30 certificates..	$75.00
31 or more certificates...	$100.00

4-Hour Expedite Service: Order may be picked up or mailed within 4-hours.

CERTIFICATES ONLY (per entity name):

1 to 10 certificates...	$50.00
11 or more certificates...	$100.00

BASIC INSTRUCTIONS:

1. All orders may be received in writing with fees enclosed at the above address. Telephone orders with payment by VISA or Mastercard may be called into our Customer Service Department at (775)684-5708. Trust account and credit card customers may fax *expedite orders only* to (775)684-5645. Trust account orders must be received on company letterhead.

2. Other than orders specified as a pick-up, all orders are mailed out via first-class mail, unless a prepaid envelope, express mail number or Federal Express number is provided.

3. We *do not* fax orders back to customers. Each order will be returned to one address only.

State of Nevada
Secretary of State
101 North Carson Street, Suite 3
Carson City, Nevada 89701-4786

Phone: (775) 684 5708

SPECIAL SERVICES
24-HOUR
EXPEDITE SERVICE

IMPORTANT: To ensure expedited service, please mark "Expedite" in a conspicuous place at top of the service request. Please indicate method of delivery.

EXPEDITE SERVICE:

The Secretary of State offers a 24-hour expedite service on most filings processed by this office. If you choose to utilize the 24-hour expedite service, please enclose with your filing an additional $50.00 per filing and/or order. Please note that this expedite fee is in addition to the standard filing fee charged on each filing and/or order.

EXPEDITE FEES:

The expedite fee for most services provided by the Secretary of State of State is $50.00 per filing. There are, however, several services that have different expedite fees. The main filings and the associated expedite fees are as follows:

Articles of Incorporation	$50.00
Articles of Organization, Limited Liability Companies	$50.00
Articles of Organization, Limited Liability Partnerships	$50.00
Certificate of Limited Partnership	$50.00
Foreign Qualifications	$50.00
Amendments and Mergers	$50.00
Reinstatement	$50.00
Preclearance of any document	$50.00
Apostilles	$25.00
Certificate of Good Standing	$25.00
Annual Lists and late lists	$25.00
Name Reservation	$10.00
Resident Agent Changes	$10.00
Resident Agent Resignation	$10.00

For information regarding the expedite fee for services not listed above, please call this office at (775)684-5708.

TIME CONSTRAINTS:

Each filing submitted receives same day filing date and may be picked up within 24 hours. Filings to be mailed will be mailed out no later than the next business day following receipt.

Expedite period begins when filing or service request is received in this office in fileable form.

The Secretary of State reserves the right to extend the expedite period in times of extreme volume, staff shortages, or equipment malfuction. These extensions are few and will rarely extend more than a few hours.

Nevada Secretary of State Form MM1999.XX
Revised on: 02/16/99

Appendix B
State Addresses

Included in this appendix are the addresses, phone numbers, and websites of the state offices in which a corporation must be registered. Once you have formed your Nevada corporation, you will need to register it as a foreign corporation doing business in your home state.

You should contact the office in your state for the latest forms and fee schedule.

ALABAMA

Secretary of State
Corporate Section
P.O. Box 5616
Montgomery, AL 36130-5616
334-242-5324

Website: http://www.sos.state.al.us

ALASKA

Department of Commerce and Economic
Development
Division of B.S.C.
Attention: Corporation Section
P.O. Box 110807
Juneau, AK 99811-0807
907-465-2521
Fax: 907-465-2549

Website:
http://www.commerce.state.ak.us/bsc/llc.htm

ARIZONA

Arizona Corporation Commission
1200 W. Washington
Phoenix, AZ 85007-2929
602-542-3135
800-345-5819 (Arizona residents only)
or
400 W. Congress
Tucson, AZ 85701-1347
520-628-6560

Website: http://www.cc.state.az.us/corp/index.ssi

ARKANSAS

Secretary of State
Corporation Division
State Capital, Room 58
Little Rock, AR 72201-1094
501-682-5151

Website: http://www.sosweb.state.ar.us

CALIFORNIA

Office of the Secretary of State
Limited Liability Company Unit
1500 - 11th Street, 3rd Floor
P.O. Box 944228
Sacramento, CA 94244-2280
916-653-3795

Website: http://www.ss.ca.gov/

COLORADO

Secretary of State
Corporations Office
1560 Broadway, Suite 200
Denver, CO 80202
303-894-2251
Fax: 303-894-2242

Website:
http://www.state.co.us/gov_dir/sos/pubs.html

CONNECTICUT

Secretary of State
30 Trinity Street
P.O. Box 150470
Hartford, CT 06106-0470
860-566-4128

Website: http://www.state.ct.us/sots/

DELAWARE

State of Delaware
Division of Corporations
P.O.Box 898
Dover, DE 19903
302-739-3073
Name Reservation: 900-420-8042

Website: http://www.state.de.us/corp

DISTRICT OF COLUMBIA

Department of Consumer and Regulatory Affairs
Corporation Division
614 H. Street, N.W. - Room 407
Washington, D.C. 20001
202-727-7283

Website: http://www.dcra.org/formlist.htm

FLORIDA

Secretary of State
Division of Corporations
P.O. Box 6327
Tallahassee, FL 32314
904-488-9000
904-487-6052

Website: http://www.dos.state.fl.us

GEORGIA

Secretary of State
2 Martin Luther King, Jr. Drive
Suite 315, West Tower
Atlanta, GA 30330
404-656-2817
Fax: 404-651-9059

Website: http://www.SOS.State.Ga.US/

HAWAII

Business Registration Division
Department of Commerce
and Consumer Affairs
1010 Richards Street
P.O. Box 40
Honolulu, HI 96810
808-586-2727

Website: http://www.hawaii.gov/dcca/dcca.html

IDAHO

Secretary of State
700 W. Jefferson, Basement West
Boise, ID 83720-0080
208-334-2301

Website: http://www.idsos.state.id.us/

ILLINOIS

Secretary of State
Business Services Dept.
328 Howlett Building, Room 359
Springfield, IL 62756
LLC Division: 217-524-8008
Name availability: 217-782-9520

Website: http://www.sos.state.il.us

INDIANA

Secretary of State
Room 155, State House
302 W. Washington, Room E018
Indianapolis, IN 46204
317-232-6576 or
317-232-6531 or
800-726-8000

Website: http://www.state.in.us/sos

IOWA

Secretary of State
Corporations Division
Hoover Building
Des Moines, IA 50319
515-281-5204
Fax: 515-242-6556

Website: http://www.sos.state.ia.us/

KANSAS

Secretary of State
Corporation Division
State Capitol, 2nd Floor 300 SW 10th St.
Topeka, KS 66612-1594
913-296-4564

Website: http://www.state.ks.us/public/sos/

KENTUCKY

Commonwealth of Kentucky
Office of the Secretary of State
P.O.Box 718
Frankfort, KY 40602
502-564-2848
502-564-7330

Website: http://www.sos.state.ky.us

LOUISIANA

Secretary of State
Corporations Division
P.O. Box 94125
Baton Rouge, LA 70804-9125
504-925-4704

Website: http://www.sec.state.la.us/

MAINE

Secretary of State
Bureau of Corporations, Elections, and
Commissions
101 State House Station
Augusta, ME 04333-0101
Forms: 207-287-4195
Business answers: 800-872-3838
Fax: 207-287-5874

Website: http://www.state.me.us/sos/sos.htm

MARYLAND

State Department of Assessments and Taxation
Corporate Charter Division
301 West Preston Street, Rm. 809
Baltimore, MD 21201
410-225 -1340 or
410-767-1330

Website: http://www.dat.state.md.us/charter.html

MASSACHUSETTS

Secretary of the Commonwealth
Corporations Division
One Ashburton Place
17th Floor
Boston, MA 02108
617-727-9640 or 617-727-9440
Citizen Information Service
800-392-6090

Website:
http://www.state.ma.us/sec/cor/coridx.htm

MICHIGAN

Michigan Department of Commerce
Corporation and Securities Bureau
Corporation Division
P.O. Box 30054
Lansing, MI 48909-7554
517-334-6302

Website: http://www.cis.state.mi.us/corp/

MINNESOTA

Secretary of State
Division of Corporations
180 State Office Building
100 Constitution Ave.
St. Paul, MN 55155-1299
612-296-2803

Website: http://www.sos.state.mn.us/bus.html

MISSISSIPPI

Secretary of State
Business Services Division
P.O. Box 136
Jackson, MS 39205-0136
601-359-1333 or
800-256-3494
Fax: 601-359-1499

Website: http://www.sos.state.ms.us/

MISSOURI

Secretary of State, Corporation Division
P.O. Box 778
Jefferson City, MO 65102
573-751-2359 or
573-751-4153

Website:
http://mosl.sos.state.mo.us/bus-ser/soscor.html

MONTANA

Secretary of State
P.O. Box 202801
Helena, MT 59620-2801
406-444-2034
Fax: 406-444-3976

Web site: http://www.mt.gov/sos/index.htm

NEBRASKA

Secretary of State
Suite 1301 State Capitol
Lincoln, NE 68509
402-471-4079
Fax: 402-471-3666

Website:
http://www.nol.org/home/SOS/htm/services.htm

NEVADA

Secretary of State
Capitol Complex
Carson City, NV 89710
702-687-5203 or
702-687-5105
Fax: 702-687-5071

Website: http://sos.state.nv.us

NEW HAMPSHIRE

Secretary of State
Corporate Division
25 Capitol St. 3rd Fl.
Concord, NH 03301-6312
603-271-3244

Website: [none]

NEW JERSEY

Secretary of State
Division of Commercial Recording
P. O. Box 300
Trenton, NJ 08625
609-530-6400

Website: http://www.state.nj.us/state/

NEW MEXICO

State Corporation Commission
Corporation Department
P.O. Drawer 1269
Santa Fe, NM 87504-1269
505-827-4511 or 505-827-4504

Website: http://www.sos.state.nm.us/

NEW YORK

Department of State
Division of Corporations and State Records
162 Washington Avenue
Albany, NY 12231-0001
518-473-2492 or 518-474-6200

Website: http://www.dos.state.ny.us/

NORTH CAROLINA

Corporations Division
Department of Secretary of State
300 North Salisbury Street
Raleigh, NC 27603-5909
919-733-4201

Website: http://www.state.nc.us/secstate/

NORTH DAKOTA

Secretary of State
Capitol Building
600 East Boulevard Avenue
Bismarck, ND 58505-0500
701-328-2900
Fax: 701-328-2992

Website: http://www.state.nd.us/sec

OHIO

Secretary of State
Corporations Division
30 E. Broad St.
State Office Tower, 14th Floor
Columbus, OH 43266-0418
614-466-3910

Website: http://www.state.oh.us/sos/

OKLAHOMA

Secretary of State-Corporation Division
2300 N. Lincoln Blvd.
101 State Capitol Building
Oklahoma City, OK 73105
405-521-3911

Website: http://www.occ.state.ok.us/

OREGON

Corporation Division
State of Oregon
158 - 12th St. NE
Salem, OR 97310
503-986-2200
Fax: 503-378-4381

Website: http://www.sos.state.or.us/

PENNSYLVANIA

Department of State
Corporation Bureau
P. O. Box 8722
Harrisburg, PA 17105-8722
717-787-1057

Website: http://www.dos.state.pa.us/corp.htm

RHODE ISLAND

Secretary of State
100 N. Main St.
Providence, RI 02903
401-222-3040
Fax: 401-277-1309

Website:
http://www.state.ri.us/STDEPT/sdlink.htm

SOUTH CAROLINA

Secretary of State
P.O. Box 11350
Columbia, SC 29211
803-734-2158

Website:
http://www.leginfo.state.sc.us/secretary.html

SOUTH DAKOTA

Secretary of State
State Capital
500 E. Capital Street
Pierre, SD 57501
605-773-3537

Website:
http://www.state.sd.us/state/executive/sos/sos.htm

TENNESSEE

Department of State
Division of Services
Suite 1800
James K. Polk Building
Nashville, TN 37243-0306
615-741-0537

Website: http://www.state.tn.us/sos/index.htm

TEXAS

Secretary of State
Corporation Division
P.O. Box 13697
Austin, TX 78711
512-463-5555
To obtain forms: 900-263-0060

Website: http://www.sos.state.tx.us/1

UTAH

Department of Commerce
Division of Corporations and Commercial Code
P.O. Box 45801
160 E. 300 South, 2nd Floor
Salt Lake City, UT 84145-0801
801-530-4849

Website: http://www.ce.ex.state.ut.us/nav/library

VERMONT

Secretary of State
109 State St.
Montpelier, VT 05609-1104
802-828-2363

Website: http://www.sec.state.vt.us/

VIRGINIA

State Corporation Commission
Jefferson Building
P.O. Box 1197
Richmond, VA 23219
804-371-9733

Website: http://www.state.va.us/scc/index.html

WASHINGTON

Secretary of State
Corporation Division
P.O. Box 40234
Olympia, WA 98504-0234
360-753-7115

Website: http://www.wa.gov/sec/

West Virginia

Secretary of State
State Capital W-139
Charleston, WV 25305
304-558-8000

Website: http://www.state.wv.us/sos/

Wisconsin

Dept. of Financial Institutions
P.O. Box 7846
Madison, WI 53707
608-266-3590

Website: http://www.wdfi.org/corp/corp.htm

Wyoming

Secretary of State
State Capitol Building
Cheyenne, WY 82002
Tel: 307-777-7311 or 307-777-7312
Fax: 307-777-5339

Website: http://soswy.state.wy.us/
e-mail: Corporations@missc.state.wy.us

APPENDIX C
NEVADA
REGISTERED AGENTS

The following is a list of companies which can serve as a registered agent for your Nevada corporation or LLC.

AA Resident Agents, Inc.
333 North Rancho Drive, Suite 410
Las Vegas, NV 89106
Telephone: (877) 727-7847
Fax: (702) 636-4904

AAA $25 Corporations for America
Terry Chilcoat
1499 #5 Main Street
Gardnerville, NV 89410
Telephone: (888) 423-8600 or (775) 888-9970

AAAA $25 R/A's of America
Terry Chilcoat
1177 Fairview Drive Suite 996
Carson City, NV 89702-0662
PO Box 662
Carson City, NV 89702-0662
Telephone: (888) 228-8300 or (775) 888-6898

AAAAA $25 Corporations for Dummies
Terry Chilcoat
1504 #8-RS273 Main Street
Gardnerville, NV 89410
Telephone: (800) 545-8759 or (775) 883-6227

Aalpha Corporate Services, Inc.
Bill Mc Farland
4960 South Virginia Street, Suite 3001
Reno, NV 89502
Telephone: (800) 933-9442 or (775) 851-1551
Fax: (800) 757-2705
Website: http://www.incorporate.org
Email: aalpha@incorporate.org

Aalpha Incorporation & Resident Agent Service Inc.
Phil Leonard
4960 South Virginia Street, Suite 302
Reno, NV 89502
Telephone: (800) 933-9442 or (775) 851-1551
Fax: (800) 757-2705
Website: http://www.incorporate.org
Email: agent@incorporate.org

Access Tahoe Corporate Agents, Inc.
Michael Hannan
805 Tahoe Blvd.
Incline Village, NV 89451
PO Box 4475
Incline Village, NV 89450-4475
Telephone: (800) 335-0088 or (775) 883-9222
Fax: (775) 833-9394
Website: www.tahoe-taxhaven.com
Email: medicallp@aol.com

Acorn Corporate Services, Inc.
3885 South Decatur Blvd. Suite 2010
Las Vegas, NV 89103
Telephone: (888) 969-2677 or (702) 310-9910
Fax: (702) 310-9911
Website: www.acorncorp.com
Email: info@acorncorp.com

Affordable Business Services Inc.
Patricia Roth
1061 East Flamingo Road, Suite 11
Las Vegas, NV 89119
Telephone: (888) 289-2039 or (702) 862-4736
Website: http://www.affordablebusiness.com

Agency Services of Nevada
c/o Law Offices of Turner Law Limited
245 East Liberty Street, Suite 200
Reno, NV 89501
P.O. Box 6477
Reno, NV 89513
Telephone: (888) 828-8208 or (775) 786-1836
Fax: (775) 786-6755

Alpine Incorporators, Inc.
Edward P. York, Ph.D., President
3410 Bryan Street
Reno NV 89503-1909
Telephone: (888) 345-1071 or (775) 787-1071
Fax: (775) 787-1346
Website: http://www.alpineincorporators.com
Email: Ed@alpineincorporators.com

American Corporate Register, Inc.
Phil Herr
4960 South Virginia Street, Suite 300
Reno NV, 89502
Telephone: (800) 944-1120 or (775) 828-9188
Fax: (800) 757-2705
Website: http://www.incnevada.com
Email: phil@incnevada.com

American Resident Agents Association
Juli Barsoom
4960 South Virginia Street, Suite 302
Reno, NV 89502
Telephone: (800) 933-9442 or (775) 851-1551
Fax: (800) 757-2705
Website: http://www.incorporate.org
Email: association@incorporate.org

American Resident Agents Association
Pearl Bloom
316 California, Suite 656
Reno, NV 89509
Telephone: (800) 737-3824 or (775) 329-9222
Fax: (800) 757-2705
Website: http://www.incorporate.org
Email: corp@incorporate.org

Beckley, Doug
Mail Boxes Etc.
1350 East Flamingo Road, Suite 13B
Las Vegas, NV 89119
Telephone: (888) 751-0415 or (702) 732-0024
Website: http://mbenv.com

Cal-Neva Prosperity Group, LLC
Frank Laereman
1545 South Wells Avenue, Suite 112
Reno, NV 89509
Telephone: (702) 327-4246

Capitol Document Services, Inc.
202 South Minnesota Street
Carson City, NV 89703
Telephone: (800) 899-0490 or (775) 884-0490
Fax: (888) 231-4790 or (775) 884-0493
Website: http://www.capitolservices.com

Carson Mail Depot
John O. Rough
1945 North Carson Street
Carson City, NV 89701
Telephone: (888) 702-4748 or (775) 884-4748
Fax: (775) 884-4211
Email: jrough@pyramid.net

Carson Registered Agents, Inc.
200 North Stewart Street
The Presidential Suite
Carson City, NV 89701
Telephone: (775) 883-1944
Fax: (775) 883-0267
Website: http://www.inc-america.com
Email: sss@inc-america.com

CATS - Corporation Services of Nevada, Inc.
3311 South Rainbow Blvd, Suite 133
Las Vegas, NV 89146
Telephone: (702) 367-1931
Fax: (702) 871-4086
Email: catsnv@ibm.net

CHQ Incorporated
1555 East Flamingo Road, Suite 155
Las Vegas, NV 89119
PO Box 19118
Paradise Valley, NV 89132
Telephone: (800) 334-3808 or (702) 796-1527
Fax: (702) 796-6694
Website: www.chqinc.com

Communities Outreach Ministries, Inc.
Charles Moore
2721 Coran Lane
Las Vegas, NV 89106
112 Harvard Avenue, No.196
Claremont, CA 91711
Telephone: (909) 670-1520
Fax: (909) 670-1520

Company Corporation Agency, Inc., The
Oliver Meservy
1155 West 4th Street, Suite 214
Reno, NV 98503-5149
Telephone: (877) 329-6500 or (702) 329-6500
Fax: (877) 682-6777
Email: corpagents@aol.com

Contractor's License Center, Inc.
4440 South Maryland Parkway, Suite 205
Las Vegas, NV 89119
Telephone: (800) 970-7277 or (702) 733-9598
Fax: (702) 733-9610

Corporate Advisory Service Inc.
Michael D. Taylor
251 Jeanell Drive, Suite 3
Carson City NV 89703
Telephone: (800) 533-2677 or (775) 885-2677
Fax: (775) 882-5121
Website: http://casinc@nanosecond.com
Email: casinc@nanosecond.com

Corporate Counsel Service
Jo Ann Amick
723 So. Casino Center Blvd., 2nd Floor
Las Vegas, NV 89101-6716
P.O. Box 7346
Las Vegas, Nevada 89125-2346
Telephone: (800) 354-4004 or (702) 474-7568
Fax: (702) 471-1012
Website: http://www.corporateserviceslv.com
Email: csg@wizard,com

Corporate Office Services, Inc.
Vera Turpen
1005 Terminal Way, Suite 110
Reno, NV 89502
Telephone: (800) 872-0858 or (775) 324-7676
Fax: (775) 324-6266
Website: www.nevcorp.com

Corporate Plus, Inc.
4535 West Sahara Avenue Suite 111
Las Vegas, NV 89102
Telephone: (702) 222-3654
Fax: (702) 222-3622
Email: corp@wizard.com

Corporate Resolve Inc.
Joe Norris/Barbara Dean
3655 Research Way, Suite A
Carson City, NV 89706
Telephone: (888) 661-8261/(888) 661-8262 or (775) 882-1629
Fax: (775) 882-0676
Website: http://www.corporateresolve.com
Email: bd@usatinc.com/ceo@usatinc.com

Corporate Services Company
Jo Ann Amick
723 So. Casino Center Blvd., 2nd Floor
Las Vegas, NV 89101-6716
P.O. Box 7348
Las Vegas, NV 89125-2346
Telephone: (800)354-4004 or (702) 384-7582
Fax: (702) 471-1012
Website: www.corporateserviceslv.com
Email: csg@wizard.com

Corporate Services Group, LLC
Jo Ann Amick
723 So. Casino Center Blvd., 2nd Floor
Las Vegas NV 89101-6716
P.O. Box 7346
Las Vegas, NV 89125-6716
Telephone: (800) 354-4004 or (702) 474-7568
Fax: (702) 471-1012
Website: http://www.corporateserviceslv.com
Email: csg@wizard.com

Corporate Services of Nevada
502 North Division Street
Carson City NV 89703
Telephone: (800) 655-0538 or (775) 883-3711
Fax: (775) 883-2723
Website: www.nevadacorps.com
Email: corpsvcs@msn.com

Corporate Solutions of Las Vegas
4970 South Arville Street, Suite 107
Las Vegas, NV 89118
Telephone : (800) 863-2527
Fax: (702) 257-9602
Website: http://www.incorporatelasvegasnv.com
Email: csofn@aol.com

Corporation Makers, Inc.
1900 Sierra Oaks Lane
Las Vegas, NV 89134
Telephone: (800) 267-7657
Fax: (702) 243-5159
Website: www.corpmakers.com
Email: corpmakers@aol.com

Corporation Trust Company of Nevada, The
Vi Miller
One East First Street
Reno, NV 89501
Telephone: (775) 688-3061
Fax: (775) 688-3067

Corporations Nevada, Inc.
Edward Earl Denton, JD, President
2620 South Maryland Parkway, Suite 807
Las Vegas, NV 89109
3702 South Virginia Street, Suite G-12,#503f
Reno, NV 89502
Telephone: (888) 682-6777 or (702) 880-7100
Fax: (888) 682-6777
Website: http://www.corporationsnevada.com
Email: corporationsnevada@earthlink.net

Create New Business, Inc.
A. Stith
774 Mays Blvd., #10-480
Incline Village, NV 89451
Telephone: (775) 321-9661
Email: cnb@crl.com

CSC Services of Nevada, Inc.
502 East John Street, Suite E
Carson City, NV 89706-3078
Telephone: (800) 222-2122 or (775) 882-3072
Fax: (775) 882-3354
Website: http://www.incspot.com
Email: info@cscinfo.com

Edge Business Services Corp.
Justin Guidi
9645 Gateway Drive, Suite B
Reno, NV 89511
Telephone: (775) 852-3339
Fax: (775) 852-9199
Website: http://edgebusiness.com
Email: signup@edgebusiness.com

Excelsior Financial Corp.
Matt Held
3681 South Sagebrush
Pahrump, NV 89041

Eyeball Services Inc.
Trevillison Linda Prieto
4420 Arville Street, # 20
Las Vegas, NV 89103
Telephone: (888) 4 EYEBALL or (702) 248-3530
Fax: (702) 257-2788
Email: EYEBALLINC@AOL.COM

1ST Class Only- A Mail Forwarding Co.
Terry Chilcoat
1504 #8-01000 Main Street
Gardnerville, NV 89410-5273
Telephone: (800) 848-4900

Frost, LaVonne (Lilli)
711 South Carson Street, Suite 1
Carson City, NV 89701
Telephone: (877) 442-4363 or (775) 883-5755
Fax: (775) 883-4775
Website: http://members.aol.com/lilli2k
Email: lilli2k@aol.com

GKL Resident Agents/Filings, Inc.
Gregory K. Lee
1100 East William Street, Suite 207
Carson City, NV 89701
PO Box 3679
Carson City, NV 89702-36791
Telephone: (888) 682-4368 or (775) 841-0644
Fax: (775) 841-2065
Email: gklnv@gbis.com

Hamilton, John
Mail Boxes, Etc.
7500 West Lake Mead Blvd., Suite C9
Las Vegas, NV 89128
Telephone: (702) 240-2800
Fax: (702) 360-9351
Website: http://mbenv.com

Hartley, P.A.
3642 Boulder Highway, #387
Las Vegas, NV 89121
Telephone: (702) 431-5386
Fax: (702) 432-8157

Infinity Capital Management
Ronald Serota
2950 East Flamingo Road, Suite D-5
Las Vegas, NV 89121
1982 North Rainbow Blvd. Suite D-5
Las Vegas, NV 89108
Telephone: (800) 628-5829 or (702) 228-3499
Fax: (702) 383-5079
Website: http://www.infinitycapital.com
Email: info@infinitycapital.com

Laughlin Associates, Inc.
Brent Buscay
2533 North Carson Street
Carson City, NV 89706
Telephone: (800) 648-0966 or (775) 883-8484
Fax: (775) 883-4874
Website: http://www.laughlinassociates.com
Email: info@laughlinassociates.com

Laughlin Associates, Inc.
Lewis Laughlin, President & CEO
2533 North Carson Street
Carson City, NV 89706
Telephone: (800) 648-0966 or (775) 883-8484
Fax: (775) 883-4874
Website: http://www.laughlinassociates.com
Email: info@laughlinassociates.com

Mail Boxes, Etc.
3540 West Sahara #6E
Las Vegas, NV 89102
Telephone: (702) 367-6252
Fax: (702) 367-6421
Email: mbe135@ivdi.net.

Malikowski Law Offices, Ltd.
Paul J. Malikowski, Esq.
33 West Eighth Street
Reno, NV 89503
Telephone: (888) 936-8337 or (775) 688-3220
Fax: (775) 688-3218
Website: www.nvlaw.com
Email: paul@nvlaw.com

McMillan Interests LLC
2950 East Flamingo Road, Suite B
Las Vegas, NV 89121
Telephone: (800) 454-9674 or (702) 892-0990
Fax: (702) 459-4889

National Business Incorporators, Inc.
1516 East Tropicana Avenue, Suite B1
Las Vegas, NV 89119
Telephone: (888) 624-8999 or (702) 891-9800
Website: www.NBIcorp.com

National Corporate Research, Ltd.
Clare Oliva
202 South Minnesota Street
Carson City, NV 89703
225 West 34th Street, Suite 910
New York, NY 10122
Telephone: (800) 221-0102 or (212) 947-7200
Fax: (212) 564-6083
Website: www.nationalcorp.com
Email: info@nationalcorp.com

National Registered Agent Services
400 West King Street
Carson City, NV 89703
Telephone: (800) 562-6429

Nevada & Offshore Business Formation, Inc.
Alan Teegardin
1321 Bridle Way
Minden, NV 89423
Telephone: (888) 463-8462 or (775) 882-0724
Fax: (775) 882-6818
Website: www.nobfi.com
Email: agents@nobfi.com

Nevada Agency and Trust Company, The
50 West Liberty #880
Reno, NV 89501
Telephone: (775) 322-0626
Fax: (775) 322-5623

Nevada Business Services
Mary Ann Dickens
675 Fairview Drive, Suite 246
Carson City, NV 89701
Telephone: (775) 882-1390
Fax: (775) 882-8924
Email: madickens@usa.net

Nevada Corporate Center, Inc.
800 Southwood Blvd., Suite 207
Incline Village, NV 89452
PO Box 8340
Incline Village, NV 89450
Telephone: (877) 638-2677 or (775) 345-6600
Fax: (775) 332-2902
Website: http://nevadacorporatecenter.com

Nevada Corporate Filings Plus
William Levine
3355 Spring Mountain Road, # 54
Las Vegas, NV 89102-8635
Telephone: (702) 362-4616
Fax: (702) 362-1071
Website: www.corpfilingsplus.com
Email: rosowskyd@ivcm.com

Nevada Corporate Planners, Inc.
3885 South Decatur, Suite 3010
Las Vegas, NV 89103
Telephone: (888) 627-7007 or (702) 367-7373
Fax: (702) 220-6444
Website: www.nvinc.com
Email: solution@skylink.net

Nevada Corporate Services, Inc.
1800 East Sahara, Suite 107
Las Vegas, NV 89104
Telephone: (800) 658-5105 or (702) 947-4100
Fax: (702) 947-4110
Email: incorporate@ivcm.com

Nevada First Holdings, Inc.
Wayne McMiniment
5130 South Pecos Road, Suite 2C
Las Vegas, NV 89120
Telephone: (800) 770-7570 or (702) 320-5315
Fax: (702) 320-5320
Website: http://www.nevada first.com.
Email: WAYNE@NEVADAFIRST.COM

Nevada Incorporating Company
Jo Ann Amick
723 So. Casino Center Blvd., 2nd Floor
Las Vegas, NV 89101-6716
P.O. Box 1635
Las Vegas, NV 89125-1635
Telephone: (800) 354-4004 or (702) 384-8727
Fax: (702) 471-1012
Website: http://www.corporateserviceslv.com
Email: csg@wizard.com

Nevada Insurance Agency Company
1385 Haskell Street
PO Box 7500
Reno, NV 89510

Nevada Offshore Banking Consultants
Terry Chilcoat
1504 #8-01004 Main Street
Gardnerville, NV 89410
Telephone: (800) 558-1958 or (775) 888-2002

Nevada State Incorporating and Resident Agent Services
Jack McQuirk
1050 Chaparral Drive
Carson City, NV 89703
Telephone: (877) 325-0258 or (775) 841-6277
Fax: (775) 883-4740
Website: www.alpine.net/~eznvcorp
Email: eznvcorp@alpine.net

Paracorp Incorporated
Nancy Gaches
318 North Carson Street, Suite 208
Carson City, NV 89701
Telephone: (888) 972-7273 or (775) 883-0104
Fax: (888) 886-7168
Website: http://www.parasec.com
Email: ngaches@parasec.com

Repackaging America Inc.
Ray Reynolds
3305 West Spring Mountain Road Suite 60-24
Las Vegas, NV 89102
438 East Katella Avenue Suite B
Orange, CA 92867
Telephone: (702) 222-1413 or (714) 771-9716 ext. 211
Fax: (714) 771-4725

Resident Agency National
377 South Nevada Street
Carson City, NV 89703-4290
Telephone: (775) 882-7549
Fax: (775) 882-4283

Resident Agent of Nevada, Inc.
Elizabeth Gebhardt
250 South Martin
PO Box 6928
Lake Tahoe, NV 89449
Telephone: (775) 588-5609
Fax: (775) 588-0805

Resident Agent Services, Inc.
Michele Marchesi
1801 Highway 50 East, Suite B
Carson City, NV 89701
Telephone: (775) 882-0771
Fax: (775) 885-2198
Website: http://agents@incorporators.com
Email: agents@incorporators.com; agents@incorp.com

Resident Agents of Nevada, Inc.
Tricia Bozin
711 South Carson Street, Suite 4
Carson City, NV 89701
Telephone: (888) 663-8232 or (775) 882-4641
Fax: (775) 882-6818
Website: www.nevada.org
Email: agents@nevada.org

Resident Agents of Nevada, Inc. (Las Vegas)
Tricia Bozin
302 East Carson Avenue, Suite 1010
Las Vegas, NV 89101
Telephone: (888) 663-8232
Fax: (775) 882-6818
Website: www.nevada.org
Email: agents@nevada.org

Rhema International, Inc.
Wayne Wakefield
280 Brinkby Avenue, Suite 201
Reno, NV 89509
Telephone: (800) 449-2997 or (775) 828-2997
Fax: (775) 828-2996
Website: http://rhema-int.com
Email: rhema@rhema-int.com

Sage International Inc.
C.W. Allen
1135 Terminal Way #209
Reno, NV 89502
Telephone: (800) 254-5779
Website: http://www.sageintl.com
Email: corpinfo@sageintl.com

Shield Corporate Services, Inc.
311 South Division Street
Carson City, NV 89703
Telephone: (800) 541-4811 or (775) 882-6661
Fax: (775) 882-5857
Website: http://shieldcorp.com
Email: ShieldCorp@aol.com

Sierra Best Corporate Service
Lila Williams Young
711 South Carson Street, Suite 1
Carson City, NV 89701
Telephone: (888) 346-2409 or (775) 882-4834
Fax: (775) 883-5566
Email: LYOUNG1745@AOL.COM

Skinner, Sutton & Watson, Attorneys at Law
Garrett Sutton, Esq.
548 California Avenue
Reno, NV 89509
Telephone: (800) 977-7577 or (775) 324-4100
Fax: (775) 333-8171
Website: http://sswlegal.com
Email: ssw2@ix.netcom.com

State Agent and Transfer Syndicate, Inc.
John E. "Jed" Block
318 North Carson Street, Suite 214
Carson City, NV 89701-4269
Telephone: (800) 253-1013 or (775) 882-1013
Fax: (775) 882-8628
Website: http://www.stagent.com
Email: NVStagent@AOL.com

Trost, Janet, Attorney at Law
518 South Ninth Street
Las Vegas, NV 89101
Telephone; (702) 257-2889
Fax: (702) 257-2778
Email: JanetTrost@aol.com

Unisearch, Inc.
Carol Blynn
8175 South Virginia Street, Suite 850-409
Reno, NV 89511-8981
Telephone: (800) 260-1131 or (775) 851-4500
Fax: (800) 260-8118 or (775) 851-1330
Website: http://www.unisearch.com
Email: carolb@unisearch.com

Val-U-Corp Services, Inc.
Dan Kramer
1802 North Carson Street Suite 212
Carson City, NV 89701
Telephone: (800) 555-9141 or (775) 887-8853
Fax: (775) 887-0738
Website: http://www.val-u-corp.com
Email: val-u-corp@val-u-corp.com

Vegas Connection Resident Agent
Kim Pinkerton
2067 Las Vegas Blvd. North #66
North Las Vegas, NV 89030
Telephone: (702) 657-5035
Fax: (702) 657-5035
Email: Vegasconn@aol.com

Whites-Listings, Inc.
Jo Ann Amick
723 South Casino Center Blvd., 2nd Floor
Las Vegas, NV 89101-6716
P.O. Box 7346
Las Vegas, NV 89125-2346
Telephone: (800) 354-4004 or (702) 474-7568
Fax: (702) 471-1012
Website: http://www.corporateserviceslv.com
Email: csg@wizard.com

APPENDIX D
FORMS

This appendix contains the blank forms which can be used to form a Nevada corporation or LLC. Be sure to read the text before using any of these forms. If you do not understand any of the forms you should consult an attorney.

DEAN HELLER
Secretary of State

101 North Carson Street, Suite 3
Carson City, Nevada 89701-4786
(775) 684 5708

Credit Card Checklist
(For Counter, Telephone, Fax and Mail Requests)

Service Type: Counter _____   Telephone _____   Mail _____   Fax _____

Expedite Service: (Requires additional fees)   **PLEASE EXPEDITE** _____

Card Type: (the Secretary of State accepts only VISA or MasterCard)

VISA _____   or MasterCard _____

Customer Credit Card Number: (Must be 16 digits)

Expiration Date:

Month_____   Year_____

Amount:

$_____ _____, _____ _____ _____. _____ _____

Cardholder Information:

Name _____

Street _____

City, State, Zip _____

Telephone _____

Reference Number: (supplied by machine) _____

Approval Number: (supplied by machine) _____

Employee Initials: _____

AUTHORIZATION: CUSTOMER AUTHORIZES THE SECRETARY OF STATE TO BILL AN AMOUNT NOT TO EXCEED $_____._____ TO BE CHARGED TO THE ABOVE CREDIT CARD NUMBER.

_____
(Cardholder signature)

Nevada Secretary of State Form CRCARD1999.01
Revised on: 02/16/99

REQUEST FOR CORPORATE FORMS

To: Department of Corporate Filings

Please send us any of the following which are available without charge and advise of the cost of any for which there is a charge.

Form for registering a foreign ☐ corporation ☐ LLC to do business in this state.

Copy of statutes applicable to foreign businesses doing business in this state.

Please send to: _____
Name (Printed of typed)

_____
Address

_____
City, State & Zip

| Form **SS-4**
(Rev. February 1998)
Department of the Treasury
Internal Revenue Service | **Application for Employer Identification Number**
(For use by employers, corporations, partnerships, trusts, estates, churches,
government agencies, certain individuals, and others. See instructions.)
▶ **Keep a copy for your records.** | EIN

OMB No. 1545-0003 |

<table>
<tr><td rowspan="8" style="writing-mode:vertical-rl">Please type or print clearly.</td><td colspan="2">**1**   Name of applicant (legal name) (see instructions)</td></tr>
<tr><td>**2**   Trade name of business (if different from name on line 1)</td><td>**3**   Executor, trustee, "care of" name</td></tr>
<tr><td>**4a** Mailing address (street address) (room, apt., or suite no.)</td><td>**5a** Business address (if different from address on lines 4a and 4b)</td></tr>
<tr><td>**4b** City, state, and ZIP code</td><td>**5b** City, state, and ZIP code</td></tr>
<tr><td colspan="2">**6**   County and state where principal business is located</td></tr>
<tr><td colspan="2">**7**   Name of principal officer, general partner, grantor, owner, or trustor—SSN or ITIN may be required (see instructions) ▶</td></tr>
</table>

8a Type of entity (Check only one box.) (see instructions)

    Caution: *If applicant is a limited liability company, see the instructions for line 8a.*

☐ Sole proprietor (SSN) _____   ☐ Estate (SSN of decedent) _____

☐ Partnership   ☐ Personal service corp.   ☐ Plan administrator (SSN) _____

☐ REMIC   ☐ National Guard   ☐ Other corporation (specify) ▶ _____

☐ State/local government   ☐ Farmers' cooperative   ☐ Trust

☐ Church or church-controlled organization   ☐ Federal government/military

☐ Other nonprofit organization (specify) ▶ _____ (enter GEN if applicable) _____

☐ Other (specify) ▶

| **8b** If a corporation, name the state or foreign country
(if applicable) where incorporated | State | Foreign country |

9 Reason for applying (Check only one box.) (see instructions)   ☐ Banking purpose (specify purpose) ▶ _____

☐ Started new business (specify type) ▶_____   ☐ Changed type of organization (specify new type) ▶ _____

    ☐ Purchased going business

☐ Hired employees (Check the box and see line 12.)   ☐ Created a trust (specify type) ▶ _____

☐ Created a pension plan (specify type) ▶   ☐ Other (specify) ▶

| **10** Date business started or acquired (month, day, year) (see instructions) | **11** Closing month of accounting year (see instructions) |

12 First date wages or annuities were paid or will be paid (month, day, year). **Note:** *If applicant is a withholding agent, enter date income will first be paid to nonresident alien. (month, day, year)* . . . . ▶

13 Highest number of employees expected in the next 12 months. **Note:** *If the applicant does not expect to have any employees during the period, enter -0-. (see instructions)* . . . . ▶	Nonagricultural	Agricultural	Household

14 Principal activity (see instructions) ▶

15 Is the principal business activity manufacturing? . . . . ☐ Yes   ☐ No
If "Yes," principal product and raw material used ▶

16 To whom are most of the products or services sold? Please check one box.   ☐ Business (wholesale)
☐ Public (retail)   ☐ Other (specify) ▶   ☐ N/A

17a Has the applicant ever applied for an employer identification number for this or any other business? . . . . ☐ Yes   ☐ No
Note: *If "Yes," please complete lines 17b and 17c.*

17b If you checked "Yes" on line 17a, give applicant's legal name and trade name shown on prior application, if different from line 1 or 2 above.
Legal name ▶   Trade name ▶

17c Approximate date when and city and state where the application was filed. Enter previous employer identification number if known.

Approximate date when filed (mo., day, year)	City and state where filed	Previous EIN

Under penalties of perjury, I declare that I have examined this application, and to the best of my knowledge and belief, it is true, correct, and complete.	Business telephone number (include area code)
	Fax telephone number (include area code)
Name and title (Please type or print clearly.) ▶	

Signature ▶   Date ▶

Note: *Do not write below this line. For official use only.*

Please leave blank ▶	Geo.	Ind.	Class	Size	Reason for applying

| **For Paperwork Reduction Act Notice, see page 4.** | Cat. No. 16055N | Form **SS-4** (Rev. 2-98) |

General Instructions

Section references are to the Internal Revenue Code unless otherwise noted.

Purpose of Form

Use Form SS-4 to apply for an employer identification number (EIN). An EIN is a nine-digit number (for example, 12-3456789) assigned to sole proprietors, corporations, partnerships, estates, trusts, and other entities for tax filing and reporting purposes. The information you provide on this form will establish your business tax account.

Caution: *An EIN is for use in connection with your business activities only. Do **NOT** use your EIN in place of your social security number (SSN).*

Who Must File

You must file this form if you have not been assigned an EIN before and:

● You pay wages to one or more employees including household employees.

● You are required to have an EIN to use on any return, statement, or other document, even if you are not an employer.

● You are a withholding agent required to withhold taxes on income, other than wages, paid to a nonresident alien (individual, corporation, partnership, etc.). A withholding agent may be an agent, broker, fiduciary, manager, tenant, or spouse, and is required to file **Form 1042,** Annual Withholding Tax Return for U.S. Source Income of Foreign Persons.

● You file **Schedule C,** Profit or Loss From Business, **Schedule C-EZ,** Net Profit From Business, or **Schedule F,** Profit or Loss From Farming, of **Form 1040,** U.S. Individual Income Tax Return, **and** have a Keogh plan or are required to file excise, employment, or alcohol, tobacco, or firearms returns.

The following must use EINs even if they do not have any employees:

● State and local agencies who serve as tax reporting agents for public assistance recipients, under Rev. Proc. 80-4, 1980-1 C.B. 581, should obtain a separate EIN for this reporting. See **Household employer** on page 3.

● Trusts, except the following:

   1. Certain grantor-owned trusts. (See the **Instructions for Form 1041.)**

   2. Individual Retirement Arrangement (IRA) trusts, unless the trust has to file **Form 990-T,** Exempt Organization Business Income Tax Return. (See the **Instructions for Form 990-T.)**

● Estates

● Partnerships

● REMICs (real estate mortgage investment conduits) (See the **Instructions for Form 1066,** U.S. Real Estate Mortgage Investment Conduit Income Tax Return.)

● Corporations

● Nonprofit organizations (churches, clubs, etc.)

● Farmers' cooperatives

● Plan administrators (A plan administrator is the person or group of persons specified as the administrator by the instrument under which the plan is operated.)

When To Apply for a New EIN

New Business. If you become the new owner of an existing business, **do not** use the EIN of the former owner. IF YOU ALREADY HAVE AN EIN, USE THAT NUMBER. If you do not have an EIN, apply for one on this form. If you become the "owner" of a corporation by acquiring its stock, use the corporation's EIN.

Changes in Organization or Ownership. If you already have an EIN, you may need to get a new one if either the organization or ownership of your business changes. If you incorporate a sole proprietorship or form a partnership, you must get a new EIN. However, **do not** apply for a new EIN if:

● You change only the name of your business,

● You elected on **Form 8832,** Entity Classification Election, to change the way the entity is taxed, or

● A partnership terminates because at least 50% of the total interests in partnership capital and profits were sold or exchanged within a 12-month period. (See Regulations section 301.6109-1(d)(2)(iii).) The EIN for the terminated partnership should continue to be used. This rule applies to terminations occurring after May 8, 1997. If the termination took place after May 8, 1996, and before May 9, 1997, a new EIN must be obtained for the new partnership unless the partnership and its partners are consistent in using the old EIN.

Note: *If you are electing to be an "S corporation," be sure you file **Form 2553,** Election by a Small Business Corporation.*

File Only One Form SS-4. File only one Form SS-4, regardless of the number of businesses operated or trade names under which a business operates. However, each corporation in an affiliated group must file a separate application.

EIN Applied for, But Not Received. If you do not have an EIN by the time a return is due, write "Applied for" and the date you applied in the space shown for the number. **Do not** show your social security number (SSN) as an EIN on returns.

If you do not have an EIN by the time a tax deposit is due, send your payment to the Internal Revenue Service Center for your filing area. (See **Where To Apply** below.) Make your check or money order payable to Internal Revenue Service and show your name (as shown on Form SS-4), address, type of tax, period covered, and date you applied for an EIN. Send an explanation with the deposit.

For more information about EINs, see **Pub. 583,** Starting a Business and Keeping Records, and **Pub. 1635,** Understanding your EIN.

How To Apply

You can apply for an EIN either by mail or by telephone. You can get an EIN immediately by calling the Tele-TIN number for the service center for your state, or you can send the completed Form SS-4 directly to the service center to receive your EIN by mail.

Application by Tele-TIN. Under the Tele-TIN program, you can receive your EIN by telephone and use it immediately to file a return or make a payment. To receive an EIN by telephone, complete Form SS-4, then call the Tele-TIN number listed for your state under **Where To Apply.** The person making the call must be authorized to sign the form. (See **Signature** on page 4.)

An IRS representative will use the information from the Form SS-4 to establish your account and assign you an EIN. Write the number you are given on the upper right corner of the form and sign and date it.

*Mail or fax (facsimile) the signed SS-4 **within 24 hours** to the Tele-TIN Unit at the service center address for your state.* The IRS representative will give you the fax number. The fax numbers are also listed in Pub. 1635.

Taxpayer representatives can receive their client's EIN by telephone if they first send a fax of a completed **Form 2848,** Power of Attorney and Declaration of Representative, or **Form 8821,** Tax Information Authorization, to the Tele-TIN unit. The Form 2848 or Form 8821 will be used solely to release the EIN to the representative authorized on the form.

Application by Mail. Complete Form SS-4 at least 4 to 5 weeks before you will need an EIN. Sign and date the application and mail it to the service center address for your state. You will receive your EIN in the mail in approximately 4 weeks.

Where To Apply

The Tele-TIN numbers listed below will involve a long-distance charge to callers outside of the local calling area and can be used only to apply for an EIN. THE NUMBERS MAY CHANGE WITHOUT NOTICE. Call 1-800-829-1040 to verify a number or to ask about the status of an application by mail.

If your principal business, office or agency, or legal residence in the case of an individual, is located in:	Call the Tele-TIN number shown or file with the Internal Revenue Service Center at:
Florida, Georgia, South Carolina	Attn: Entity Control Atlanta, GA 39901 770-455-2360
New Jersey, New York City and counties of Nassau, Rockland, Suffolk, and Westchester	Attn: Entity Control Holtsville, NY 00501 516-447-4955
New York (all other counties), Connecticut, Maine, Massachusetts, New Hampshire, Rhode Island, Vermont	Attn: Entity Control Andover, MA 05501 978-474-9717
Illinois, Iowa, Minnesota, Missouri, Wisconsin	Attn: Entity Control Stop 6800 2306 E. Bannister Rd. Kansas City, MO 64999 816-926-5999
Delaware, District of Columbia, Maryland, Pennsylvania, Virginia	Attn: Entity Control Philadelphia, PA 19255 215-516-6999
Indiana, Kentucky, Michigan, Ohio, West Virginia	Attn: Entity Control Cincinnati, OH 45999 606-292-5467

Kansas, New Mexico, Oklahoma, Texas	Attn: Entity Control Austin, TX 73301 512-460-7843
Alaska, Arizona, California (counties of Alpine, Amador, Butte, Calaveras, Colusa, Contra Costa, Del Norte, El Dorado, Glenn, Humboldt, Lake, Lassen, Marin, Mendocino, Modoc, Napa, Nevada, Placer, Plumas, Sacramento, San Joaquin, Shasta, Sierra, Siskiyou, Solano, Sonoma, Sutter, Tehama, Trinity, Yolo, and Yuba), Colorado, Idaho, Montana, Nebraska, Nevada, North Dakota, Oregon, South Dakota, Utah, Washington, Wyoming	Attn: Entity Control Mail Stop 6271 P.O. Box 9941 Ogden, UT 84201 801-620-7645
California (all other counties), Hawaii	Attn: Entity Control Fresno, CA 93888 209-452-4010
Alabama, Arkansas, Louisiana, Mississippi, North Carolina, Tennessee	Attn: Entity Control Memphis, TN 37501 901-546-3920
If you have no legal residence, principal place of business, or principal office or agency in any state	Attn: Entity Control Philadelphia, PA 19255 215-516-6999

Specific Instructions

The instructions that follow are for those items that are not self-explanatory. Enter N/A (nonapplicable) on the lines that do not apply.

Line 1. Enter the legal name of the entity applying for the EIN exactly as it appears on the social security card, charter, or other applicable legal document.

Individuals. Enter your first name, middle initial, and last name. If you are a sole proprietor, enter your individual name, not your business name. Enter your business name on line 2. Do not use abbreviations or nicknames on line 1.

Trusts. Enter the name of the trust.

Estate of a decedent. Enter the name of the estate.

Partnerships. Enter the legal name of the partnership as it appears in the partnership agreement. **Do not** list the names of the partners on line 1. See the specific instructions for line 7.

Corporations. Enter the corporate name as it appears in the corporation charter or other legal document creating it.

Plan administrators. Enter the name of the plan administrator. A plan administrator who already has an EIN should use that number.

Line 2. Enter the trade name of the business if different from the legal name. The trade name is the "doing business as" name.

Note: *Use the full legal name on line 1 on all tax returns filed for the entity. However, if you enter a trade name on line 2 and choose to use the trade name instead of the legal name, enter the trade name on all returns you file. To prevent processing delays and errors, **always** use either the legal name or the trade name only on all tax returns.*

Line 3. Trusts enter the name of the trustee. Estates enter the name of the executor, administrator, or other fiduciary. If the entity applying has a designated person to receive tax information, enter that person's name as the "care of" person. Print or type the first name, middle initial, and last name.

Line 7. Enter the first name, middle initial, last name, and SSN of a principal officer if the business is a corporation; of a general partner if a partnership; of the owner of a single member entity that is disregarded as an entity separate from its owner; or of a grantor, owner, or trustor if a trust. If the person in question is an alien individual with a previously assigned individual taxpayer identification number (ITIN), enter the ITIN in the space provided, instead of an SSN. You are not required to enter an SSN or ITIN if the reason you are applying for an EIN is to make an entity classification election (see Regulations section 301.7701-1 through 301.7701-3), and you are a nonresident alien with no effectively connected income from sources within the United States.

Line 8a. Check the box that best describes the type of entity applying for the EIN. If you are an alien individual with an ITIN previously assigned to you, enter the ITIN in place of a requested SSN.

Caution: *This is not an election for a tax classification of an entity. See "Limited liability company" below.*

If not specifically mentioned, check the "Other" box, enter the type of entity and the type of return that will be filed (for example, common trust fund, Form 1065). Do not enter N/A. If you are an alien individual applying for an EIN, see the **Line 7** instructions above.

Sole proprietor. Check this box if you file Schedule C, C-EZ, or F (Form 1040) and have a Keogh plan, or are required to file excise, employment, or alcohol, tobacco, or firearms returns, or are a payer of gambling winnings. Enter your SSN (or ITIN) in the space provided. If you are a nonresident alien with no effectively connected income from sources within the United States, you do not need to enter an SSN or ITIN.

REMIC. Check this box if the entity has elected to be treated as a real estate mortgage investment conduit (REMIC). See the **Instructions for Form 1066** for more information.

Other nonprofit organization. Check this box if the nonprofit organization is other than a church or church-controlled organization and specify the type of nonprofit organization (for example, an educational organization).

If the organization also seeks tax-exempt status, you must file either **Package 1023,** Application for Recognition of Exemption, or **Package 1024,** Application for Recognition of Exemption Under Section 501(a). Get **Pub. 557,** Tax Exempt Status for Your Organization, for more information.

Group exemption number (GEN). If the organization is covered by a group exemption letter, enter the four-digit GEN. (Do not confuse the GEN with the nine-digit EIN.) If you do not know the GEN, contact the parent organization. Get Pub. 557 for more information about group exemption numbers.

Withholding agent. If you are a withholding agent required to file Form 1042, check the "Other" box and enter "Withholding agent."

Personal service corporation. Check this box if the entity is a personal service corporation. An entity is a personal service corporation for a tax year only if:

● The principal activity of the entity during the testing period (prior tax year) for the tax year is the performance of personal services substantially by employee-owners, and

● The employee-owners own at least 10% of the fair market value of the outstanding stock in the entity on the last day of the testing period.

Personal services include performance of services in such fields as health, law, accounting, or consulting. For more information about personal service corporations, see the **Instructions for Form 1120,** U.S. Corporation Income Tax Return, and **Pub. 542,** Corporations.

Limited liability company (LLC). See the definition of limited liability company in the **Instructions for Form 1065.** An LLC with two or more members can be a partnership or an association taxable as a corporation. An LLC with a single owner can be an association taxable as a corporation or an entity disregarded as an entity separate from its owner. See Form 8832 for more details.

● If the entity is classified as a partnership for Federal income tax purposes, check the "partnership" box.

● If the entity is classified as a corporation for Federal income tax purposes, mark the "Other corporation" box and write "limited liability co." in the space provided.

● If the entity is disregarded as an entity separate from its owner, check the "Other" box and write in "disregarded entity" in the space provided.

Plan administrator. If the plan administrator is an individual, enter the plan administrator's SSN in the space provided.

Other corporation. This box is for any corporation other than a personal service corporation. If you check this box, enter the type of corporation (such as insurance company) in the space provided.

Household employer. If you are an individual, check the "Other" box and enter "Household employer" and your SSN. If you are a state or local agency serving as a tax reporting agent for public assistance recipients who become household employers, check the "Other" box and enter "Household employer agent." If you are a trust that qualifies as a household employer, you do not need a separate EIN for reporting tax information relating to household employees; use the EIN of the trust.

QSSS. For a qualified subchapter S subsidiary (QSSS) check the "Other" box and specify "QSSS."

Line 9. Check only **one** box. Do not enter N/A.

Started new business. Check this box if you are starting a new business that requires an EIN. If you check this box, enter the type of business being started. **Do not** apply if you already have an EIN and are only adding another place of business.

Hired employees. Check this box if the existing business is requesting an EIN because it has hired or is hiring employees and is therefore required to file employment tax returns. **Do not** apply if you already have an EIN and are only hiring employees. For information on the applicable employment taxes for family members, see **Circular E,** Employer's Tax Guide (Publication 15).

Created a pension plan. Check this box if you have created a pension plan and need this number for reporting purposes. Also, enter the type of plan created.

Note: *Check this box if you are applying for a trust EIN when a new pension plan is established.*

Banking purpose. Check this box if you are requesting an EIN for banking purposes only, and enter the banking purpose (for example, a bowling league for depositing dues or an investment club for dividend and interest reporting).

Changed type of organization. Check this box if the business is changing its type of organization, for example, if the business was a sole proprietorship and has been incorporated or has become a partnership. If you check this box, specify in the space provided the type of change made, for example, "from sole proprietorship to partnership."

Purchased going business. Check this box if you purchased an existing business. **Do not** use the former owner's EIN. **Do not** apply for a new EIN if you already have one. Use your own EIN.

Created a trust. Check this box if you created a trust, and enter the type of trust created. For example, indicate if the trust is a nonexempt charitable trust or a split-interest trust.

Note: *Do not check this box if you are applying for a trust EIN when a new pension plan is established. Check "Created a pension plan."*

Exception. Do **not** file this form for certain grantor-type trusts. The trustee does not need an EIN for the trust if the trustee furnishes the name and TIN of the grantor/owner and the address of the trust to all payors. See the Instructions for Form 1041 for more information.

Other (specify). Check this box if you are requesting an EIN for any reason other than those for which there are checkboxes, and enter the reason.

Line 10. If you are starting a new business, enter the starting date of the business. If the business you acquired is already operating, enter the date you acquired the business. Trusts should enter the date the trust was legally created. Estates should enter the date of death of the decedent whose name appears on line 1 or the date when the estate was legally funded.

Line 11. Enter the last month of your accounting year or tax year. An accounting or tax year is usually 12 consecutive months, either a calendar year or a fiscal year (including a period of 52 or 53 weeks). A calendar year is 12 consecutive months ending on December 31. A fiscal year is either 12 consecutive months ending on the last day of any month other than December or a 52-53 week year. For more information on accounting periods, see **Pub. 538,** Accounting Periods and Methods.

Individuals. Your tax year generally will be a calendar year.

Partnerships. Partnerships generally must adopt one of the following tax years:
● The tax year of the majority of its partners,
● The tax year common to all of its principal partners,
● The tax year that results in the least aggregate deferral of income, or
● In certain cases, some other tax year.

See the **Instructions for Form 1065,** U.S. Partnership Return of Income, for more information.

REMIC. REMICs must have a calendar year as their tax year.

Personal service corporations. A personal service corporation generally must adopt a calendar year unless:
● It can establish a business purpose for having a different tax year, or
● It elects under section 444 to have a tax year other than a calendar year.

Trusts. Generally, a trust must adopt a calendar year except for the following:
● Tax-exempt trusts,
● Charitable trusts, and
● Grantor-owned trusts.

Line 12. If the business has or will have employees, enter the date on which the business began or will begin to pay wages. If the business does not plan to have employees, enter N/A.

Withholding agent. Enter the date you began or will begin to pay income to a nonresident alien. This also applies to individuals who are required to file Form 1042 to report alimony paid to a nonresident alien.

Line 13. For a definition of agricultural labor (farmwork), see **Circular A,** Agricultural Employer's Tax Guide (Publication 51).

Line 14. Generally, enter the exact type of business being operated (for example, advertising agency, farm, food or beverage establishment, labor union, real estate agency, steam laundry, rental of coin-operated vending machine, or investment club). Also state if the business will involve the sale or distribution of alcoholic beverages.

Governmental. Enter the type of organization (state, county, school district, municipality, etc.).

Nonprofit organization (other than governmental). Enter whether organized for religious, educational, or humane purposes, and the principal activity (for example, religious organization—hospital, charitable).

Mining and quarrying. Specify the process and the principal product (for example, mining bituminous coal, contract drilling for oil, or quarrying dimension stone).

Contract construction. Specify whether general contracting or special trade contracting. Also, show the type of work normally performed (for example, general contractor for residential buildings or electrical subcontractor).

Food or beverage establishments. Specify the type of establishment and state whether you employ workers who receive tips (for example, lounge—yes).

Trade. Specify the type of sales and the principal line of goods sold (for example, wholesale dairy products, manufacturer's representative for mining machinery, or retail hardware).

Manufacturing. Specify the type of establishment operated (for example, sawmill or vegetable cannery).

Signature. The application must be signed by (a) the individual, if the applicant is an individual, (b) the president, vice president, or other principal officer, if the applicant is a corporation, (c) a responsible and duly authorized member or officer having knowledge of its affairs, if the applicant is a partnership or other unincorporated organization, or (d) the fiduciary, if the applicant is a trust or an estate.

How To Get Forms and Publications

Phone. You can order forms, instructions, and publications by phone. Just call 1-800-TAX-FORM (1-800-829-3676). You should receive your order or notification of its status within 7 to 15 workdays.

Personal computer. With your personal computer and modem, you can get the forms and information you need using:
● IRS's Internet Web Site at **www.irs.ustreas.gov**
● Telnet at **iris.irs.ustreas.gov**
● File Transfer Protocol at **ftp.irs.ustreas.gov**

You can also dial direct (by modem) to the Internal Revenue Information Services (IRIS) at 703-321-8020. IRIS is an on-line information service on FedWorld.

For small businesses, return preparers, or others who may frequently need tax forms or publications, a CD-ROM containing over 2,000 tax products (including many prior year forms) can be purchased from the Government Printing Office.

CD-ROM. To order the CD-ROM call the Superintendent of Documents at 202-512-1800 or connect to **www.access.gpo.gov/su_docs**

Privacy Act and Paperwork Reduction Act Notice. We ask for the information on this form to carry out the Internal Revenue laws of the United States. We need it to comply with section 6109 and the regulations thereunder which generally require the inclusion of an employer identification number (EIN) on certain returns, statements, or other documents filed with the Internal Revenue Service. Information on this form may be used to determine which Federal tax returns you are required to file and to provide you with related forms and publications. We disclose this form to the Social Security Administration for their use in determining compliance with applicable laws. We will be unable to issue an EIN to you unless you provide all of the requested information which applies to your entity.

You are not required to provide the information requested on a form that is subject to the Paperwork Reduction Act unless the form displays a valid OMB control number. Books or records relating to a form or its instructions must be retained as long as their contents may become material in the administration of any Internal Revenue law. Generally, tax returns and return information are confidential, as required by section 6103.

The time needed to complete and file this form will vary depending on individual circumstances. The estimated average time is:

Recordkeeping	7 min.
Learning about the law or the form	19 min.
Preparing the form	45 min.
Copying, assembling, and sending the form to the IRS	20 min.

If you have comments concerning the accuracy of these time estimates or suggestions for making this form simpler, we would be happy to hear from you. You can write to the Tax Forms Committee, Western Area Distribution Center, Rancho Cordova, CA 95743-0001. **Do not** send this form to this address. Instead, see **Where To Apply** on page 2.

BANKING RESOLUTION OF

_____

The undersigned, being the
      ☐ corporate secretary of the above corporation,
      ☐ member of the above limited liability company,
      ☐ manager of the above limited liability company

hereby certifies that on the _____ day of _____, _____ the company duly adopted the following resolution:

RESOLVED that the company open bank accounts with _____ _____ and that the ☐ officers of the corporation or ☐ members ☐ managers of the limited liability company are authorized to take such action as is necessary to open such accounts; that the bank's printed form of resolution is hereby adopted and incorporated into these minutes by reference and shall be placed in the minute book; that any ____ of the following persons shall have signature authority over the account:

_____   _____

_____   _____

and that said resolution has not been modified or rescinded.

Date: _____

_____
      ☐   Corporate Secretary
      ☐   Member
      ☐   Manager

RESOLUTION TO REIMBURSE EXPENSES
of

_____

     RESOLVED that the company shall reimburse the following parties for the organizational expenses of the organizers of this company and that the company shall amortize or deduct these expenses as allowed by IRS regulations.

Name	Expense	Amount
_____	_____	$_____
_____	_____	$_____
_____	_____	$_____
_____	_____	$_____
_____	_____	$_____
_____	_____	$_____
_____	_____	$_____

Date:_____

_____

_____

_____

_____

_____

BILL OF SALE

The undersigned, in consideration of

hereby grants, bargains, sells, transfers and delivers unto said corporation the following goods and chattels:

To have and to hold the same forever.

And the undersigned, their heirs, successors and administrators, covenant and warrant that they are the lawful owners of the said goods and chattels and that they are free from all encumbrances. That the undersigned have the right to sell this property and that they will warrant and defend the sale of said property against the lawful claims and demands of all persons. IN WITNESS whereof the undersigned have executed this Bill of Sale this _____ day of _____, _____.

_____

_____

_____

NEVADA BUSINESS REGISTRATION

Please read instructions before completing this form. Information on this form must be printed or typed.

PLEASE UNDERSTAND THAT EACH AGENCY MAY NEED TO REQUEST ADDTIONAL INFORMATION PARTICULAR TO THE NEEDS OF YOUR BUSINESS IN ORDER TO ACT ON YOUR APPLICATION. THE COMPLETION OF THIS FORM DOES NOT RELIEVE YOU OF ANY STATUTORY OR REGULATORY REQUIREMENTS RELATING TO YOUR BUSINESS.

1 ☐ New Business ☐ Change in Ownership ☐ Change in Location ☐ Change in Name ☐ Change in Mail Address ☐ Other—

2 Corporate Name

3 Federal Tax Identification Number

4 Corporate Address

5 Doing Business in Nevada as: Business Telephone # : ( ) Cellular # : ( ) Fax #: ( )

6 Mailing Address Street Number, Direction (N, S, E, W) and Name Suite, Unit or Apartment Number City, State, and Zip Code

7 Location (s) of Business Operations Street Number, Direction (N, S, E, W) and Name Suite, Unit or Apartment Number City, State, and Zip Code

8 Location of Business Records: Street Number, Direction (N, S, E, W) and Name Suite, Unit or Apartment Number City, State, and Zip Code Telephone #:

9 Type of Business Entity:
☐ Sole Proprietor ☐ S. Corp. ☐ Association ☐ Partnership ☐ Limited Liability ☐ Publicly-Traded Corporation ☐ Privately-Held Corporation ☐ Other

10 Name of Owner(s), Partners, Corporate Officers, etc. (If Individual Ownership, list only one Owner.)

Name of Owner, Partner, Officer, etc. (Last, First, MI):	Residence Address (Street)		SSN:	Date of Birth
Title	Percent Owned	City, State, Zip		Res. Phone
Name of Owner, Partner, Officer, etc. (Last, First, MI):	Residence Address (Street)		SSN:	Date of Birth
Title	Percent Owned	City, State, Zip		Res. Phone
Name of Owner, Partner, Officer, etc. (Last, First, MI):	Residence Address (Street)		SSN:	Date of Birth
Title	Percent Owned	City, State, Zip		Res. Phone
Name of Owner, Partner, Officer, etc. (Last, First, MI):	Residence Address (Street)		SSN:	Date of Birth
Title	Percent Owned	City, State, Zip		Res. Phone
Name of Local Contact (Last,First, MI)	Residence Address (Street), City, State, Zip			Res. Phone

11

Date Business Started in Nevada	Date first worker hired in Nevada	Date and amount of first Nevada payroll:	Number of Employees

PLEASE CHECK ALL THAT APPLY

12
☐ Mining ☐ Domestics ☐ Outside Dining ☐ Water Appropriation ☐ Adult Materials/Activity ☐ Supply/Use Temporary Workers
☐ Service ☐ Agriculture ☐ Home Occupation ☐ Hazardous Material ☐ Amusement Machines ☐ Alcohol
☐ Tobacco ☐ Manufacturing ☐ Retail Sales--New ☐ Construction/Erection ☐ Leased or Leasing Employees ☐ Gaming
☐ Delivery ☐ Transportation ☐ Retail Sales--Used ☐ Telephone Solicitation ☐ Leasing (Other than Employees) ☐ Other---
☐ Wholesale ☐ Not for Profit ☐ Live Entertainment ☐ Environmental Discharge ☐ Regulated by Federal/State Permit #---

13 Describe the Nature of Your Business

14 **IF YOU HAVE ACQUIRED A NEVADA BUSINESS OR CHANGED OWNERSHIP, PLEASE COMPLETE THIS SECTION :**

Date Acquired: Acquired by: ☐ Purchase ☐ Lease ☐ Other ☐ In Whole ☐ In Part

Name(s) of Previous Owners(s) Business Name and ESD Account Number of Previous Owner(s)

Address (Street) City State Zip Code

15 I am applying for: ☐ Unemployment Insurance (Employment Security) ☐ State Business License ☐ State Sales/ Use Tax Permit ☐ Local Business License

16 ** Do not sign until reading signature instructions. If the Business is a general partnership or joint venture, more than one signature is required.

I CERTIFY THE INFORMATION PROVIDED IN THIS REGISTRATION FORM IS TRUE, CORRECT AND COMPLETE TO THE BEST OF MY KNOWLEDGE AND BELIEF

Signature / Original **	Print Name	Date and Time
Signature / Original **	Print Name	Date and Time

DEAN HELLER
Secretary of State

101 North Carson Street, Suite 3
Carson City, Nevada 89701-4786
(775) 684 5708

| | **Articles of Incorporation** (PURSUANT TO NRS 78) | Office Use Only: |

Important: Read attached instructions before completing form.

1. _Name of Corporation:_	
2. _Resident Agent Name and Street Address:_ *(must be a Nevada address where process may be served)*	Name _____ _____, **NEVADA** _____ Street Address City Zip Code
3. _Shares:_ *(No. of shares corporation authorized to issue)*	Number of shares with par value: _____ Par value: _____ Number of shares without par value: _____
4. _Governing Board:_ *(Check one)*	Shall be styled as _____ Directors or _____ Trustees
Names, Addresses, Number of Board of Directors/Trustees:	The First Board of Directors/Trustees shall consist of _____ members whose names and addresses are as follows: Name _____ Name _____ Address City, State, Zip Address City, State, Zip
5. _Purpose:_ *(Optional--See Instructions)*	The purpose of this Corporation shall be:
6. _Other Matters:_ *(See instructions)*	Number of additional pages attached: _____
7. _Names, Addresses and Signatures of Incorporators:_ *(Signatures must be notarized)* *Attach additional pages if there are more than 2 incorporators.*	Name _____ Name _____ Address City, State, Zip Address City, State, Zip Signature Signature
Notary:	This instrument was acknowledged before me on This instrument was acknowledged before me on _____,_____ by _____,_____ by Name of person Name of person As incorporator As incorporator of _____ of _____ (Name of party on behalf of whom instrument executed) (Name of party on behalf of whom instrument executed) Notary Public Signature Notary Public Signature (affix notary stamp or seal) (affix notary stamp or seal)
8. _Certificate of Acceptance of Appointment of Resident Agent:_	I, _____ hereby accept appointment as Resident Agent for the above named corporation. Signature of Resident Agent Date

This form must be accompanied by appropriate fees. See attached fee schedule.

Nevada Secretary of State Form CORPART1999.01
Revised on: 02/12/99

DEAN HELLER
Secretary of State

101 North Carson Street, Suite 3
Carson City, Nevada 89701-4786
(775) 684 5708

<table>
<tr><td>

Instructions for
Articles of Incorporation
(PURSUANT TO NRS 78)

</td></tr>
</table>

IMPORTANT: READ ALL INSTRUCTIONS CAREFULLY BEFORE COMPLETING FORM.

1. *Name of the Corporation.* A name appearing to be that of a natural person and containing a given name or initials must not be used as a corporate name except with the addition of a corporate ending such as Incorporated, Inc., Limited, Ltd., Company, Co., Corporation, Corp. or other words that identifies it as not being a natural person. The name must be distinguishable from the names of corporations, limited liability companies, limited partnerships or limited liability partnerships on file in the office of the Secretary of State. A name may be reserved, if available, for 90 days by submitting a written request with a $20.00 filing fee.

2. *Resident Agent.* Persons wishing to incorporate in the State of Nevada must designate a person as a resident agent who resides or is located in this state. Every resident agent must have a street address in this state for the service of process, and may have a separate mailing address such as a post office box, which may be different from the street address.

3. State the number of shares the corporation shall have the authority to issue with par value and its par value appropriate space provided. State the number of shares without par value in the space provided for shares without par value.

4. Indicate whether the governing board will be styled as directors or trustees. Indicate the number of members of the first board. State the names and addresses of the first board. Use a separate 8 ½ x 11 sheet as necessary for additional directors. Directors or trustees must be at least 18 year of age.

5. This section is optional and is required only if the corporation is to engage in insurance or banking. Pre-approval from the State Insurance Commissioner or the State Financial Institutions Division is necessary if you have either of these purposes.

6. On a separate 8 ½ x 11, white sheet you may state additional information you wish to be part of the articles. This is an optional provision. If the additional information is contradictory to information on the form, the entire filing will be returned for correction.

7. Names and addresses of the incorporators are required. Each incorporator must sign and each signature must be notarized. Additional 8 ½ x 11 white sheet will be necessary if more than 2 incorporators.

8. Resident agent must complete and sign certificate of acceptance at bottom of form or attach a separate signed certificate of acceptance.

IMPORTANT

INITIAL LIST OF OFFICERS: Pursuant to NRS 78.150, each corporation organized under the laws of this state shall, on or before the first day of the second month after the filing of its articles of incorporation, and annually thereafter, file its list of officers, directors and resident agent. The fee is $85.00 per year. Forms will be mailed to you upon the organization of your corporation and annually thereafter to the corporation's resident agent.

COPIES: You *must* send in the number of copies you would like certified and returned to you in addition to the original article to be filed. A filing fee of $10.00 for each certification is required. Copies received without the required fee shall be returned uncertified. NRS 78.105 requires that a corporation receive at least one certified copy to be kept in the office of the resident agent. The Secretary of State keeps the original filing.

FILING FEE: Filing fee is based on the number of shares authorized. Please see the attached fee schedule. Filing may be expedited for an additional $50.00 expedite fee.

Filing may be submitted at the office of the Secretary of State or by mail at the following addresses:

<table>
<tr>
<td>

Secretary of State
New Filings Division
101 N. Carson Street, Suite 3
Carson City, NV 89701-4786
775-684-5708 Fax 775-684-5725

</td>
<td>

Secretary of State-Satellite Office
Commercial Recordings Division
555 E. Washington Avenue, 2nd Floor
Las Vegas, NV 89101
702-486-2880 Fax 702-486-2888

</td>
</tr>
</table>

Nevada Secretary of State Form CORPINST1999.01
Revised on: 02/12/99

BYLAWS OF

_____

A NEVADA CORPORATION

ARTICLE I - OFFICES

The principal office of the Corporation shall be located in the City of _____ and the State of Nevada. The Corporation may also maintain offices at such other places as the Board of Directors may, from time to time, determine.

ARTICLE II - SHAREHOLDERS

Section 1 - Annual Meetings: The annual meeting of the shareholders of the Corporation shall be held each year on _____ at _____m. at the principal office of the Corporation or at such other places as the Board may authorize, for the purpose of electing directors, and transacting such other business as may properly come before the meeting.

Section 2 - Special Meetings: Special meetings of the shareholders may be called at any time by the Board, the President, or by the holders of twenty-five percent (25%) of the shares then outstanding and entitled to vote.

Section 3 - Place of Meetings: All meetings of shareholders shall be held at the principal office of the Corporation, or at such other places as the board shall designate in the notice of such meetings.

Section 4 - Notice of Meetings: Written or printed notice stating the place, day, and hour of the meeting and, in the case of a special meeting, the purpose of the meeting, shall be delivered personally or by mail not less than ten days, nor more than sixty days, before the date of the meeting. Notice shall be given to each Member of record entitled to vote at the meeting. If mailed, such notice shall be deemed to have been delivered when deposited in the United States Mail with postage paid and addressed to the Member at his address as it appears on the records of the Corporation.

Section 5 - Waiver of Notice: A written waiver of notice signed by a Member, whether before or after a meeting, shall be equivalent to the giving of such notice. Attendance of a Member at a meeting shall constitute a waiver of notice of such meeting, except when the Member attends for the express purpose of objecting, at the beginning of the meeting, to the transaction of any business because the meeting is not lawfully called or convened.

Section 6 - Quorum: Except as otherwise provided by Statute, or the Articles of Incorporation, at all meetings of shareholders of the Corporation, the presence at the commencement of such meetings in person or by proxy of shareholders of record holding a majority of the total number of shares of the Corporation then issued and outstanding and entitled to vote, but in no event less than one-third of the shares entitled to vote at the meeting, shall constitute a quorum for the transaction of any business. If any shareholder leaves after the commencement of a meeting, this shall have no effect on the existence of a quorum, after a quorum has been established at such meeting.

Despite the absence of a quorum at any annual or special meeting of shareholders, the shareholders, by a majority of the votes cast by the holders of shares entitled to vote thereon, may adjourn the meeting. At any such adjourned meeting at which a quorum is present, any business may be transacted at the meeting as originally called as if a quorum had been present.

Section 7 - Voting: Except as otherwise provided by Statute or by the Articles of Incorporation, any corporate action, other than the election of directors, to be taken by vote of the shareholders, shall be authorized by a majority of votes cast at a meeting of shareholders by the holders of shares entitled to vote thereon.

Except as otherwise provided by Statute or by the Articles of Incorporation, at each meeting of shareholders, each holder of record of stock of the Corporation entitled to vote thereat, shall be entitled to one vote for each share of stock registered in his name on the stock transfer books of the corporation.

Each shareholder entitled to vote may do so by proxy; provided, however, that the instrument authorizing such proxy to act shall have been executed in writing by the shareholder himself. No proxy shall be valid after the expiration of eleven months from the date of its execution, unless the person executing it shall have specified therein, the length of time it is to continue in force. Such instrument shall be exhibited to the Secretary at the meeting and shall be filed with the records of the corporation.

Any resolution in writing, signed by all of the shareholders entitled to vote thereon, shall be and constitute action by such shareholders to the effect therein expressed, with the same force and effect as if the same had been duly passed by unanimous vote at a duly called meeting of shareholders and such resolution so signed shall be inserted in the Minute Book of the Corporation under its proper date.

ARTICLE III - BOARD OF DIRECTORS

Section 1 - Number, Election and Term of Office: The number of the directors of the Corporation shall be (____) This number may be increased or decreased by the amendment of these bylaws by the Board but shall in no case be less than ____ director(s). The members of the Board, who need not be shareholders, shall be elected by a majority of the votes cast at a meeting of shareholders entitled to vote in the election. Each director shall hold office until the annual meeting of the shareholders next succeeding his election, and until his successor is elected and qualified, or until his prior death, resignation or removal.

Section 2 - Vacancies: Any vacancy in the Board shall be filled for the unexpired portion of the term by a majority vote of the remaining directors, though less than a quorum, at any regular meeting or special meeting of the Board called for that purpose. Any such director so elected may be replaced by the shareholders at a regular or special meeting of shareholders.

Section 3 - Duties and Powers: The Board shall be responsible for the control and management of the affairs, property and interests of the Corporation, and may exercise all powers of the Corporation, except as limited by statute.

Section 4 - Annual Meetings: An annual meeting of the Board shall be held immediately following the annual meeting of the shareholders, at the place of such annual meeting of shareholders. The Board from time to time, may provide by resolution for the holding of other meetings of the Board, and may fix the time and place thereof.

Section 5 - Special Meetings: Special meetings of the Board shall be held whenever called by the President or by one of the directors, at such time and place as may be specified in the respective notice or waivers of notice thereof.

Section 6 - Notice and Waiver: Notice of any special meeting shall be given at least five days prior thereto by written notice delivered personally, by mail or by telegram to each Director at his address. If mailed, such notice shall be deemed to be delivered when deposited in the United States Mail with postage prepaid. If notice is given by telegram, such notice shall be deemed to be delivered when the telegram is delivered to the telegraph company.

Any Director may waive notice of any meeting, either before, at, or after such meeting, by signing a waiver of notice. The attendance of a Director at a meeting shall constitute a waiver of notice of such meeting and a waiver of any and all objections to the place of such meeting, or the manner in which it has been called or convened, except when a Director states at the beginning of the meeting any objection to the transaction of business because the meeting is not lawfully called or convened.

Section 7 - Chairman: The Board may, at its discretion, elect a Chairman. At all meetings of the Board, the Chairman of the Board, if any and if present, shall preside. If there is no Chairman, or he is absent, then the President shall preside, and in his absence, a Chairman chosen by the directors shall preside.

Section 8 - Quorum and Adjournments: At all meetings of the Board, the presence of a majority of the entire Board shall be necessary and sufficient to constitute a quorum for the transaction of business, except as otherwise provided by law, by the Articles of Incorporation, or by these bylaws. A majority of the directors present at the time and place of any regular or special meeting, although less than a quorum, may adjourn the same from time to time without notice, until a quorum shall be present.

Section 9 - Board Action: At all meetings of the Board, each director present shall have one vote, irrespective of the number of shares of stock, if any, which he may hold. Except as otherwise provided by Statute, the action of a majority of the directors present at any meeting at which a quorum is present shall be the act of the Board. Any action authorized, in writing, by all of the Directors entitled to vote thereon and filed with the minutes of the Corporation shall be the act of the Board with the same force and effect as if the same had been passed by unanimous vote at a duly called meeting of the Board. Any action taken by the Board may be taken without a meeting if agreed to in writing by all members before or after the action is taken and if a record of such action is filed in the minute book.

Section 10 - Telephone Meetings: Directors may participate in meetings of the Board through use of a telephone if such can be arranged so that all Board members can hear all other members. The use of a telephone for participation shall constitute presence in person.

Section 11 - Resignation and Removal: Any director may resign at any time by giving written notice to another Board member, the President or the Secretary of the Corporation. Unless otherwise specified in such written notice, such resignation shall take effect upon receipt thereof by the Board or by such officer, and the acceptance of such resignation shall not be necessary to make it effective. Any director may be removed with or without cause at any time by the affirmative vote of shareholders holding of record in the aggregate at least a majority of the outstanding shares of the Corporation at a special meeting of the shareholders called for that purpose, and may be removed for cause by action of the Board.

Section 12 - Compensation: No stated salary shall be paid to directors, as such for their services, but by resolution of the Board a fixed sum and/or expenses of attendance, if any, may be allowed for attendance at each regular or special meeting of the Board. Nothing herein contained shall be construed to preclude any director from serving the Corporation in any other capacity and receiving compensation therefor.

ARTICLE IV - OFFICERS

Section 1 - Number, Qualification, Election and Term: The officers of the Corporation shall consist of a President, a Secretary, a Treasurer, and such other officers, as the Board may from time to time deem advisable. Any officer may be, but is not required to be, a director of the Corporation. The officers of the Corporation shall be elected by the Board at the regular annual meeting of the Board. Each officer shall hold office until the annual meeting of the Board next succeeding his election, and until his successor shall have been elected and qualified, or until his death, resignation or removal.

Section 2 - Resignation and Removal: Any officer may resign at any time by giving written notice of such resignation to the President or the Secretary of the Corporation or to a member of the Board. Unless otherwise specified in such written notice, such resignation shall take effect upon receipt thereof by the Board member or by such officer, and the acceptance of such resignation shall not be necessary to make it effective. Any officer may be removed, either with or without cause, and a successor elected by a majority vote of the Board at any time.

Section 3 - Vacancies: A vacancy in any office may at any time be filled for the unexpired portion of the term by a majority vote of the Board.

Section 4 - Duties of Officers: Officers of the Corporation shall, unless otherwise provided by the Board, each have such powers and duties as generally pertain to their respective offices as well as such powers and duties as may from time to time be specifically decided by the Board. The President shall be the chief executive officer of the Corporation.

Section 5 - Compensation: The officers of the Corporation shall be entitled to such compensation as the Board shall from time to time determine.

Section 6 - Delegation of Duties: In the absence or disability of any Officer of the Corporation or for any other reason deemed sufficient by the Board of Directors, the Board may delegate his powers or duties to any other Officer or to any other Director.

Section 7 - Shares of Other Corporations: Whenever the Corporation is the holder of shares of any other Corporation, any right or power of the Corporation as such shareholder (including the attendance, acting and voting at shareholders' meetings and execution of waivers, consents, proxies or other instruments) may be exercised on behalf of the Corporation by the President, any Vice President, or such other person as the Board may authorize.

ARTICLE V - COMMITTEES

The Board of Directors may, by resolution, designate an Executive Committee and one or more other committees. Such committees shall have such functions and may exercise such power of the Board of Directors as can be lawfully delegated, and to the extent provided in the resolution or resolutions creating such committee or committees. Meetings of committees may be held without notice at such time and at such place as shall from time to time be determined by the committees. The committees of the corporation shall keep regular minutes of their proceedings, and report these minutes to the Board of Directors when required.

ARTICLE VI - BOOKS, RECORDS AND REPORTS

Section 1 - Annual Report: The Corporation shall send an annual report to the Members of the Corporation not later than _____ months after the close of each fiscal year of the Corporation. Such report shall include a balance sheet as of the close of the fiscal year of the Corporation and a revenue and disbursement statement for the year ending on such closing date. Such financial statements shall be prepared from and in accordance with the books of the Corporation, and in conformity with generally accepted accounting principles applied on a consistent basis.

Section 2 - Permanent Records: The corporation shall keep current and correct records of the accounts, minutes of the meetings and proceedings and membership records of the corporation. Such records shall be kept at the registered office or the principal place of business of the corporation. Any such records shall be in written form or in a form capable of being converted into written form.

Section 3 - Inspection of Corporate Records: Any person who is a Voting Member of the Corporation shall have the right at any reasonable time, and on written demand stating the purpose thereof, to examine and make copies from the relevant books and records of accounts, minutes, and records of the Corporation. Upon the written request of any Voting Member, the Corporation shall mail to such Member a copy of the most recent balance sheet and revenue and disbursement statement.

ARTICLE VII- SHARES OF STOCK

Section 1 - Certificates: Each shareholder of the corporation shall be entitled to have a certificate representing all shares which he or she owns. The form of such certificate shall be adopted by a majority vote of the Board of Directors and shall be signed by the President and Secretary of the Corporation and sealed with the seal of the corporation. No certificate representing shares shall be issued until the full amount of consideration therefore has been paid.

Section 2 - Stock Ledger: The corporation shall maintain a ledger of the stock records of the Corporation. Transfers of shares of the Corporation shall be made on the stock ledger of the Corporation only at the direction of the holder of record upon surrender of the outstanding certificate(s). The Corporation shall be entitled to treat the holder of record of any share or shares as the absolute owner thereof for all purposes and, accordingly, shall not be bound to recognize any legal, equitable or other claim to, or interest in, such share or shares on the part of any other person, whether or not it shall have express or other notice thereof, except as otherwise expressly provided by law.

ARTICLE VIII - DIVIDENDS

Upon approval by the Board of Directors the corporation may pay dividends on its shares in the form of cash, property or additional shares at any time that the corporation is solvent and if such dividends would not render the corporation insolvent.

ARTICLE IX - FISCAL YEAR

The fiscal year of the Corporation shall be the period selected by the Board of Directors as the tax year of the Corporation for federal income tax purposes.

ARTICLE X - CORPORATE SEAL

The Board of Directors may adopt, use and modify a corporate seal. Failure to affix the seal to corporate documents shall not affect the validity of such document.

ARTICLE XI - AMENDMENTS

The Articles of Incorporation may be amended by the Shareholders as provided by Nevada statutes. These Bylaws may be altered, amended, or replaced by the Board of Directors; provided, however, that any Bylaws or amendments thereto as adopted by the Board of Directors may be altered, amended, or repealed by vote of the Shareholders. Bylaws adopted by the Members may not be amended or repealed by the Board.

ARTICLE XII - INDEMNIFICATION

Any officer, director or employee of the Corporation shall be indemnified to the full extent allowed by the laws of the State of Nevada.

Certified to be the Bylaws of the corporation adopted by the Board of Directors on _____, _____.

_____
Secretary

BYLAWS OF

A NEVADA PROFESSIONAL ASSOCIATION

ARTICLE I - OFFICES

The principal office of the Corporation shall be located in the City of _____ and the State of Nevada. The Corporation may also maintain offices at such other places as the Board of Directors may, from time to time, determine.

ARTICLE II - PURPOSES

The business purpose of the Corporation shall be to engage in all aspects of the practice of _____ and its fields of specialization. The Corporation shall render professional services only through its legally authorized officers, agents and employees.

ARTICLE III - SHAREHOLDERS

Section 1 - Qualifications: Only persons who are duly licensed and in good standing in the profession by the State of Nevada may be shareholders of the Corporation. Neither the Corporation nor the shareholders may transfer any shares to persons who are not duly licensed. All share certificates of the corporation shall contain a notice that the transfer is restricted by the bylaws of the Corporation. If any shareholder shall become disqualified to practice the profession, he or she shall immediately make arrangements to transfer his or her shares to a qualified person or to the Corporation and shall no longer participate in the profits of the Corporation related to the profession.

Section 2 - Annual Meetings: The annual meeting of the shareholders of the Corporation shall be held each year on_____at _____m. at the principal office of the Corporation or at such other places as the Board may authorize, for the purpose of electing directors, and transacting such other business as may properly come before the meeting.

Section 3 - Special Meetings: Special meetings of the shareholders may be called at any time by the Board, the President, or by the holders of twenty-five percent (25%) of the shares then outstanding and entitled to vote.

Section 4 - Place of Meetings: All meetings of shareholders shall be held at the principal office of the Corporation, or at such other places as the Board shall designate in the notice of such meetings.

Section 5 - Notice of Meetings: Written or printed notice stating the place, day, and hour of the meeting and, in the case of a special meeting, the purpose of the meeting, shall be delivered personally or by mail not less than ten days, nor more than sixty days, before the date of the meeting. Notice shall be given to each Member of record entitled to vote at the meeting. If mailed, such notice shall be deemed to have been delivered when deposited in the United States Mail with postage paid and addressed to the Member at his address as it appears on the records of the Corporation.

Section 6 - Waiver of Notice: A written waiver of notice signed by a Member, whether before or after a meeting, shall be equivalent to the giving of such notice. Attendance of a Member at a meeting shall constitute a waiver of notice of such meeting, except when the Member attends for the express purpose of objecting, at the eginning of the meeting, to the transaction of any business because the meeting is not lawfully called or convened.

Section 7 - Quorum: Except as otherwise provided by Statute, or the by Articles of Incorporation, at all meetings of shareholders of the Corporation, the presence at the commencement of such meetings of shareholders of record holding a majority of the total number of shares of the Corporation then issued and outstanding and entitled to vote, but in no event less than one-third of the shares entitled to vote at the meeting, shall constitute a quorum for the transaction of any business. If any shareholder leaves after the commencement of a meeting, this shall have no effect on the existence of a quorum, after a quorum has been established at such meeting.

Despite the absence of a quorum at any annual or special meeting of shareholders, the shareholders, by a majority of the votes cast by the holders of shares entitled to vote thereon, may adjourn the meeting. At any such adjourned meeting at which a quorum is present, any business may be transacted at the meeting as originally called as if a quorum had been present.

Section 8 - Voting: Except as otherwise provided by Statute or by the Articles of Incorporation, any corporate action, other than the election of directors, to be taken by vote of the shareholders, shall be authorized by a majority of votes cast at a meeting of shareholders by the holders of shares entitled to vote thereon.

Except as otherwise provided by Statute or by the Articles of Incorporation, at each meeting of shareholders, each holder of record of stock of the Corporation entitled to vote thereat, shall be entitled to one vote for each share of stock registered in his name on the stock transfer books of the corporation.

Any resolution in writing, signed by all of the shareholders entitled to vote thereon, shall be and constitute action by such shareholders to the effect therein expressed, with the same force and effect as if the same had been duly passed by unanimous vote at a duly called meeting of shareholders and such resolution so signed shall be inserted in the Minute Book of the Corporation under its proper date.

Section 9 - Proxies: Shareholders may not at any time vote by proxy or enter into any voting trust or other agreement vesting another person with the voting power of his stock.

ARTICLE IV - BOARD OF DIRECTORS

Section 1 Qualifications: Only persons who are duly licensed and in good standing in the profession by the State of Nevada may be directors of the Corporation. If any director shall become disqualified from practicing the profession, he or she shall immediately resign his or her directorship and any other employment with the Corporation.

Section 2 - Number, Election and Term of Office: The number of the directors of the Corporation shall be (____) This number may be increased or decreased by the amendment of these bylaws by the Board but shall in no case be less than one director. The members of the Board, who need not be shareholders, shall be elected by a majority of the votes cast at a meeting of shareholders entitled to vote in the election. Each director shall hold office until the annual meeting of the shareholders next succeeding his election, and until his successor is elected and qualified, or until his prior death, resignation or removal.

Section 3 - Vacancies: Any vacancy in the Board shall be filled for the unexpired portion of the term by a majority vote of the remaining directors, though less than a quorum, at any regular meeting or special meeting of the Board called for that purpose. Any such director so elected may be replaced by the shareholders at a regular or special meeting of shareholders.

Section 4 - Duties and Powers: The Board shall be responsible for the control and management of the affairs, property and interests of the Corporation, and may exercise all powers of the Corporation, except as limited by statute.

Section 5 - Annual Meetings: An annual meeting of the Board shall be held immediately following the annual meeting of the shareholders, at the place of such annual meeting of shareholders. The Board, from time to time, may provide by resolution for the holding of other meetings of the Board, and may fix the time and place thereof.

Section 6 - Special Meetings: Special meetings of the Board shall be held whenever called by the President or by one of the directors, at such time and place as may be specified in the respective notice or waivers of notice thereof.

Section 7 - Notice and Waiver: Notice of any special meeting shall be given at least five days prior thereto by written notice delivered personally, by mail or by telegram to each director at his address. If mailed, such notice shall be deemed to be delivered when deposited in the United States Mail with postage prepaid. If notice is given by telegram, such notice shall be deemed to be delivered when the telegram is delivered to the telegraph company.

Any director may waive notice of any meeting, either before, at, or after such meeting, by signing a waiver of notice. The attendance of a director at a meeting shall constitute a waiver of notice of such meeting and a waiver of any and all objections to the place of such meeting, or the manner in which it has been called or convened, except when a director states at the beginning of the meeting any objection to the transaction of business because the meeting is not lawfully called or convened.

Section 8 - Chairman: The Board may, at its discretion, elect a Chairman. At all meetings of the Board, the Chairman of the Board, if any and if present, shall preside. If there is no Chairman, or he is absent, then the President shall preside, and in his absence, a Chairman chosen by the directors shall preside.

Section 9 - Quorum and Adjournments: At all meetings of the Board, the presence of a majority of the entire Board shall be necessary and sufficient to constitute a quorum for the transaction of business, except as otherwise provided by law, by the Articles of Incorporation, or by these bylaws. A majority of the directors present at the time and place of any regular or special meeting, although less than a quorum, may adjourn the same from time to time without notice, until a quorum shall be present.

Section 10 - Board Action: At all meetings of the Board, each director present shall have one vote, irrespective of the number of shares of stock, if any, which he may hold. Except as otherwise provided by Statute, the action of a majority of the directors present at any meeting at which a quorum is present shall be the act of the Board. Any action authorized, in writing, by all of the Directors entitled to vote thereon and filed with the minutes of the Corporation shall be the act of the Board with the same force and effect as if the same had been passed by unanimous vote at a duly called meeting of the Board. Any action taken by the Board may be taken without a meeting if agreed to in writing by all members before or after the action is taken and if a record of such action is filed in the Minute Book.

Section 11 - Telephone Meetings: Directors may participate in meetings of the Board through use of a telephone if such can be arranged so that all Board members can hear all other members. The use of a telephone for participation shall constitute presence in person.

Section 12 - Resignation and Removal: Any director may resign at any time by giving written notice to another Board member, the President or the Secretary of the Corporation. Unless otherwise specified in such written notice, such resignation shall take effect upon receipt thereof by the Board or by such officer, and the acceptance of such resignation shall not be necessary to make it effective. Any director may be removed with or without cause at any time by the affirmative vote of shareholders holding of record in the aggregate at least a majority of the outstanding shares of the Corporation at a special meeting of the shareholders called for that purpose, and may be removed for cause by action of the Board.

Section 13 - Compensation: No stated salary shall be paid to directors, as such for their services, but by resolution of the Board a fixed sum and/or expenses of attendance, if any, may be allowed for attendance at each regular or special meeting of the Board. Nothing herein contained shall be construed to preclude any director from serving the Corporation in any other capacity and receiving compensation therefor.

ARTICLE V - OFFICERS

Section 1 Qualifications: Only persons who are duly licensed and in good standing in the profession by the State of Nevada may be officers of the Corporation. If any director shall become disqualified from practicing the profession, he or she shall immediately resign his or her directorship and any other employment with the corporation.

Section 2 - Number, Election and Term: The officers of the Corporation shall consist of a President, a Secretary, a Treasurer, and such other officers, as the Board may from time to time deem advisable. Any officer may be, but is not required to be, a director of the Corporation. Any two or more offices may be held by the same person. The officers of the Corporation shall be elected by the Board at the regular annual meeting of the Board. Each officer shall hold office until the annual meeting of the Board next succeeding his election, and until his successor shall have been elected and qualified, or until his death, resignation or removal.

Section 3 - Resignation and Removal: Any officer may resign at any time by giving written notice of such resignation to the President or the Secretary of the Corporation or to a member of the Board. Unless otherwise specified in such written notice, such resignation shall take effect upon receipt thereof by the Board member or by such officer, and the acceptance of such resignation shall not be necessary to make it effective. Any officer may be removed, either with or without cause, and a successor elected by a majority vote of the Board at any time.

Section 4 - Vacancies: A vacancy in any office may at any time be filled for the unexpired portion of the term by a majority vote of the Board.

<u>Section 5 - Duties of Officers</u>: The officers of the Corporation shall, unless otherwise provided by the Board, each have such powers and duties as generally pertain to their respective offices as well as such powers and duties as may from time to time be specifically decided by the Board. The President shall be the chief executive officer of the Corporation.

<u>Section 6 - Compensation</u>: The officers of the Corporation shall be entitled to such compensation as the Board shall from time to time determine.

<u>Section 7 - Delegation of Duties</u>: In the absence or disability of any Officer of the Corporation or for any other reason deemed sufficient by the Board of Directors, the Board may delegate his powers or duties to any other Officer or to any other director.

<u>Section 8 - Shares of Other Corporations</u>: Whenever the Corporation is the holder of shares of any other Corporation, any right or power of the Corporation as such shareholder (including the attendance, acting and voting at shareholders' meetings and execution of waivers, consents, proxies or other instruments) may be exercised on behalf of the Corporation by the President, any Vice President, or such other person as the Board may authorize.

ARTICLE VI - COMMITTEES

The Board of Directors may, by resolution, designate an Executive Committee and one or more other committees. Such committees shall have such functions and may exercise such power of the Board of Directors as can be lawfully delegated, and to the extent provided in the resolution or resolutions creating such committee or committees. Meetings of committees may be held without notice at such time and at such place as shall from time to time be determined by the committees. The committees of the corporation shall keep regular minutes of their proceedings, and report these minutes to the Board of Directors when required.

ARTICLE VII - BOOKS, RECORDS AND REPORTS

<u>Section 1 - Annual Report</u>: The Corporation shall send an annual report to the Members of the Corporation not later than four months after the close of each fiscal year of the Corporation. Such report shall include a balance sheet as of the close of the fiscal year of the Corporation and a revenue and disbursement statement for the year ending on such closing date. Such financial statements shall be prepared from and in accordance with the books of the Corporation, and in conformity with generally accepted accounting principles applied on a consistent basis.

<u>Section 2 - Permanent Records</u>: The Corporation shall keep current and correct records of the accounts, minutes of the meetings and proceedings and membership records of the Corporation. Such records shall be kept at the registered office or the principal place of business of the Corporation. Any such records shall be in written form or in a form capable of being converted into written form.

<u>Section 3 - Inspection of Corporate Records</u>: Any person who is a Voting Member of the Corporation shall have the right at any reasonable time, and on written demand stating the purpose thereof, to examine and make copies from the relevant books and records of accounts, minutes, and records of the Corporation. Upon the written request of any Voting Member, the Corporation shall mail to such Member a copy of the most recent balance sheet and revenue and disbursement statement.

ARTICLE VIII- SHARES OF STOCK

<u>Section 1 - Authorized shares</u>: The Corporation shall be authorized to issue _____ shares of stock in one class only, each with a par value of $_____.

<u>Section 2 - Certificates</u>: Each shareholder of the Corporation shall be entitled to have a certificate representing all shares which he or she owns. The form of such certificate shall be adopted by a majority vote of the Board of Directors and shall be signed by the President and Secretary of the Corporation and sealed with the seal of the Corporation. No certificate representing shares shall be issued until the full amount of consideration therefore has been paid.

<u>Section 3 - Stock Ledger</u>: The Corporation shall maintain a ledger of the stock records of the Corporation. Transfers of shares of the Corporation shall be made on the stock ledger of the Corporation only at the direction of the holder of record upon surrender of the outstanding certificate(s). The Corporation shall be entitled to treat the holder of record of any share or shares as the absolute owner thereof for all purposes and, accordingly, shall not be bound to recognize any legal, equitable or other claim to, or interest in, such share or shares on the part of any other person, whether or not it shall have express or other notice thereof, except as otherwise expressly provided by law.

ARTICLE IX - DIVIDENDS

Upon approval by the Board of Directors the corporation may pay dividends on its shares in the form of cash, property or additional shares at any time that the Corporation is solvent and if such dividends would not render the Corporation insolvent.

ARTICLE X - FISCAL YEAR

The fiscal year of the Corporation shall be the period selected by the Board of Directors as the tax year of the Corporation for federal income tax purposes.

ARTICLE XI - CORPORATE SEAL

The Board of Directors may adopt, use and modify a corporate seal. Failure to affix the seal to corporate documents shall not affect the validity of such document.

ARTICLE XII - AMENDMENTS

The Articles of Incorporation may be amended by the shareholders as provided by Nevada statutes. These bylaws may be altered, amended, or replaced by the Board of Directors; provided, however, that any bylaws or amendments thereto as adopted by the Board of Directors may be altered, amended, or repealed by vote of the shareholders. Bylaws adopted by the Members may not be amended or repealed by the Board.

ARTICLE XIII - INDEMNIFICATION

Any officer, director or employee of the Corporation shall be indemnified to the full extent allowed by the laws of the State of Nevada.

Certified to be the bylaws of the corporation adopted by the Board of Directors on _____,
_____.

_____
Secretary

Instructions for Form 2553

(Revised September 1997)

**Department of the Treasury
Internal Revenue Service**

Election by a Small Business Corporation

Section references are to the Internal Revenue Code unless otherwise noted.

General Instructions

Purpose.— To elect to be an S corporation, a corporation must file Form 2553. The election permits the income of the S corporation to be taxed to the shareholders of the corporation rather than to the corporation itself, except as noted below under **Taxes an S Corporation May Owe.**

Who May Elect.— A corporation may elect to be an S corporation only if it meets all of the following tests:

1. It is a domestic corporation.

2. It has no more than 75 shareholders. A husband and wife (and their estates) are treated as one shareholder for this requirement. All other persons are treated as separate shareholders.

3. Its only shareholders are individuals, estates, certain trusts described in section 1361(c)(2)(A), or, for tax years beginning after 1997, exempt organizations described in section 401(a) or 501(c)(3). Trustees of trusts that want to make the election under section 1361(e)(3) to be an electing small business trust should see Notice 97-12, 1997-3 I.R.B. 11.

Note: *See the instructions for Part III regarding qualified subchapter S trusts.*

4. It has no nonresident alien shareholders.

5. It has only one class of stock (disregarding differences in voting rights). Generally, a corporation is treated as having only one class of stock if all outstanding shares of the corporation's stock confer identical rights to distribution and liquidation proceeds. See Regulations section 1.1361-1(1) for more details.

6. It is not one of the following ineligible corporations:

a. A bank or thrift institution that uses the reserve method of accounting for bad debts under section 585;

b. An insurance company subject to tax under the rules of subchapter L of the Code;

c. A corporation that has elected to be treated as a possessions corporation under section 936; or

d. A domestic international sales corporation (DISC) or former DISC.

7. It has a permitted tax year as required by section 1378 or makes a section 444 election to have a tax year other than a permitted tax year. Section 1378 defines a permitted tax year as a tax year ending December 31, or any other tax year for which the corporation establishes a business purpose to the satisfaction of the IRS. See Part II for details on requesting a fiscal tax year based on a business purpose or on making a section 444 election.

8. Each shareholder consents as explained in the instructions for column K.

See sections 1361, 1362, and 1378 for additional information on the above tests.

An election can be made by a parent S corporation to treat the assets, liabilities, and items of income, deduction, and credit of an eligible wholly-owned subsidiary as those of the parent. For details, see Notice 97-4, 1997-2 I.R.B. 24.

Taxes an S Corporation May Owe.— An S corporation may owe income tax in the following instances:

1. If, at the end of any tax year, the corporation had accumulated earnings and profits, and its passive investment income under section 1362(d)(3) is more than 25% of its gross receipts, the corporation may owe tax on its excess net passive income.

2. A corporation with net recognized built-in gain (as defined in section 1374(d)(2)) may owe tax on its built-in gains.

3. A corporation that claimed investment credit before its first year as an S corporation will be liable for any investment credit recapture tax.

4. A corporation that used the LIFO inventory method for the year immediately preceding its first year as an S corporation may owe an additional tax due to LIFO recapture.

For more details on these taxes, see the Instructions for Form 1120S.

Where To File.— File this election with the Internal Revenue Service Center listed below.

If the corporation's principal business, office, or agency is located in	Use the following Internal Revenue Service Center address
New Jersey, New York (New York City and counties of Nassau, Rockland, Suffolk, and Westchester)	Holtsville, NY 00501
New York (all other counties), Connecticut, Maine, Massachusetts, New Hampshire, Rhode Island, Vermont	Andover, MA 05501
Florida, Georgia, South Carolina	Atlanta, GA 39901
Indiana, Kentucky, Michigan, Ohio, West Virginia	Cincinnati, OH 45999
Kansas, New Mexico, Oklahoma, Texas	Austin, TX 73301
Alaska, Arizona, California (counties of Alpine, Amador, Butte, Calaveras, Colusa, Contra Costa, Del Norte, El Dorado, Glenn, Humboldt, Lake, Lassen, Marin, Mendocino, Modoc, Napa, Nevada, Placer, Plumas, Sacramento, San Joaquin, Shasta, Sierra, Siskiyou, Solano, Sonoma, Sutter, Tehama, Trinity, Yolo, and Yuba), Colorado, Idaho, Montana, Nebraska, Nevada, North Dakota, Oregon, South Dakota, Utah, Washington, Wyoming	Ogden, UT 84201
California (all other counties), Hawaii	Fresno, CA 93888
Illinois, Iowa, Minnesota, Missouri, Wisconsin	Kansas City, MO 64999
Alabama, Arkansas, Louisiana, Mississippi, North Carolina, Tennessee	Memphis, TN 37501
Delaware, District of Columbia, Maryland, Pennsylvania, Virginia	Philadelphia, PA 19255

When To Make the Election.— Complete and file Form 2553 **(a)** at any time before the 16th day of the 3rd month of the tax year, if filed during the tax year the election is to take effect, or **(b)** at any time during the preceding tax year. An election made no later than 2 months and 15 days after the beginning of a tax year that is less than 2½ months long is treated as timely made for that tax year. An election made after the 15th day of the 3rd month but before the end of the tax year is effective for the next year. For example, if a calendar tax year

corporation makes the election in April 1998, it is effective for the corporation's 1999 calendar tax year.

However, an election made after the due date will be accepted as timely filed if the corporation can show that the failure to file on time was due to reasonable cause. To request relief for a late election, the corporation generally must request a private letter ruling and pay a user fee in accordance with Rev. Proc. 97-1, 1997-1 I.R.B. 11 (or its successor). But if the election is filed within 6 months of its due date and the original due date for filing the corporation's initial Form 1120S has not passed, the ruling and user fee requirements do not apply. To request relief in this case, write "FILED PURSUANT TO REV. PROC. 97-40" at the top of page 1 of Form 2553, attach a statement explaining the reason for failing to file the election on time, and file Form 2553 as otherwise instructed. See Rev. Proc. 97-40, 1997-33 I.R.B. 50, for more details.

See Regulations section 1.1362-6(b)(3)(iii) for how to obtain relief for an inadvertent invalid election if the corporation filed a timely election, but one or more shareholders did not file a timely consent.

Acceptance or Nonacceptance of Election.— The service center will notify the corporation if its election is accepted and when it will take effect. The corporation will also be notified if its election is not accepted. The corporation should generally receive a determination on its election within 60 days after it has filed Form 2553. If box Q1 in Part II is checked on page 2, the corporation will receive a ruling letter from the IRS in Washington, DC, that either approves or denies the selected tax year. When box Q1 is checked, it will generally take an additional 90 days for the Form 2553 to be accepted.

Do not file Form 1120S for any tax year before the year the election takes effect. If the corporation is now required to file **Form 1120,** U.S. Corporation Income Tax Return, or any other applicable tax return, continue filing it until the election takes effect.

Care should be exercised to ensure that the IRS receives the election. If the corporation is not notified of acceptance or nonacceptance of its election within 3 months of date of filing (date mailed), or within 6 months if box Q1 is checked, take follow-up action by corresponding with the service center where the corporation filed the election. If the IRS questions whether Form 2553 was filed, an acceptable proof of filing is **(a)** certified or registered mail receipt (timely filed) from the U.S. Postal Service or its equivalent from a designated private delivery service (see Notice 97-26, 1997-17 I.R.B. 6); **(b)** Form 2553 with accepted stamp; **(c)** Form 2553 with stamped IRS received date; or **(d)** IRS letter stating that Form 2553 has been accepted.

End of Election.— Once the election is made, it stays in effect until it is terminated. If the election is terminated in a tax year beginning after 1996, the corporation (or a successor corporation) can make another election on Form 2553 only with IRS consent for any tax year before the 5th tax year after the first tax year in which the termination took effect. See Regulations section 1.1362-5 for more details.

Cat. No. 49978N

Specific Instructions

Part I

Note: *All corporations must complete Part I.*
Name and Address of Corporation.— Enter the true corporate name as stated in the corporate charter or other legal document creating it. If the corporation's mailing address is the same as someone else's, such as a shareholder's, enter "c/o" and this person's name following the name of the corporation. Include the suite, room, or other unit number after the street address. If the Post Office does not deliver to the street address and the corporation has a P.O. box, show the box number instead of the street address. If the corporation changed its name or address after applying for its employer identification number, be sure to check the box in item G of Part I.

Item A. Employer Identification Number (EIN).— If the corporation has applied for an EIN but has not received it, enter "applied for." If the corporation does not have an EIN, it should apply for one on **Form SS-4,** Application for Employer Identification Number. You can order Form SS-4 by calling 1-800-TAX-FORM (1-800-829-3676).

Item D. Effective Date of Election.— Enter the beginning effective date (month, day, year) of the tax year requested for the S corporation. Generally, this will be the beginning date of the tax year for which the beginning effective date is required to be shown in item I, Part I. For a new corporation (first year the corporation exists) it will generally be the date required to be shown in item H, Part I. The tax year of a new corporation starts on the date that it has shareholders, acquires assets, or begins doing business, whichever happens first. If the effective date for item D for a newly formed corporation is later than the date in item H, the corporation should file Form 1120 or Form 1120-A for the tax period between these dates.

Column K. Shareholders' Consent Statement.— Each shareholder who owns (or is deemed to own) stock at the time the election is made must consent to the election. If the election is made during the corporation's tax year for which it first takes effect, any person who held stock at any time during the part of that year that occurs before the election is made, must consent to the election, even though the person may have sold or transferred his or her stock before the election is made.

An election made during the first 2½ months of the tax year is effective for the following tax year if any person who held stock in the corporation during the part of the tax year before the election was made, and who did not hold stock at the time the election was made, did not consent to the election.

Each shareholder consents by signing and dating in column K or signing and dating a separate consent statement described below. The following special rules apply in determining who must sign the consent statement.

• If a husband and wife have a community interest in the stock or in the income from it, both must consent.

• Each tenant in common, joint tenant, and tenant by the entirety must consent.

• A minor's consent is made by the minor, legal representative of the minor, or a natural or adoptive parent of the minor if no legal representative has been appointed.

• The consent of an estate is made by the executor or administrator.

• The consent of an electing small business trust is made by the trustee.

• If the stock is owned by a trust (other than an electing small business trust), the deemed owner of the trust must consent. See section 1361(c)(2) for details regarding trusts that are permitted to be shareholders and rules for determining who is the deemed owner.

*Continuation sheet or separate consent statement.—*If you need a continuation sheet or use a separate consent statement, attach it to Form 2553. The separate consent statement must contain the name, address, and EIN of the corporation and the shareholder information requested in columns J through N of Part I. If you want, you may combine all the shareholders' consents in one statement.

Column L.— Enter the number of shares of stock each shareholder owns and the dates the stock was acquired. If the election is made during the corporation's tax year for which it first takes effect, do not list the shares of stock for those shareholders who sold or transferred all of their stock before the election was made. However, these shareholders must still consent to the election for it to be effective for the tax year.

Column M.— Enter the social security number of each shareholder who is an individual. Enter the EIN of each shareholder that is an estate, a qualified trust, or an exempt organization.

Column N.— Enter the month and day that each shareholder's tax year ends. If a shareholder is changing his or her tax year, enter the tax year the shareholder is changing to, and attach an explanation indicating the present tax year and the basis for the change (e.g., automatic revenue procedure or letter ruling request).

Signature.— Form 2553 must be signed by the president, treasurer, assistant treasurer, chief accounting officer, or other corporate officer (such as tax officer) authorized to sign.

Part II

Complete Part II if you selected a tax year ending on any date other than December 31 (other than a 52-53-week tax year ending with reference to the month of December).

Box P1.— Attach a statement showing separately for each month the amount of gross receipts for the most recent 47 months as required by section 4.03(3) of Rev. Proc. 87-32, 1987-2 C.B. 396. A corporation that does not have a 47-month period of gross receipts cannot establish a natural business year under section 4.01(1).

Box Q1.— For examples of an acceptable business purpose for requesting a fiscal tax year, see Rev. Rul. 87-57, 1987-2 C.B. 117.

In addition to a statement showing the business purpose for the requested fiscal year, you must attach the other information necessary to meet the ruling request requirements of Rev. Proc. 97-1 (or its successor). Also attach a statement that shows separately the amount of gross receipts from sales or services (and inventory costs, if applicable) for each of the 36 months preceding the effective date of the election to be an S corporation. If the corporation has been in existence for fewer than 36 months, submit figures for the period of existence.

If you check box Q1, you will be charged a $250 user fee (subject to change). Do not pay the fee when filing Form 2553. The service center will send Form 2553 to the IRS in

Washington, DC, who, in turn, will notify the corporation that the fee is due.

Box Q2.— If the corporation makes a back-up section 444 election for which it is qualified, then the election will take effect in the event the business purpose request is not approved. In some cases, the tax year requested under the back-up section 444 election may be different than the tax year requested under business purpose. See **Form 8716,** Election To Have a Tax Year Other Than a Required Tax Year, for details on making a back-up section 444 election.

Boxes Q2 and R2.— If the corporation is not qualified to make the section 444 election after making the item Q2 back-up section 444 election or indicating its intention to make the election in item R1, and therefore it later files a calendar year return, it should write "Section 444 Election Not Made" in the top left corner of the first calendar year Form 1120S it files.

Part III

Certain qualified subchapter S trusts (QSSTs) may make the QSST election required by section 1361(d)(2) in Part III. Part III may be used to make the QSST election only if corporate stock has been transferred to the trust on or before the date on which the corporation makes its election to be an S corporation. However, a statement can be used instead of Part III to make the election.

Note: *Use Part III* **only** *if you make the election in Part I (i.e., Form 2553 cannot be filed with only Part III completed).*

The deemed owner of the QSST must also consent to the S corporation election in column K, page 1, of Form 2553. See section 1361 (c)(2).

Paperwork Reduction Act Notice.— We ask for the information on this form to carry out the Internal Revenue laws of the United States. You are required to give us the information. We need it to ensure that you are complying with these laws and to allow us to figure and collect the right amount of tax.

You are not required to provide the information requested on a form that is subject to the Paperwork Reduction Act unless the form displays a valid OMB control number. Books or records relating to a form or its instructions must be retained as long as their contents may become material in the administration of any Internal Revenue law. Generally, tax returns and return information are confidential, as required by section 6103.

The time needed to complete and file this form will depend on individual circumstances. The estimated average time is:

Recordkeeping	6 hr., 28 min.
Learning about the law or the form	3 hr., 41 min.
Preparing, copying, assembling, and sending the form to the IRS	3 hr., 56 min.

If you have comments concerning the accuracy of these time estimates or suggestions for making this form simpler, we would be happy to hear from you. You can write to the Tax Forms Committee, Western Area Distribution Center, Rancho Cordova, CA 95743-0001. **DO NOT** send the form to this address. Instead, see **Where To File** on page 1.

Printed on recycled paper

*U.S. Government Printing Office: 1997 - 432-190/60241

Form **2553**

(Rev. September 1997)

Department of the Treasury
Internal Revenue Service

Election by a Small Business Corporation

(Under section 1362 of the Internal Revenue Code)

▶ For Paperwork Reduction Act Notice, see page 2 of instructions.

▶ See separate instructions.

OMB No. 1545-0146

Notes:

1. This election to be an S corporation can be accepted only if all the tests are met under **Who May Elect** on page 1 of the instructions; all signatures in Parts I and III are originals (no photocopies); and the exact name and address of the corporation and other required form information are provided.

2. Do not file **Form 1120S**, U.S. Income Tax Return for an S Corporation, for any tax year before the year the election takes effect.

3. If the corporation was in existence before the effective date of this election, see **Taxes an S Corporation May Owe** on page 1 of the instructions.

Part I	**Election Information**		
Please Type or Print	Name of corporation (see instructions)	**A** Employer identification number	
	Number, street, and room or suite no. (If a P.O. box, see instructions.)	**B** Date incorporated	
	City or town, state, and ZIP code	**C** State of incorporation	

D Election is to be effective for tax year beginning (month, day, year) . . . . ▶ / /

E Name and title of officer or legal representative who the IRS may call for more information

F Telephone number of officer or legal representative
( )

G If the corporation changed its name or address after applying for the EIN shown in **A** above, check this box . . . . ▶ ☐

H If this election takes effect for the first tax year the corporation exists, enter month, day, and year of the **earliest** of the following: (1) date the corporation first had shareholders, (2) date the corporation first had assets, or (3) date the corporation began doing business . . . . ▶ / /

I Selected tax year: Annual return will be filed for tax year ending (month and day) ▶..

If the tax year ends on any date other than December 31, except for an automatic 52-53-week tax year ending with reference to the month of December, you **must** complete Part II on the back. If the date you enter is the ending date of an automatic 52-53-week tax year, write "52-53-week year" to the right of the date. See Temporary Regulations section 1.441-2T(e)(3).

J Name and address of each shareholder; shareholder's spouse having a community property interest in the corporation's stock; and each tenant in common, joint tenant, and tenant by the entirety. (A husband and wife (and their estates) are counted as one shareholder in determining the number of shareholders without regard to the manner in which the stock is owned.)	K Shareholders' Consent Statement. Under penalties of perjury, we declare that we consent to the election of the above-named corporation to be an S corporation under section 1362(a) and that we have examined this consent statement, including accompanying schedules and statements, and to the best of our knowledge and belief, it is true, correct, and complete. We understand our consent is binding and may not be withdrawn after the corporation has made a valid election. (Shareholders sign and date below.)		L Stock owned		M Social security number or employer identification number (see instructions)	N Share-holder's tax year ends (month and day)
	Signature	Date	Number of shares	Dates acquired		

Under penalties of perjury, I declare that I have examined this election, including accompanying schedules and statements, and to the best of my knowledge and belief, it is true, correct, and complete.

Signature of officer ▶   Title ▶   Date ▶

See Parts II and III on back.   Cat. No. 18629R   Form **2553** (Rev. 9-97)

187

Part II   **Selection of Fiscal Tax Year** (All corporations using this part must complete item O and item P, Q, or R.)

O   Check the applicable box to indicate whether the corporation is:

    1. ☐ A new corporation adopting the tax year entered in item I, Part I.

    2. ☐ An existing corporation retaining the tax year entered in item I, Part I.

    3. ☐ An existing corporation changing to the tax year entered in item I, Part I.

P   Complete item P if the corporation is using the expeditious approval provisions of Rev. Proc. 87-32, 1987-2 C.B. 396, to request **(1)** a natural business year (as defined in section 4.01(1) of Rev. Proc. 87-32) or **(2)** a year that satisfies the ownership tax year test in section 4.01(2) of Rev. Proc. 87-32. Check the applicable box below to indicate the representation statement the corporation is making as required under section 4 of Rev. Proc. 87-32.

    1. Natural Business Year ▶ ☐ I represent that the corporation is retaining or changing to a tax year that coincides with its natural business year as defined in section 4.01(1) of Rev. Proc. 87-32 and as verified by its satisfaction of the requirements of section 4.02(1) of Rev. Proc. 87-32. In addition, if the corporation is changing to a natural business year as defined in section 4.01(1), I further represent that such tax year results in less deferral of income to the owners than the corporation's present tax year. I also represent that the corporation is not described in section 3.01(2) of Rev. Proc. 87-32. (See instructions for additional information that must be attached.)

    2. Ownership Tax Year ▶ ☐ I represent that shareholders holding more than half of the shares of the stock (as of the first day of the tax year to which the request relates) of the corporation have the same tax year or are concurrently changing to the tax year that the corporation adopts, retains, or changes to per item I, Part I. I also represent that the corporation is not described in section 3.01(2) of Rev. Proc. 87-32.

Note: If you do not use item P and the corporation wants a fiscal tax year, complete either item Q or R below. Item Q is used to request a fiscal tax year based on a business purpose and to make a back-up section 444 election. Item R is used to make a regular section 444 election.

Q   Business Purpose—To request a fiscal tax year based on a business purpose, you must check box Q1 and pay a user fee. See instructions for details. You may also check box Q2 and/or box Q3.

    1. Check here ▶ ☐ if the fiscal year entered in item I, Part I, is requested under the provisions of section 6.03 of Rev. Proc. 87-32. Attach to Form 2553 a statement showing the business purpose for the requested fiscal year. See instructions for additional information that must be attached.

    2. Check here ▶ ☐ to show that the corporation intends to make a back-up section 444 election in the event the corporation's business purpose request is not approved by the IRS. (See instructions for more information.)

    3. Check here ▶ ☐ to show that the corporation agrees to adopt or change to a tax year ending December 31 if necessary for the IRS to accept this election for S corporation status in the event (1) the corporation's business purpose request is not approved and the corporation makes a back-up section 444 election, but is ultimately not qualified to make a section 444 election, or (2) the corporation's business purpose request is not approved and the corporation did not make a back-up section 444 election.

R   Section 444 Election—To make a section 444 election, you must check box R1 and you may also check box R2.

    1. Check here ▶ ☐ to show the corporation will make, if qualified, a section 444 election to have the fiscal tax year shown in item I, Part I. To make the election, you must complete **Form 8716,** Election To Have a Tax Year Other Than a Required Tax Year, and either attach it to Form 2553 or file it separately.

    2. Check here ▶ ☐ to show that the corporation agrees to adopt or change to a tax year ending December 31 if necessary for the IRS to accept this election for S corporation status in the event the corporation is ultimately not qualified to make a section 444 election.

Part III   **Qualified Subchapter S Trust (QSST) Election Under Section 1361(d)(2)***

Income beneficiary's name and address	Social security number
Trust's name and address	Employer identification number

Date on which stock of the corporation was transferred to the trust (month, day, year) . . . . ▶   /   /

In order for the trust named above to be a QSST and thus a qualifying shareholder of the S corporation for which this Form 2553 is filed, I hereby make the election under section 1361(d)(2). Under penalties of perjury, I certify that the trust meets the definitional requirements of section 1361(d)(3) and that all other information provided in Part III is true, correct, and complete.

_____   _____
Signature of income beneficiary or signature and title of legal representative or other qualified person making the election   Date

*Use Part III to make the QSST election only if stock of the corporation has been transferred to the trust on or before the date on which the corporation makes its election to be an S corporation. The QSST election must be made and filed separately if stock of the corporation is transferred to the trust after the date on which the corporation makes the S election.

✿ **Printed on recycled paper**   *U.S. Government Printing Office: 1997 - 432-190/60239

188

WAIVER OF NOTICE

OF THE ORGANIZATIONAL MEETING

OF

_____

We, the undersigned incorporators named in the certificate of incorporation of the above-named corporation hereby agree and consent that the organization meeting of the corporation be held on the date and time and place stated below and hereby waive all notice of such meeting and of any adjournment thereof.

Place of meeting: _____

Date of Meeting: _____

Time of meeting: _____

Dated: _____

_____
Incorporator

_____
Incorporator

_____
Incorporator

Minutes of the Organizational Metting of

Incorporators and Directors of

_____

The organization meeting of the above corporation was held on
_____, _____ at _____
_____ at _____ o'clock ___m.

The following persons were present:

_____   _____

_____   _____

_____   _____

The Waiver of Notice of this meeting was signed by all directors and incorporators named in the Articles of Incorporation and filed in the minute book.

The meeting was called to order by _____ an Incorporator named in the Articles of Incorporation. _____ was nominated and elected Chairman and acted as such until relieved by the president. _____ was nominated and elected temporary secretary, and acted as such until relieved by the permanent secretary.

A copy of the Articles of Incorporation which was filed with the Secretary of State of the State of _____ on _____, _____ was examined by the Directors and Incorporators and filed in the minute book.

The election of officers for the coming year was then held and the following were duly nominated and elected by the Board of Directors to be the officers of the corporation, to serve until such time as their successors are elected and qualified:

President: _____
Vice President: _____
Secretary: _____
Treasurer: _____

The proposed Bylaws for the corporation were then presented to the meeting and discussed. Upon motion duly made, seconded and carried, the Bylaws were adopted and added to the minute book.

A corporate seal for the corporation was then presented to the meeting and upon motion duly made, seconded and carried, it was adopted as the seal of the corporation. An impression thereof was then made in the margin of these minutes

The necessity of opening a bank account was then discussed and upon motion duly made, seconded and carried, the following resolution was adopted:

RESOLVED that the corporation open bank accounts with _____ _____ and that the officers of the corporation are authorized to take such action as is necessary to open such accounts; that the bank's printed form of resolution is hereby adopted and incorporated into these minutes by reference and shall be placed in the minute book; that any ____ of the following persons shall have signature authority over the account:

_____   _____
_____   _____
_____

Proposed stock certificates and stock transfer ledger were then presented to the meeting and examined. Upon motion duly made, seconded and carried the stock certificates and ledger were adopted as the certificates and transfer book to be used by the corporation. A sample stock certificate marked "VOID" and the stock transfer ledger were then added to the minute book. Upon motion duly made, seconded and carried, it was then resolved that the stock certificates, when issued, would be signed by the President and the Secretary of the corporation.

The tax status of the corporation was then discussed and it was moved, seconded and carried that the stock of the corporation be issued under § 1244 of the Internal Revenue Code and that the officers of the corporation take the necessary action to:

1.   Obtain an employer tax number by filing form SS-4,

2.   ☐   Become an S-Corporation for tax purposes,
        ☐   Remain a C-Corporation for tax purposes,

The expenses of organizing the corporation were then discussed and it was moved, seconded and carried that the corporation pay in full from the corporate funds the expenses and reimburse any advances made by the incorporators upon proof of payment.

The Directors named in the Articles of Incorporation then tendered their resignations, effective upon the adjournment of this meeting. Upon motion duly made, seconded and carried, the following named persons were elected as Directors of the corporation, each to hold office until the first annual meeting of shareholders, and until a successor of each shall have been elected and qualified.

_____

_____

_____

There were presented to the corporation, the following offer(s) to purchase shares of capital stock:

FROM	NO. OF SHARES	CONSIDERATION

The offers were discussed and after motion duly made, seconded and carried were approved. It was further resolved that the Board of Directors has determined that the consideration was valued at least equal to the value of the shares to be issued and that upon tender of the consideration, fully paid non-assessable shares of the corporation be issued.

There being no further business before the meeting, on motion duly made, seconded and carried, the meeting adjourned.

DATED: _____

_____

President

_____

Secretary

Offer to Purchase Stock

Date: _____

To the Board of Directors of

_____

    The undersigned, hereby offers to purchase _____ shares of the _____ stock of your corporation at a total purchase price of _____.

Very truly yours,

_____

- -

Offer to Sell Stock
Pursuant to Sec. 1244 I.R.C.

Date: _____

To: _____

Dear

    The corporation hereby offers to sell to you _____ shares of its common stock at a price of \$_____ per share. These shares are issued pursuant to Section 1244 of the Internal Revenue Code,

    Your signature below shall constitute an acceptance of our offer as of the date it is received by the corporation.

Very truly yours,

_____

By:_____

Accepted:

_____

RESOLUTION
of

_____

a Nevada Corporation

     RESOLVED that the corporation elects "S-Corporation" status for tax purposes under the Internal Revenue Code and that the officers of the corporation are directed to file IRS Form 2553 and to take any further action necessary for the corporation to qualify for S-corporation status.

Shareholders' Consent

The undersigned shareholders being all of the shareholders of the above corporation, a Nevada corporation hereby consent to the election of the corporation to obtain S-corporation status

Name and Address of Shareholder	Shares Owned	Date Acquired
_____	_____	_____
_____	_____	_____
_____	_____	_____

Date:_____

_____

_____

_____

_____

_____

Stock Ledger

Certificates Issued   *Transfer of Shares*

Cert. No.	No. of Shares	Date of Acquisition	Shareholder Name and Address	From Whom Transferred	Amount Paid	Date of Transfer	To Whom Transferred	Cert. No. Surrendered	No. of Shares Transferred	Cert. No.

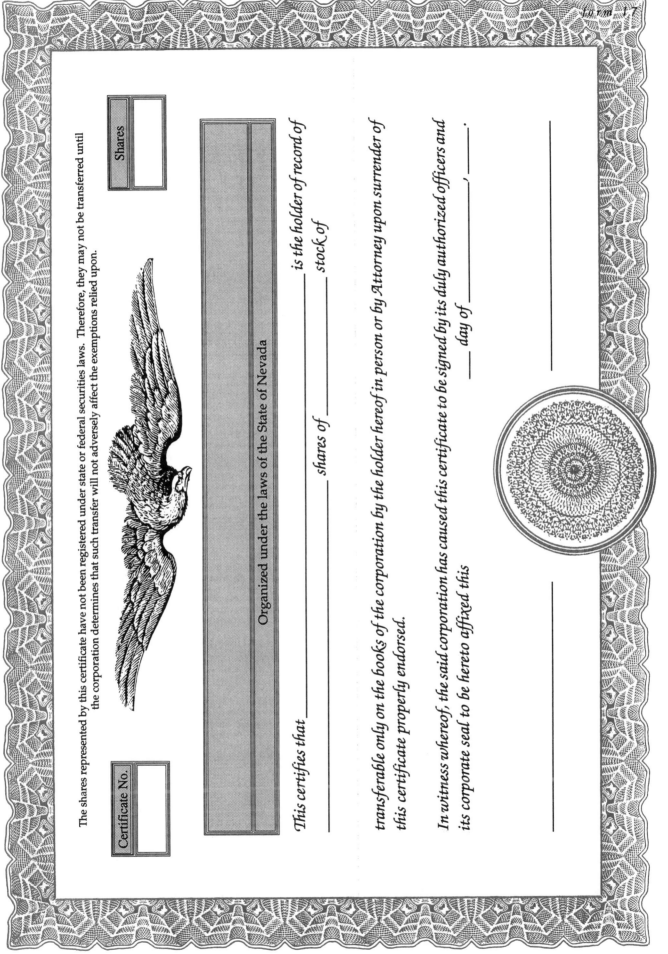

The shares represented by this certificate have not been registered under state or federal securities laws. Therefore, they may not be transferred until the corporation determines that such transfer will not adversely affect the exemptions relied upon.

Shares

Certificate No.

Organized under the laws of the State of Nevada

This certifies that

is the holder of record of

_____ shares of _____ stock of

transferable only on the books of the corporation by the holder hereof in person or by Attorney upon surrender of this certificate properly endorsed.

In witness whereof, the said corporation has caused this certificate to be signed by its duly authorized officers and its corporate seal to be hereto affixed this _____ day of _____, _____.

For value received, _____ hereby sell, assign and transfer unto _____

_____ ,

_____

_____ shares represented by this certificate and do hereby irrevocably constitute and appoint

_____ attorney to transfer the said shares on

the books of the corporation with full power of substitution in the premises.

Dated _____

_____

Witness:

_____

The shares represented by this certificate have not been registered under state or federal securities laws. Therefore, they may not be transferred until the corporation determines that such transfer will not adversely affect the exemptions relied upon.

Certificate No.

Shares

Organized under the laws of the State of Nevada

This certifies that _____ is the holder of record of

_____ shares of _____ stock of

transferable only on the books of the corporation by the holder hereof in person or by Attorney upon surrender of this certificate properly endorsed.

In witness whereof, the said corporation has caused this certificate to be signed by its duly authorized officers and its corporate seal to be hereto affixed this _____ day of _____, _____.

_____

203

For value received, _____ hereby sell, assign and transfer unto _____

_____,

_____

_____ *shares represented by this certificate and do hereby irrevocably constitute and appoint* _____ *attorney to transfer the said shares on* *the books of the corporation with full power of substitution in the premises.*

Dated _____

_____

Witness:

_____

Certificate No.

Shares

The shares represented by this certificate have not been registered under state or federal securities laws. Therefore, they may not be transferred until the corporation determines that such transfer will not adversely affect the exemptions relied upon.

Organized under the laws of the State of Nevada

This certifies that _____ is the holder of record of

_____ shares of _____ stock of

transferable only on the books of the corporation by the holder hereof in person or by Attorney upon surrender of this certificate properly endorsed.

In witness whereof, the said corporation has caused this certificate to be signed by its duly authorized officers and its corporate seal to be hereto affixed this _____ day of _____, _____.

_____   _____

For value received, _____ *hereby sell, assign and transfer unto* _____

_____,

_____

_____ *shares represented by this certificate and do hereby irrevocably constitute and appoint*

_____ *attorney to transfer the said shares on*

the books of the corporation with full power of substitution in the premises.

Dated _____

_____

Witness:

_____

The shares represented by this certificate have not been registered under state or federal securities laws. Therefore, they may not be transferred until the corporation determines that such transfer will not adversely affect the exemptions relied upon.

Shares

Certificate No.

Organized under the laws of the State of Nevada

This certifies that _____

is the holder of record of

_____ shares of _____ stock of

transferable only on the books of the corporation by the holder hereof in person or by Attorney upon surrender of this certificate properly endorsed.

In witness whereof, the said corporation has caused this certificate to be signed by its duly authorized officers and its corporate seal to be hereto affixed this _____ day of _____, _____.

_____

_____

For value received, _____ hereby sell, assign and transfer unto _____

_____,

_____

_____ *shares represented by this certificate and do hereby irrevocably constitute and appoint*

_____ *attorney to transfer the said shares on*

the books of the corporation with full power of substitution in the premises.

Dated _____

_____

Witness:

_____

The shares represented by this certificate have not been registered under state or federal securities laws. Therefore, they may not be transferred until the corporation determines that such transfer will not adversely affect the exemptions relied upon.

Certificate No.

Shares

Organized under the laws of the State of Nevada

This certifies that _____ is the holder of record of

_____ shares of _____ stock of

transferable only on the books of the corporation by the holder hereof in person or by Attorney upon surrender of this certificate properly endorsed.

In witness whereof, the said corporation has caused this certificate to be signed by its duly authorized officers and its corporate seal to be hereto affixed this _____ day of _____, _____.

For value received, _____ hereby sell, assign and transfer unto _____

_____ ,

_____

_____ *shares represented by this certificate and do hereby irrevocably constitute and appoint*

_____ *attorney to transfer the said shares on*

the books of the corporation with full power of substitution in the premises.

Dated _____

_____

Witness:

_____

WAIVER OF NOTICE OF THE ANNUAL MEETING OF THE BOARD OF DIRECTORS OF

_____

The undersigned, being all the Directors of the Corporation, hereby agree and consent that an annual meeting of the Board of Directors of the Corporation be held on the _____ day of _____, _____ at ____ o'clock ___m at _____ _____ and do hereby waive all notice whatsoever of such meeting and of any adjournment or adjournments thereof.

We do further agree and consent that any and all lawful business may be transacted at such meeting or at any adjournment or adjournments thereof as may be deemed advisable by the Directors present. Any business transacted at such meeting or at any adjournment or adjournments thereof shall be as valid and legal as if such meeting or adjourned meeting were held after notice.

Date: _____

_____
Director

_____
Director

_____
Director

_____
Director

Minutes of the Annual Meeting of the Board of Directors of

_____

The annual meeting of the Board of Directors of the Corporation was held on the date and at the time and place set forth in the written waiver of notice signed by the directors, and attached to the minutes of this meeting.

The following were present, being all the directors of the Corporation:

_____   _____

_____   _____

The meeting was called to order and it was moved, seconded and unanimously carried that _____ act as Chairman and that _____ act as Secretary.

The minutes of the last meeting of the Board of Directors which was held on _____, _____ were read and approved by the Board.

Upon motion duly made, seconded and carried, the following were elected officers for the following year and until their successors are elected and qualify:

President:
Vice President:
Secretary
Treasurer:

There being no further business to come before the meeting, upon motion duly made, seconded and unanimously carried, it was adjourned.

_____
Secretary

Directors:

_____

_____

_____

_____

Waiver of Notice of the Annual Meeting of the Shareholders of

_____

The undersigned, being all the shareholders of the Corporation, hereby agree and consent that an annual meeting of the shareholders of the Corporation be held on the ____ day of _____, _____ at ____ o'clock ___m at _____ _____ and do hereby waive all notice whatsoever of such meeting and of any adjournment or adjournments thereof.

We do further agree and consent that any and all lawful business may be transacted at such meeting or at any adjournment or adjournments thereof. Any business transacted at such meeting or at any adjournment or adjournments thereof shall be as valid and legal as if such meeting or adjourned meeting were held after notice.

Date: _____

_____
Shareholder

_____
Shareholder

_____
Shareholder

_____
Shareholder

MINUTES OF THE ANNUAL MEETING OF
SHAREHOLDERS OF

_____

    The annual meeting of Shareholders of the Corporation was held on the date and at the time and place set forth in the written waiver of notice signed by the shareholders, and attached to the minutes of this meeting.

    There were present the following shareholders:

<u>Shareholder</u>   <u>No. of Shares</u>

_____   _____

_____   _____

_____   _____

_____   _____

    The meeting was called to order and it was moved, seconded and unanimously carried that _____ act as Chairman and that _____ act as Secretary.

    A roll call was taken and the Chairman noted that all of the outstanding shares of the Corporation were represented in person or by proxy. Any proxies were attached to these minutes.

    The minutes of the last meeting of the shareholders which was held on _____, _____ were read and approved by the shareholders.

    Upon motion duly made, seconded and carried, the following were elected directors for the following year:

_____   _____

_____   _____

    There being no further business to come before the meeting, upon motion duly made, seconded and unanimously carried, it was adjourned.

                               _____
                               Secretary

Shareholders:

_____

_____

_____

_____

Waiver of Notice of Special Meeting of the Board of Directors of

_____

The undersigned, being all the Directors of the Corporation, hereby agree and consent that a special meeting of the Board of Directors of the Corporation be held on the _____ day of _____, _____ at ____ o'clock __m at _____ _____ and do hereby waive all notice whatsoever of such meeting and of any adjournment or adjournments thereof.

The purpose of the meeting is:

We do further agree and consent that any and all lawful business may be transacted at such meeting or at any adjournment or adjournments thereof as may be deemed advisable by the Directors present. Any business transacted at such meeting or at any adjournment or adjournments thereof shall be as valid and legal as if such meeting or adjourned meeting were held after notice.

Date: _____

_____
Director

_____
Director

_____
Director

_____
Director

MINUTES OF SPECIAL MEETING OF THE BOARD OF DIRECTORS OF

_____

A special meeting of the Board of Directors of the Corporation was held on the date and at the time and place set forth in the written waiver of notice signed by the directors, and attached to the minutes of this meeting.

The following were present, being all the directors of the Corporation:

_____   _____

_____   _____

The meeting was called to order and it was moved, seconded and unanimously carried that _____ act as Chairman and that _____ act as Secretary.

The minutes of the last meeting of the Board of Directors which was held on _____, _____ were read and approved by the Board.

Upon motion duly made, seconded and carried, the following resolution was adopted:

There being no further business to come before the meeting, upon motion duly made, seconded and unanimously carried, it was adjourned.

_____
Secretary

Directors:

_____

_____

_____

_____

WAIVER OF NOTICE OF SPECIAL MEETING OF
THE SHAREHOLDERS OF

_____

The undersigned, being all the shareholders of the Corporation, hereby agree and consent that a special meeting of the shareholders of the Corporation be held on the ____ day of _____, _____ at ___ o'clock __m at _____ _____ and do hereby waive all notice whatsoever of such meeting and of any adjournment or adjournments thereof.

The purpose of the meeting is

We do further agree and consent that any and all lawful business may be transacted at such meeting or at any adjournment or adjournments thereof. Any business transacted at such meeting or at any adjournment or adjournments thereof shall be as valid and legal as if such meeting or adjourned meeting were held after notice.

Date: _____

_____
Shareholder

_____
Shareholder

_____
Shareholder

_____
Shareholder

MINUTES OF SPECIAL MEETING OF
SHAREHOLDERS OF

_____

A special meeting of Shareholders of the Corporation was held on the date and at the time and place set forth in the written waiver of notice signed by the shareholders, and attached to the minutes of this meeting.

There were present the following shareholders:

Shareholder   No. of Shares

_____   _____

_____   _____

_____   _____

_____   _____

The meeting was called to order and it was moved, seconded and unanimously carried that _____ act as Chairman and that _____ act as Secretary.

A roll call was taken and the Chairman noted that all of the outstanding shares of the Corporation were represented in person or by proxy. Any proxies were attached to these minutes.

The minutes of the last meeting of the shareholders which was held on _____, _____ were read and approved by the shareholders.

Upon motion duly made, seconded and carried, the following resolution was adopted:

There being no further business to come before the meeting, upon motion duly made, seconded and unanimously carried, it was adjourned.

_____
Secretary

Shareholders:

_____

_____

_____

_____

DEAN HELLER
Secretary of State

101 North Carson Street, Suite 3
Carson City, Nevada 89701-4786
(775) 684 5708

| **Limited Liability Company** **Articles of Organization** (PURSUANT TO NRS 86) | Office Use Only: |

Important: Read attached instructions before completing form.

1. **Name of Limited Liability Company:**	
2. **Resident Agent Name and Street Address:** *(must be a Nevada address where process may be served)*	Name _____ _____, **NEVADA** _____ Street Address City Zip Code
3. **Dissolution Date:** *(OPTIONAL--See Instructions)*	Latest date upon which the company is to dissolve (if existence is not perpetual): _____
4. **Management:** *(Check one)*	Company shall be managed by _____ Manager(s) **OR** _____ Members
Names Addresses, of Manager(s) or Members: *(Attach additional pages as necessary)*	Name _____ Name _____ Street Address _____ Street Address _____ City, State, Zip _____ City, State, Zip _____
5. **Other Matters:** *(See instructions)*	Number of additional pages attached: _____
6. **Names, Addresses and Signatures of Organizer(s):** *(Signatures must be notarized)* Attach additional pages if there are more than 2 organizers.	Name _____ Name _____ Street Address _____ Street Address _____ City, State, Zip _____ City, State, Zip _____ Signature _____ Signature _____
Notary:	This instrument was acknowledged before me on This instrument was acknowledged before me on _____,_____by _____,_____by Name of person Name of person As organizer As organizer of _____ of _____ (Name of party on behalf of whom instrument executed) (Name of party on behalf of whom instrument executed) Notary Public Signature Notary Public Signature (affix notary stamp or seal) (affix notary stamp or seal)
7. **Certificate of Acceptance of Appointment of Resident Agent:**	I, _____hereby accept appointment as Resident Agent for the above named limited liability company. Signature of Resident Agent Date

This form must be accompanied by appropriate fees. See attached fee schedule.

Nevada Secretary of State Form CORPART1999.01
Revised on: 02/16/99

DEAN HELLER
Secretary of State

101 North Carson Street, Suite 3
Carson City, Nevada 89701-4786
(775) 684 5708

Instructions for Limited Liability Company Articles of Organization
(PURSUANT TO NRS 86)

IMPORTANT: READ ALL INSTRUCTIONS CAREFULLY BEFORE COMPLETING FORM.

1.   *Name of the Limited-Liability Company.* The name must contain the words Limited-Liability Company, Limited Company or Limited or the abbreviations L.L.C., LLC or LC . The word "company" may also be abbreviated. The name must be distinguishable from the name of a limited-liability company, limited partnership, limited liability partnership, or corporation already on file in this office. A name may be reserved, if available, for 90 days by submitting a written request with a $20.00 filing fee to the office of the Secretary of State. For details you may call (775) 684-5708 or write to the Secretary of State, 101 North Carson Street, Suite 3, Carson City, NV, 89701-4786.

2.   *Resident Agent.* Persons wishing to file articles of organization in the State of Nevada must designate a person as a resident agent who resides or is located in this state. Every resident agent must have a street address in the state of Nevada for the service of process, and may have a separate mailing address such as a post office box, which may be different from the street address

3.   *Dissolution Date.* State the latest date upon which the company is to dissolve. This provision is optional.

4.   Limited-liability companies may be managed by one or more manager(s) or one or more members. Please state whether the company is managed by members or managers. If the company is to be managed by one or more managers, the name and post office or street address, either resident or business, of each manager must be set forth. If the company is to be managed by the members, the name and post office or street address, either residence or business, of each member must be set forth.

5.   On a separate 8 ½" x 11" sheet, state any other provisions which the members elect to set out in the articles of organization for the regulation of the internal affairs of the company, including any provisions which under NRS Chapter 86 are required or permitted to be set out in the operating agreement of the company.

6.   One or more persons may organize a limited-liability company. Indicate the names and addresses of the organizers executing the articles. Remember that organizer's signatures must be acknowledged.

7.   Resident agent must complete and sign certificate of acceptance at bottom of form or attach a separate signed certificate of acceptance.

IMPORTANT

COPIES: Pursuant to NRS 86.561 you *must* send in the number of copies you would like certified and returned to you in addition to the original articles to be filed. A filing fee of $10.00 for each certification is required. NRS 86.241 requires that a corporation have at least one certified copy to be kept in the office of the resident agent. The Secretary of State keeps the original filing.

FILING FEE: $125.00 Filing is required. Filing may be expedited for an additional $50.00 expedite fee.

Filing may be submitted at the office of the Secretary of State or by mail at the following addresses:

Secretary of State	Secretary of State-Satellite Office
New Filings Division	Commercial Recordings Division
101 N. Carson Street, Suite 3	555 E. Washington Avenue, 2nd Floor
Carson City, NV 89701-4786	Las Vegas, NV 89101
775-684-5708 Fax 775-684-5725	702-486-2880 Fax 702-486-2888

Nevada Secretary of State Form LLCINST1999.01
Revised on: 02/16/99

Form **8832**
(December 1996)

Department of the Treasury
Internal Revenue Service

Entity Classification Election

OMB No. 1545-1516

Please Type or Print	Name of entity	Employer identification number (EIN)
	Number, street, and room or suite no. If a P.O. box, see instructions	
	City or town, state, and ZIP code. If a foreign address, enter city, province or state, postal code and country.	

1 **Type of election** (see instructions):

a ☐ Initial classification by a newly-formed entity (or change in current classification of an existing entity to take effect on January 1, 1997)

b ☐ Change in current classification (to take effect later than January 1, 1997)

2 **Form of an entity** (see instructions):

a ☐ A domestic eligible entity electing to ne classified as an association taxable as a corporation.

b ☐ A domestic eligible entity electing to be classified as a partnership.

c ☐ A domestic eligible entity with a single owner electing to be disregarded as a separate entity.

d ☐ A foreign eligible entity electing to be classified as an association taxable as a corporation.

e ☐ A foreign eligible entity electing to be classified as a partnership.

f ☐ A foreign eligible entity with a single owner electing to be disregarded as a separate entity.

3 Election is to be effective beginning (month, day, year) (see instructions) . . . . ▶ _____ / ___ / ___

4 Name and title of person whom the IRS may call for more information	**5** That person's telephone number

Consent Statement and Signature(s) (see instructions)

Under penalties of perjury, I (we) declare that I (we) consent to the election of the above-named entity to be classified as indicated above, and that I (we) have examined this consent statement, and to the best of my (our) knowledge and belief, it is true, correct and complete. If I an an officer, manager, or member signing for all members of the entity, I further declare that I am authorized to execute this consent statement on their behalf.

Signature(s)	Date	Title

For Paperwork Reduction Act Notice, see page 2.   Cat. No. 22598R   Form **8832** (12-96)

General Instructions

Section references are to the Internal Revenue Code unless otherwise noted.

Paperwork Reduction Act Notice

We ask for the information on this form to carry out the Internal Revenue laws of the United States. You are required to give us the information. We need it to ensure that you are complying with these laws and to allow us to figure and collect the right amount of tax.

You are not required to provide the information requested on a form that is subject to the Paperwork Reduction Act unless the form or its instructions must be retained as long as their contents may become material in the administration of any Internal Revenue law. Generally, tax returns and return information are confidential, as required by section 6103.

The time needed to complete and file this form will vary depending on individual circumstances. The estimated average time is:

Recordkeeping . . .1 hr., 20 min.

Learning about the law or the form . . .1 hr., 41 min.

Preparing or sending the form to the IRS. . . .17 min.

If you have comments concerning the accuracy of these time estimated or suggestions for making this form simpler, we would be happy to hear from you. You can write to the Tax Forms Committee, Western Area Distribution Center, Rancho Cordova, Ca 95743-001. **DO NOT** send the form to this address. Instead, see **Where To File** on page 3.

Purpose of Form

For Federal tax purposes, certain business entities automatically are classified as corporations. See items **1** and **3** through **8** under the definition of corporation on this page. Other business entities may choose how they are classified for Federal tax purposes. Except for a business entity automatically classified as a corporation, a business entity with at least two members can choose to be classified as either an association taxable as a corporation or a partnership, and a business entity with a single member can choose to be classified as either an association taxable as a corporation or disregarded as an entity separate from its owner.

Generally, an eligible entity that does not file this form will be classified under the default rules described below. An eligible entity that chooses not to be classified under the default rules or that wishes to change its current classification must file Form 8832 to elect a classification, The IRS will use the information entered on this form to establish the entity's filing and reporting requirements for Federal tax purposes.

Default Rules

Existing entity default rule.—

Certain domestic and foreign entities that are already in existence before January 1, 1997, and have an established Federal tax classification, generally do not need to make an election to continue that classification. However, for an eligible entity with a single owner that claimed to be a partnership under the law in effect before January 1, 1997, that entity will now be disregarded as an entity separate from its owner. If an existing entity decides to change its classification, it may do so subject to the rules in Regulations section 301.7701-3(c)(1)(iv). A foreign eligible entity is treated as being in existence prior to the effective date of this section only if the entity's classification is relevant at any time during the 60 months prior to January 1, 1997.

Domestic default rule.—Unless an election is made on Form 8832 a domestic eligible entity is:

1. A partnership if it has two or more members.

2. Disregarded as an entity separate from its owner if it has a single owner.

Foreign default rule.—Unless an election is made on Form 8832, a foreign eligible entity is:

1. A partnership if it has two or more members and at least one member does not have limited liability.

2. An association if all members have limited liability.

3. Disregarded as an entity separate from its owner if it has a single owner that does not have limited liability.

Definitions

Business entity.—A business entity is any entity recognized for Federal tax purposes that is not properly classified as a trust under Regulations section 301.7701-4 or otherwise subject to special treatment under the Code. See Regulations section 301.7701-2(a).

Corporation.—For Federal tax purposes, a corporation is any of the following:

1. A business entity organized under a Federal or state statute, or under a statute of a federally recognized Indian tribe, if the statute describes or refers to the entity as incorporated or as a corporation, body corporate, or body politic.

2. An association (as determined under regulations section 301.7701-3).

3. A business entity organized under a state statute, if the statute describes or refers to the entity as a joint-stock company or joint-stock association.

4. An insurance company.

5. A state-chartered business entity conducting banking activities, if any of its deposits are insured under the Federal Deposit Insurance Act, as amended, 12 U.S.C. 1811 et seq., or a similar Federal statute.

6. A business entity wholly owned by a state or any political subdivision thereof.

7. A business entity that is taxable as a corporation under a provision of the Code other than section 7701(a)(3).

8. A foreign business entity listed in Regulations section 301.7701-2(b)(8). However, a foreign business entity listed in those regulations generally will not be treated as a corporation if all of the following apply:

a. The entity was in existence on May 8, 1996.

b. The entity's classification was relevant (as defined below) on May 8, 1996.

c. No person (including the entity) for who the entity's classification was relevant on May 8, 1996, treats the entity as a corporation for purposes of filing that person's Federal income tax returns, information returns, and withholding documents for the tax year including May 8, 1996.

d. Any change in the entity's claimed classification within the 60 months prior to May 8, 1996, was a result of a change in the organizational documents of the entity, and the entity recognized the Federal tax consequences of any change in the entity's classification within the 60 months prior to May 8, 1996.

e. The entity had reasonable basis (within the meaning of section 6662) for treating the entity as other than a corporation on May 8, 1996.

f, Neither the entity nor any member was notified in writing on or before May 8, 1996, that the classification of the entity was under examination (in which case the entity's classification will be determined in the examination).

Binding contract rule.—If a foreign business entity described in Regulations section 301.7701-2(b)(8)(i) is formed after May 8, 1996, under a written binding contract (including an accepted bid to develop a project) in effect on May 8, 1996, and all times thereafter, in which the parties agreed to engage (directly or indirectly) in an active and substantial business operation in the jurisdiction in which the entity is formed, **8** on page 2 is applied by substituting the date of the entity's formation for May 8, 1996.

Eligible entity.—An eligible entity is a business entity that is not included in items **1** or **3** through **8** under the definition of corporation on page 2.

Limited liability.—A member of a foreign eligible has limited liability if the member has no personal liability for any debts of or claims against the entity by reason of being a member. This determination is based solely on the statute or law under which the entity is organized (and, if relevant, the entity's organizational documents). A member has personal liability if the creditors of the entity may seek satisfaction of all or any part of the debts or claims against the entity from the member as such. A member has personal liability even if the member makes an agreement under which another person (whether or not a member of the entity) assumes that liability or agrees to indemnify that member for that liability.

Partnership.—A partnership is a business entity that has at least two members and is not a corporation as defined on page 2.

Relevant.—A foreign eligible entity's classification is relevant when its classification affects the liability of any person for Federal tax or information purposes. The date the classification of a foreign eligible entity is relevant is the date an event occurs that creates an obligation to file a Federal tax return, information return or statement for which the classification of the entity must be determined.

Effect of Election

The resulting tax consequences of a change in classification remain the same no matter how a change in entity classification is achieved. For example, if an organization classified as an association elects to be classified as a partnership, the organization and its owners must recognize gain, if any, under the rules applicable to liquidations of corporations.

Who Must File

File this form for an eligible entity that is one of the following:

● A domestic entity electing to be classified as an association taxable as a corporation.

● A domestic entity electing to change its current classification (even if it is currently classified under the default rule).

● A foreign entity that has more than one owner, all owners have limited liability, and it elects to be classified as a partnership.

● A foreign entity that has at least one owner without limited liability, and it elects to be classified as an association taxable as a corporation.

● A foreign entity with a single owner having limited liability, and it elects to have the entity disregarded as an entity separate from its owner.

● A foreign entity electing to change its current classification (even if it is currently classified under the default rule).

Do not file this form for an eligible entity that is:

● Tax exempt under section 501(a), or

● A real estate investment trust (REIT), as defined in section 856.

When To File

See the instructions for line 3.

Where to File

File Form 8832 with the Internal Revenue Service Center, Philadelphia, PA 19255. Also attach a copy of Form 8832 to the entity's Federal income tax or information return for the tax year of the election. If the entity is not required to file a return for that year, a copy of its Form 8832 must be attached to the Federal income tax or information returns of all direct or indirect owners of the entity for the tax year of the owner that includes the date on which the election took effect. Although failure to attach a copy will not invalidate an other wise valid election, each member of the entity is required to file returns that are consistent with the entity's election. In addition, penalties may be assessed against persons who are required to, but who do not, attach Form 8832 to their returns. Other penalties may apply for filing Federal income tax or information returns inconsistent with the entity's election.

LIMITED LIABILITY COMPANY
MEMBER-MANAGED OPERATING AGREEMENT OF

_____

THIS AGREEMENT is made effective as of _____, _____ among the member(s) and the company.

1. Formation. A limited liability company of the above name has been formed under the laws of the state of Nevada by filing articles of organization with the secretary of state. The purpose of the business shall be to carry on any act or activity lawful under the jurisdiction in which it operates. The company may operate under a fictitious name or names as long as the company is in compliance with applicable fictitious name registration laws. The term of the company shall be perpetual or until dissolved as provided by law or by vote of the member(s) as provided in this agreement. Upon dissolution the remaining members shall have the power to continue the operation of the company as long as necessary and allowable under state law until the winding up of the affairs of the business has been completed

2. Members. The initial member(s) shall be listed on Schedule A, which shall accompany and be made a part of this agreement. Additional members may be admitted to membership upon the unanimous consent of the current members. Transfer or pledge of a member's interest may not be made except upon consent of all members.

3. Contributions. The initial capital contribution(s) shall be listed on Schedule A, which shall accompany and be made a part of this agreement. No member shall be obligated to contribute any more than the amount set forth on Schedule A unless agreed to in writing by all of the members and no member shall have any personal liability for any debt, obligation or liability of the company other than for full payment of his or her capital contribution. No member shall be entitled to interest on the capital contribution. Member voting rights shall be in proportion to the amount of their contributions.

4. Profit and Loss. The profits and losses of the business, and all other taxable or deductible items shall be allocated to the members according to the percentages on Schedule A, which shall accompany and be made a part of this agreement.

5. Distributions. The company shall have the power to make distributions to its members in such amounts and at such intervals as a majority of the members deem appropriate according to law.

6. Management. The limited liability company shall be managed by its members listed on schedule A. In the event of a dispute between members, final determination shall be made with a vote by the members, votes being proportioned according to capital contributions.

7. Registered Agent. The company shall at all times have a registered agent and registered office. The initial registered agent and registered office shall be listed on Schedule A, which shall accompany and be made a part of this agreement.

8. Assets. The assets of the company shall be registered in the legal name of the company and not in the names of the individual members.

9. Records and Accounting. The company shall keep an accurate accounting of its affairs using any method of accounting allowed by law. All members shall have a right to inspect the records during normal business hours. The members shall have the power to hire such accountants as they deem necessary or desirable.

10. Banking. The members of the company shall be authorized to set up bank accounts as in their sole discretion are deemed necessary and are authorized to execute any banking resolutions provided by the institution in which the accounts are being set up.

11. Taxes. The company shall file such tax returns as required by law. The company shall elect to be taxed as a majority of the members decide is in their best interests. The "tax matters partner," as required by the Internal Revenue Code, shall be listed on Schedule A, which shall accompany and be made a part of this agreement.

12. Separate Entity. The company is a legal entity separate from its members. No member shall have any separate liability for any debts, obligations or liability of the company except as provided in this agreement.

13. Indemnity and Exculpation. The limited liability company shall indemnify and hold harmless its members, managers, employees and agents to the fullest extent allowed by law for acts or omissions done as part of their duties to or for the company. Indemnification shall include all liabilities, expenses, attorney and accountant fees, and other costs reasonably expended. No member shall be liable to the company for acts done in good faith.

14. Meetings. The members shall have no obligation to hold annual or any other meeting, but may hold such meetings if they deem them necessary or desirable.

15. Amendment of this Agreement. This agreement may not be amended except in writing signed by all of the members.

16. Conflict of interest. No member shall be involved with any business or undertaking which competes with the interests of the company except upon agreement in writing by all of the members.

17. Deadlock. In the event that the members cannot come to an agreement on any matter the members agree to submit the issue to mediation to be paid for by the company. In the event the mediation is unsuccessful, they agree to seek arbitration under the rules of the American Arbitration Association.

18. Dissociation of a member. A member shall have the right to discontinue membership upon giving thirty days notice. A member shall cease to have the right to membership upon death, court-ordered incapacity, bankruptcy or expulsion. The company shall have the right to buy the interest of any dissociated member at fair market value.

19. Dissolution. The company shall dissolve upon the unanimous consent of all the members or upon any event requiring dissolution under state law. In the event of the death, bankruptcy, permanent incapacity, or withdrawal of a member the remaining members may elect to dissolve or to continue the continuation of the company.

20. General Provisions. This agreement is intended to represent the entire agreement between the parties. In the event that any party of this agreement is held to be contrary to law or unenforceable, said party shall be considered amended to comply with the law and such holding shall not affect the enforceability of other terms of this agreement. This agreement shall be binding upon the heirs, successors and assigns of the members.

21. Miscellaneous. _____
_____
_____
_____
_____
_____
_____

IN WITNESS whereof, the members of the limited liability company sign this agreement and adopt it as their operating agreement this _____ day of _____, _____.

_____   _____

_____   _____

_____   _____

LIMITED LIABILITY COMPANY
MANAGEMENT AGREEMENT OF

_____

THIS AGREEMENT is made effective as of _____, _____ among the member(s) and the company.

1. Formation. A limited liability company of the above name has been formed under the laws of the state of Nevada by filing articles of organization with the secretary of state. The purpose of the business shall be to carry on any act or activity lawful under the jurisdiction in which it operates. The company may operate under a fictitious name or names as long as the company is in compliance with applicable fictitious name registration laws. The term of the company shall be perpetual or until dissolved as provided by law or by vote of the member(s) as provided in this agreement. Upon dissolution the remaining members shall have the power to continue the operation of the company as long as necessary and allowable under state law until the winding up of the affairs of the business has been completed.

2. Members. The initial member(s) shall be listed on Schedule A, which shall accompany and be made a part of this agreement. Additional members may be admitted to membership upon the unanimous consent of the current members. Transfer or pledge of a member's interest may not be made except upon consent of all members.

3. Contributions. The initial capital contribution(s) shall be listed on Schedule A, which shall accompany and be made a part of this agreement. No member shall be obligated to contribute any more than the amount set forth on Schedule A unless agreed to in writing by all of the members. No member shall have any personal liability for any debt, obligation or liability of the company other than for full payment of his or her capital contribution. No member shall be entitled to interest on the capital contribution. Member voting rights shall be in proportion to the amount of their contributions.

4. Profit and Loss. The profits and losses of the business, and all other taxable or deductible items shall be allocated to the members according to the percentages on Schedule A, which shall accompany and be made a part of this agreement.

5. Distributions. The company shall have the power to make distributions to its members in such amounts and at such intervals as a majority of the members deem appropriate according to law.

6. Management. The limited liability company shall be managed by the managers listed on schedule A, which shall accompany and be made a part of this agreement. These managers may or may not be members of the company and each manager shall have an equal vote with other managers as to management decisions. managers shall serve until resignation or death or until they are removed by a majority vote of the members. Replacement managers shall be selected by a majority vote of the members. managers shall have no personal liability for expenses, obligations or liabilities of the company.

7. Registered Agent. The company shall at all times have a registered agent and registered office. The initial registered agent and registered office shall be listed on Schedule A, which shall accompany and be made a part of this agreement.

8. Assets. The assets of the company shall be registered in the legal name of the company and not in the names of the individual members.

9. Records and Accounting. The company shall keep an accurate accounting of its affairs using any method of accounting allowed by law. All members shall have a right to inspect the records during normal business hours. The members shall have the power to hire such accountants as they deem necessary or desirable.

10. Banking. The members of the company shall be authorized to set up bank accounts as in their sole discretion are deemed necessary and are authorized to execute any banking resolutions provided by the institution in which the accounts are being set up.

11. Taxes. The company shall file such tax returns as required by law. The company shall elect to be taxed as a majority of the members decide is in their best interests. The "tax matters partner," as required by the Internal Revenue Code, shall be listed on Schedule A, which shall accompany and be made a part of this agreement.

12. Separate Entity. The company is a legal entity separate from its members. No member shall have any separate liability for any debts, obligations or liability of the company except as provided in this agreement.

13. Indemnity and Exculpation. The limited liability company shall indemnify and hold harmless its members, managers, employees and agents to the fullest extent allowed by law for acts or omissions done as part of their duties to or for the company. Indemnification shall include all liabilities, expenses, attorney and accountant fees, and other costs reasonably expended. No member shall be liable to the company for acts done in good faith.

14. Meetings. The members shall have no obligation to hold annual or any other meeting, but may hold such meetings if they deem them necessary or desirable.

15. Amendment of this Agreement. This agreement may not be amended except in writing signed by all of the members.

16. Conflict of interest. No member shall be involved with any business or undertaking which competes with the interests of the company except upon agreement in writing by all of the members.

17. Deadlock. In the event that the members cannot come to an agreement on any matter the members agree to submit the issue to mediation to be paid for by the company. In the event the mediation is unsuccessful, they agree to seek arbitration under the rules of the American Arbitration Association.

18. Dissociation of a member. A member shall have the right to discontinue membership upon giving thirty days notice. A member shall cease to have the right to membership upon death, court-ordered incapacity, bankruptcy or expulsion. The company shall have the right to buy the interest of any dissociated member at fair market value.

19. Dissolution. The company shall dissolve upon the unanimous consent of all the members or upon any event requiring dissolution under state law. In the event of the death, bankruptcy, permanent incapacity, or withdrawal of a member the remaining members may elect to dissolve or to continue the continuation of the company.

20. General Provisions. This agreement is intended to represent the entire agreement between the parties. In the event that any party of this agreement is held to be contrary to law or unenforceable, said party shall be considered amended to comply with the law and such holding shall not affect the enforceability of other terms of this agreement. This agreement shall be binding upon the heirs, successors and assigns of the members.

21. Miscellaneous. _____
_____
_____
_____
_____
_____
_____

IN WITNESS whereof, the members of the limited liability company sign this agreement and adopt it as their operating agreement this _____ day of _____, _____.

_____   _____

_____   _____

_____   _____

Schedule A to
Limited Liability Company
Operating or Management Agreement of

_____

1. Initial Member(s): The initial member(s) are:

2. Capital Contribution(s): The capital contribution(s) of the member(s) is/are:

3. Profits and Losses: The profits, losses and other tax matters shall be allocated among the members in the following percentages:

4. Management: The company shall be managed by:

5. Registered Agent: the initial registered agent and registered office of the company are:

6. Tax Matters: The tax matters partner is:

MINUTES OF A MEETING OF MEMBERS OF

_____

A meeting of the members of the company was held on _____, at
_____.

The following were present, being all the members of the limited liability company:

_____   _____

_____   _____

_____   _____

The meeting was called to order and it was moved, seconded and unanimously carried that
_____ act as Chairman and that _____ act
as Secretary.

After discussion and upon motion duly made, seconded and carried the following resolution(s)
were adopted:

There being no further business to come before the meeting, upon motion duly made,
seconded and unanimously carried, it was adjourned.

_____
Secretary

Members:

_____

_____

_____

_____

CERTIFICATE OF AUTHORITY

FOR

_____

This is to certify that the above limited liability company is managed by its

□ members

□ managers

who are listed below and that each of them is authorized and empowered to transact business on behalf of the company.

Name   Address

_____   _____

_____

_____   _____

_____

_____   _____

_____

_____   _____

_____

Date: _____

Name of company:

_____

By: _____

Position: _____

INDEX

Your #1 Source for Real World Legal Information...

SPHINX® PUBLISHING

A Division of Sourcebooks, Inc.®

- Written by lawyers
- Simple English explanation of the law
- Forms and instructions included

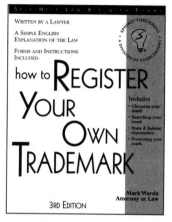

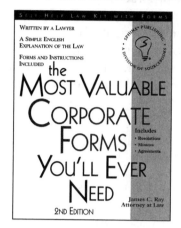

HOW TO REGISTER YOUR OWN TRADEMARK, 3RD ED.

The names of your company's products and your logos can be among your most valuable assets. This book explains how to protect them by registering them in the U.S. Patent and Trademark Office. Includes all the forms needed for registering all types of marks.

192 pages; $19.95;
ISBN 1-57248-104-8

THE MOST VALUABLE CORPORATE FORMS YOU'LL EVER NEED, 2ND ED.

Running a corporation requires many forms, and smaller organizations cannot afford to have an attorney on retainer for every occasion. This book provides over 100 forms for all types of corporate situations.

220 pages; $24.95;
ISBN 1-57071-346-4

THE MOST VALUABLE BUSINESS LEGAL FORMS YOU'LL EVER NEED, 2ND ED.

Using the right legal forms can add to your profits and help you avoid legal problems. This book provides businesses with the many and varied legal forms they will need. They are so simple and standard, you will wonder why anyone would pay a lawyer to fill them out!

140 pages; $19.95;
ISBN 1-57071-345-6

See the following order form for books written specifically for California, Florida, Georgia, Illinois, Massachusetts, Michigan, Minnesota, New York, North Carolina, Pennsylvania, and Texas! *Coming soon—Ohio and New Jersey!*

What our customers say about our books:

"It couldn't be more clear for the lay person." —R.D.

"I want you to know I really appreciate your book. It has saved me a lot of time and money." —L.T.

"Your real estate contracts book has saved me nearly $12,000.00 in closing costs over the past year." —A.B.

"...many of the legal questions that I have had over the years were answered clearly and concisely through your plain English interpretation of the law." —C.E.H.

"If there weren't people out there like you I'd be lost. You have the best books of this type out there." —S.B.

"...your forms and directions are easy to follow." —C.V.M.

Sphinx Publishing's Legal Survival Guides
are directly available from the Sourcebooks, Inc., or from your local bookstores.
For credit card orders call 1–800–43–BRIGHT, write P.O. Box 4410, Naperville, IL 60567-4410,
or fax 630-961-2168

SPHINX® PUBLISHING'S NATIONAL TITLES
Valid in All 50 States

LEGAL SURVIVAL IN BUSINESS

How to Form a Limited Liability Company	$19.95
How to Form Your Own Corporation (2E)	$19.95
How to Form Your Own Partnership	$19.95
How to Register Your Own Copyright (2E)	$19.95
How to Register Your Own Trademark (3E)	$19.95
Most Valuable Business Legal Forms You'll Ever Need (2E)	$19.95
Most Valuable Corporate Forms You'll Ever Need (2E)	$24.95
Software Law (with diskette)	$29.95

LEGAL SURVIVAL IN COURT

Crime Victim's Guide to Justice	$19.95
Debtors' Rights (3E)	$12.95
Defend Yourself against Criminal Charges	$19.95
Grandparents' Rights (2E)	$19.95
Help Your Lawyer Win Your Case (2E)	$12.95
Jurors' Rights (2E)	$9.95
Legal Malpractice and Other Claims against Your Lawyer	$18.95
Legal Research Made Easy (2E)	$14.95
Simple Ways to Protect Yourself from Lawsuits	$24.95
Victims' Rights	$12.95
Winning Your Personal Injury Claim	$19.95

LEGAL SURVIVAL IN REAL ESTATE

How to Buy a Condominium or Townhome	$16.95
How to Negotiate Real Estate Contracts (3E)	$16.95
How to Negotiate Real Estate Leases (3E)	$16.95
Successful Real Estate Brokerage Management	$19.95

LEGAL SURVIVAL IN PERSONAL AFFAIRS

Your Right to Child Custody, Visitation and Support	$19.95
The Nanny and Domestic Help Legal Kit	$19.95
How to File Your Own Bankruptcy (4E)	$19.95
How to File Your Own Divorce (3E)	$19.95
How to Make Your Own Will	$12.95
How to Write Your Own Living Will	$9.95
How to Write Your Own Premarital Agreement (2E)	$19.95
How to Win Your Unemployment Compensation Claim	$19.95
Living Trusts and Simple Ways to Avoid Probate (2E)	$19.95
Neighbor v. Neighbor (2E)	$12.95
The Power of Attorney Handbook (3E)	$19.95
Simple Ways to Protect Yourself from Lawsuits	$24.95
Social Security Benefits Handbook (2E)	$14.95
Unmarried Parents' Rights	$19.95
U.S.A. Immigration Guide (3E)	$19.95
Guia de Inmigracion a Estados Unidos (2E)	$19.95

Legal Survival Guides are directly available from Sourcebooks, Inc., or from your local bookstores.

For credit card orders call 1–800–43–BRIGHT, write P.O. Box 4410, Naperville, IL 60567-4410, or fax 630-961-2168

SPHINX® PUBLISHING ORDER FORM

BILL TO:		SHIP TO:	
Phone #	Terms	F.O.B. Chicago, IL	Ship Date

Charge my: ☐ VISA ☐ MasterCard ☐ American Express

☐ **Money Order or Personal Check**

Credit Card Number

Expiration Date

Qty	ISBN	Title	Retail	Ext.
		SPHINX PUBLISHING NATIONAL TITLES		
___	1-57071-166-6	Crime Victim's Guide to Justice	$19.95	___
___	1-57071-342-1	Debtors' Rights (3E)	$12.95	___
___	1-57071-162-3	Defend Yourself against Criminal Charges	$19.95	___
___	1-57248-082-3	Grandparents' Rights (2E)	$19.95	___
___	1-57248-087-4	Guia de Inmigracion a Estados Unidos (2E)	$19.95	___
___	1-57248-103-X	Help Your Lawyer Win Your Case (2E)	$12.95	___
___	1-57071-164-X	How to Buy a Condominium or Townhome	$16.95	___
___	1-57071-223-9	How to File Your Own Bankruptcy (4E)	$19.95	___
___	1-57071-224-7	How to File Your Own Divorce (3E)	$19.95	___
___	1-57248-083-1	How to Form a Limited Liability Company	$19.95	___
___	1-57248-100-5	How to Form a DE Corporation from Any State	$19.95	___
___	1-57248-101-3	How to Form a NV Corporation from Any State	$19.95	___
___	1-57248-099-8	How to Form a Nonprofit Corporation	$24.95	___
___	1-57071-227-1	How to Form Your Own Corporation (2E)	$19.95	___
___	1-57071-343-X	How to Form Your Own Partnership	$19.95	___
___	1-57071-228-X	How to Make Your Own Will	$12.95	___
___	1-57071-331-6	How to Negotiate Real Estate Contracts (3E)	$16.95	___
___	1-57071-332-4	How to Negotiate Real Estate Leases (3E)	$16.95	___
___	1-57071-225-5	How to Register Your Own Copyright (2E)	$19.95	___
___	1-57248-104-8	How to Register Your Own Trademark (3E)	$19.95	___
___	1-57071-349-9	How to Win Your Unemployment Compensation Claim	$19.95	___
___	1-57071-167-4	How to Write Your Own Living Will	$9.95	___
___	1-57071-344-8	How to Write Your Own Premarital Agreement (2E)	$19.95	___
___	1-57071-333-2	Jurors' Rights (2E)	$9.95	___
___	1-57248-032-7	Legal Malpractice and Other Claims against...	$18.95	___
___	1-57071-400-2	Legal Research Made Easy (2E)	$14.95	___
___	1-57071-336-7	Living Trusts and Simple Ways to Avoid Probate (2E)	$19.95	___
___	1-57071-345-6	Most Valuable Bus. Legal Forms You'll Ever Need (2E)	$19.95	___
___	1-57071-346-4	Most Valuable Corporate Forms You'll Ever Need (2E)	$24.95	___
___	1-57248-089-0	Neighbor v. Neighbor (2E)	$12.95	___
___	1-57071-348-0	The Power of Attorney Handbook (3E)	$19.95	___
___	1-57248-020-3	Simple Ways to Protect Yourself from Lawsuits	$24.95	___
___	1-57071-337-5	Social Security Benefits Handbook (2E)	$14.95	___
___	1-57071-163-1	Software Law (w/diskette)	$29.95	___
___	0-913825-86-7	Successful Real Estate Brokerage Mgmt.	$19.95	___
___	1-57248-098-X	The Nanny and Domestic Help Legal Kit	$19.95	___
___	1-57071-399-5	Unmarried Parents' Rights	$19.95	___
___	1-57071-354-5	U.S.A. Immigration Guide (3E)	$19.95	___
___	0-913825-82-4	Victims' Rights	$12.95	___
___	1-57071-165-8	Winning Your Personal Injury Claim	$19.95	___
___	1-57248-097-1	Your Right to Child Custody, Visitation and Support	$19.95	___
		CALIFORNIA TITLES		
___	1-57071-360-X	CA Power of Attorney Handbook	$12.95	___
___	1-57071-355-3	How to File for Divorce in CA	$19.95	___
___	1-57071-356-1	How to Make a CA Will	$12.95	___
___	1-57071-408-8	How to Probate an Estate in CA	$19.95	___
___	1-57071-357-X	How to Start a Business in CA	$16.95	___
___	1-57071-358-8	How to Win in Small Claims Court in CA	$14.95	___
___	1-57071-359-6	Landlords' Rights and Duties in CA	$19.95	___
		FLORIDA TITLES		
___	1-57071-363-4	Florida Power of Attorney Handbook (2E)	$12.95	___
___	1-57248-093-9	How to File for Divorce in FL (6E)	$21.95	___
___	1-57248-086-6	How to Form a Limited Liability Co. in FL	$19.95	___
___	1-57071-401-0	How to Form a Partnership in FL	$19.95	___
___	1-57071-380-4	How to Form a Corporation in FL (4E)	$19.95	___
___	1-57071-361-8	How to Make a FL Will (5E)	$12.95	___
___	1-57248-088-2	How to Modify Your FL Divorce Judgment (4E)	$22.95	___
___		*Form Continued on Following Page*	**SUBTOTAL**	___

To order, call Sourcebooks at 1-800-43-BRIGHT or FAX (630)961-2168 (Bookstores, libraries, wholesalers—please call for discount)

SPHINX® PUBLISHING ORDER FORM

Qty	ISBN	Title	Retail	Ext.
		FLORIDA TITLES (CONT'D)		
	1-57071-364-2	How to Probate an Estate in FL (3E)	$24.95	
	1-57248-081-5	How to Start a Business in FL (5E)	$16.95	
	1-57071-362-6	How to Win in Small Claims Court in FL (6E)	$14.95	
	1-57071-335-9	Landlords' Rights and Duties in FL (7E)	$19.95	
	1-57071-334-0	Land Trusts in FL (5E)	$24.95	
	0-913825-73-5	Women's Legal Rights in FL	$19.95	
		GEORGIA TITLES		
	1-57071-376-6	How to File for Divorce in GA (3E)	$19.95	
	1-57248-075-0	How to Make a GA Will (3E)	$12.95	
	1-57248-076-9	How to Start a Business in Georgia (3E)	$16.95	
		ILLINOIS TITLES		
	1-57071-405-3	How to File for Divorce in IL (2E)	$19.95	
	1-57071-415-0	How to Make an IL Will (2E)	$12.95	
	1-57071-416-9	How to Start a Business in IL (2E)	$16.95	
	1-57248-078-5	Landlords' Rights & Duties in IL	$19.95	
		MASSACHUSETTS TITLES		
	1-57071-329-4	How to File for Divorce in MA (2E)	$19.95	
	1-57248-108-0	How to Make a MA Will (2E)	$12.95	
	1-57248-109-9	How to Probate an Estate in MA (2E)	$19.95	
	1-57248-106-4	How to Start a Business in MA (2E)	$16.95	
	1-57248-107-2	Landlords' Rights and Duties in MA (2E)	$19.95	
		MICHIGAN TITLES		
	1-57071-409-6	How to File for Divorce in MI (2E)	$19.95	
	1-57248-077-7	How to Make a MI Will (2E)	$12.95	
	1-57071-407-X	How to Start a Business in MI (2E)	$16.95	
		MINNESOTA TITLES		
	1-57248-039-4	How to File for Divorce in MN	$19.95	
	1-57248-040-8	How to Form a Simple Corporation in MN	$19.95	
	1-57248-037-8	How to Make a MN Will	$9.95	
	1-57248-038-6	How to Start a Business in MN	$16.95	
		NEW YORK TITLES		
	1-57071-184-4	How to File for Divorce in NY	$19.95	
	1-57248-105-6	How to Form a Corporation in NY	$19.95	

Qty	ISBN	Title	Retail	Ext.
		NEW YORK TITLES (CONT'D)		
	1-57248-095-5	How to Make a NY Will (2E)	$12.95	
	1-57071-185-2	How to Start a Business in NY	$16.95	
	1-57071-187-9	How to Win in Small Claims Court in NY	$14.95	
	1-57071-186-0	Landlords' Rights and Duties in NY	$19.95	
	1-57071-188-7	New York Power of Attorney Handbook	$19.95	
		NORTH CAROLINA TITLES		
	1-57071-326-X	How to File for Divorce in NC (2E)	$19.95	
	1-57071-327-8	How to Make a NC Will (2E)	$12.95	
	1-57248-096-3	How to Start a Business in NC (2E)	$16.95	
	1-57248-091-2	Landlords' Rights & Duties in NC	$19.95	
		OHIO TITLES		
	1-57248-102-1	How to File for Divorce in OH	$19.95	
		PENNSYLVANIA TITLES		
	1-57071-177-1	How to File for Divorce in PA	$19.95	
	1-57248-094-7	How to Make a PA Will (2E)	$12.95	
	1-57248-112-9	How to Start a Business in PA (2E)	$16.95	
	1-57071-179-8	Landlords' Rights and Duties in PA	$19.95	
		TEXAS TITLES		
	1-57071-330-8	How to File for Divorce in TX (2E)	$19.95	
	1-57248-009-2	How to Form a Simple Corporation in TX	$19.95	
	1-57071-417-7	How to Make a TX Will (2E)	$12.95	
	1-57071-418-5	How to Probate an Estate in TX (2E)	$19.95	
	1-57071-365-0	How to Start a Business in TX (2E)	$16.95	
	1-57248-111-0	How to Win in Small Claims Court in TX (2E)	$14.95	
	1-57248-110-2	Landlords' Rights and Duties in TX (2E)	$19.95	

SUBTOTAL THIS PAGE _____

SUBTOTAL PREVIOUS PAGE _____

Illinois residents add 6.75% sales tax
Florida residents add 6% state sales tax plus applicable discretionary surtax _____

Shipping — $4.00 for 1st book, $1.00 each additional _____

TOTAL _____